HARNESSING THE POWER OF MOTHERHOOD

HARNESSING
THE POWER OF
MOTHERHOOD

*The National
Florence Crittenton Mission,
1883–1925*

Katherine G. Aiken

THE UNIVERSITY OF TENNESSEE PRESS / KNOXVILLE

Library of Congress Cataloging-in-Publication Data

Aiken, Katherine G., 1951–
Harnessing the power of motherhood : the National Florence
Crittenton Mission, 1883–1925 / Katherine G. Aiken. — 1st ed.
p. cm.
Includes bibliographical references and index.
ISBN 1-57233-017-1 (cloth: alk. paper)
1. National Florence Crittenton Mission—History. 2. Rescue
work—United States—History. 3. Unmarried mothers—Services
for—United States—History. 4. Social work with
prostitutes—United States—History. I. Title.
HQ314 .A66 1998
362.83'92'0973—ddc21
98-8979

For my parents
Dorothy Aiken Dickinson
and the late
William D. Aiken

Contents

Illustrations

Acknowledgments

It has taken me an inordinately long time to complete this book, which began, almost twenty years ago, as my doctoral dissertation on the National Florence Crittenton Mission. Since then, a stint in continuing education administration, two children, and a tenure-track job that brought with it a two-hundred-mile commute have intervened. Consequently, the list of people who have helped me is also long.

Librarians and archivists across the country have aided me in countless ways. The staff of the interlibrary loan departments at Washington State University and the University of Idaho (especially Jennifer O'Laughlin) responded to my many requests with efficiency and good humor. Research at the Burton Historical Collection of the Detroit Public Library uncovered useful information, and later, Assistant Manager David Poremba helped me obtain photographs. Librarians and archivists at the University of Illinois, Chicago Circle; the Archives of Labor and Urban Affairs, Wayne State University; Special Collections, University of Oregon Library; the Boston Public Library; the Library of Congress; the University of Virginia Library; and the Oregon Historical Society aided me. As a young graduate student on her first archival research trip, I could not have encountered a more gracious archivist than David Klaassen of the Social Welfare History Archives, University of Minnesota. More recently, Professor Klaassen and his staff went beyond the call of duty to locate photographs and to correlate my endnotes with the new arrangement of the Florence Crittenton Collection. National Florence Crittenton Mission Secretary John C. Wesley surveyed the Executive Committee of the Mission to gain permission to cite mission sources and use NFCM photographs.

I was fortunate to be a member of Robert Zieger's National Endowment for the Humanities Summer Seminar at Wayne State University in 1981. Not only was the research I conducted in Detroit critical to this study, but Zieger and the seminar members offered constructive criticism and the considerable benefits of an academic community.

My University of Idaho History Department colleagues have made my academic life there a pleasure indeed. As Department Chair, W. Kent Hackmann facilitated my work on this project and made helpful comments on the manuscript. The current Chair, Richard Spence, has continued to support my efforts and provided funding to assist with obtaining photographs. Departmental Secretary Nancy Dafoe has performed services too numerous to list. Judy Scheel worked her computer wizardry on several occasions.

A strong support group has helped me keep my perspective as I have struggled to deal with the demands of family and academia, especially Professor Kathryn Paxton George. My friend and colleague Nancy F. Renk read the entire manuscript and offered sound advice.

Meredith Morris-Babb, then of the University of Tennessee Press, was patient during a number of revisions. Director Jennifer Siler shepherded the manuscript through the final submission. Karin Kaufman's careful copyediting tightened and polished the manuscript. As a first-time author I have appreciated Managing Editor Stan Ivester's careful explanations of each step in the process. Readers for the University of Tennessee Press, Professors Marian Morton and Joseph Hawes, offered comments that led me to rethink my arguments and improve the manuscript.

Professor LeRoy Ashby suggested the National Florence Crittenton Mission as a subject, served as dissertation advisor, and has been my mentor and friend for more than two decades. He and Mary Ashby opened their home to me and other graduate students. LeRoy Ashby is the quintessential teacher/scholar whose standards of excellence and dedication continue to inspire his current and former students. His comments on several versions of this manuscript saved me from errors and led me in new directions.

My husband's parents, Charles and Sally Schwartz, provided child care whenever called upon. My siblings, Mary Louise Fishback, Sally Aiken Fitterer, and Jerome R. Aiken, continue to be great companions and friends as well as relatives. My parents supported my decision to become a historian when it was a somewhat nontraditional career path; throughout the years, their love and confidence sustained me. I regret that my father did not live to see this book completed.

Although a cliché, it is nonetheless true: I could never have written this book without the constant encouragement of my husband and partner, Joseph M. Schwartz. His considerable managerial skills allow me to combine a four-hour round-trip commute with a typically hectic family schedule. His practical and sound advice are my mainstay. He has lived with "Florence" for years without complaint, and I am grateful for his sense of humor and his love and companionship. Our children, Christopher David Schwartz and Rebecca Anne Schwartz, have grown up with this project and did little to speed its completion. They have, however, given me insight into the meaning of motherhood and much joy.

Introduction

"The problem of the unmarried mother is so tragic in itself, so potent in its possibilities for good or evil for the girl, so pitiful for the unfathered child, so vital to the welfare of the community."[1] So wrote Frances Emerson in the August 30, 1919, edition of the major social reform journal *Survey*. More than seventy years later, Vice-President Dan Quayle echoed Emerson's views when he attacked television character Murphy Brown's decision to become a single mother. Although Quayle's statement led to a storm of controversy and even ridicule, an *Atlantic Monthly* cover story entitled "Dan Quayle Was Right" concluded that the vice-president had indeed touched upon an issue of significance for a number of Americans.[2]

The problem of unmarried mothers remains an emotional and controversial one involving underlying themes of women's place in society, sexuality, and "family values"—all issues that resonate deeply in American history. As Frances Emerson noted years ago, the unmarried mother herself, the child in question, the baby's absent father, and the effect on the larger community all represent viable concerns. These concerns were of paramount importance to Americans who participated in one of the most significant of the turn-of-the-century social welfare movements, the National Florence Crittenton Mission (NFCM).

Historians have frequently recognized the pioneering role the National Florence Crittenton Mission played in rescuing prostitutes, establishing homes for unmarried mothers, and providing aid to these mothers and their children. However, historical analysis of the Florence Crittenton (FC) organization has been limited, emphasizing Florence Crittenton home residents at the expense of other aspects of the Crittenton movement. This book provides a more comprehensive discussion of the NFCM, its development, and its policies. The resulting picture is one of an organization that, because of its varied programs, defies characterization. While providing essential social welfare services for women and children, National Florence Crittenton Mission activists also addressed issues of public policy and social-work practice.

Between 1880 and 1924, the United States underwent a profound social, economic, and political transformation—a transformation that laid the foundations for modern American society. Women certainly felt the strain of this transition and struggled to keep pace with dramatic change while maintaining the sense of status and place they enjoyed as wives and mothers. Women who joined the various reform movements of the period often found themselves emphasizing their traditional roles while forging new ones. Study of the National Florence Crittenton Mission provides an opportunity to assess women's responses to these challenges while analyzing the institutional development of a significant social welfare organization.

Throughout changing political and social milieus, American women have clung tenaciously to their special role as mothers. To question the value of motherhood is to question the basic foundations of society; thus motherhood is a perfect vehicle for women's affirmation of their own power. Many women sought to harness the power of motherhood and use it to improve women's condition. While historians have sometimes emphasized the reverse of this argument—theorizing that traditional notions of woman as wife and mother have been used to keep women in a certain prescribed realm—in the case of the NFCM, the weight of the evidence is decidedly on the other side. Maternalism was a tool that Crittenton women wielded on their own behalf, and on behalf of their charges. In the process, FC volunteers helped to introduce their image of motherhood into the public arena.[3]

The National Florence Crittenton Mission began its history as a nationwide organization dedicated to "rescuing" so-called fallen women, or prostitutes. As such, the mission was part of a general reform movement that sought to address questions of urban growth, moral decline, immigration, women's place—issues of continued significance. Other national groups, most notably the Salvation Army, the Women's Christian Temperance Union (WCTU), and the Young Women's Christian Association (YWCA), engaged in rescue work, but rescue efforts were only part of their programs. The NFCM began as an institution helping "unfortunate women," and it continued along the same lines throughout its history. The organization grew to include homes in seventy-three cities, and by 1924 it was operating the largest chain of maternity homes in the country. For most Americans, *Florence Crittenton* came to mean rescue work and efforts to assist unmarried mothers.

Rescue homes for "fallen" women were a stratagem for late-nineteenth- and early-twentieth-century reformers for a number of reasons. The term *rescue* by definition implies victims, as well as an element of risk for those attempting to aid those victims. *Home* was fraught with significance for reformers during the period and still brings to mind images of a haven and special familial relationships. At the same time, homes were one of the few places in American society where women exercised control. An important theme of this study is an exploration of FC workers' attempts to translate the power they associated with the concept of home into an organizational framework with the capacity to actually allow "fallen" women to escape their situation and become rescued. Use of the term *fallen* points to Crittenton perceptions of the victims. The term is passive, as if the women described had no control over their own lives, a judgment many rescue workers embraced. This picture of the women as victims changed over time and was inextricably tied to the Crittenton workers' attitudes regarding gender roles, sexuality, and morality, and therefore represents another area of inquiry in this work.

The NFCM and its leadership provide an opportunity for the historian to examine several aspects of reform. Charles Nelson Crittenton was a harbinger, and eventually a model, of progressive reform in a variety of ways. A self-made millionaire, he experienced the deep religious conversion that seemed to catapult many individuals into the reform arena; Crittenton's story could have come straight from Charles Sheldon's best-selling novel *In His Steps*. But Crittenton combined his religious zeal with a penchant for businesslike methods and efficiency. When he realized that lack of an alternative stymied prostitutes determined to mend their ways, Crittenton set about providing that alternative—and his vision was a broad one. He devoted his life and most of his considerable resources to publicizing the plight of fallen women and convincing people to do something to rescue them. This involved Charles Crittenton in the discussion of a number of delicate subjects, and he did not shirk broaching those topics as he crisscrossed the country urging audiences to join in rescue efforts. By all accounts Charles Crittenton was a convincing speaker, but his real appeal was his sincere concern for unfortunate women. Few who heard him came away without at least some sympathy for these women, no small feat in an era when society placed a high value on women's sexual purity. The Crittenton message emphasized that true manliness required sympathy and understanding toward all women, regardless of their situation in life. His alliance with Frances Willard and the Women's Christian Temperance Union allowed Crittenton to further extend his work, but he represented only one element of the National Florence Crittenton Mission story.

For most of its early history, the NFCM was under the leadership of Dr. Kate Waller Barrett, and she provided the Crittenton organization's soul. She became one of the best known women in the United States and a leading authority on unmarried mothers, prostitution, and immigrant women. A physician, a trained nurse, a wife and mother, she was a product of changes confronting women during this period. Attired simply, and usually in black, she was the "true woman" incarnate. Her ideas directed and shaped FC work, and her tireless efforts and exhausting travel schedule allowed Barrett to ensure that Crittenton workers everywhere shared her philosophy. She was a transitional figure in women's history and illustrated the tensions women experienced as they pursued new directions. Her dedication to woman's traditional role as wife and mother bordered on the fanatic; in fact, her catch phrase, "Motherhood as a means of regeneration," was the basic tenet for all Crittenton work. She shared with many of her contemporaries an almost unreasonable faith in the power of the "home" to work wonders in the lives of fallen women, and Kate Waller Barrett believed emphatically that woman was at her best in her roles as wife and mother. Barrett's vision of home life and motherhood was a decidedly middle-class one, and she and other FC workers joined their peers in the National Congress of Mothers' and other less-organized groups to instruct working-class women in the finer points of middle-class motherhood.

At the same time, Barrett's education and training and her view of reform were more a product of the twentieth century than the nineteenth. While Regina Kunzel has argued persuasively that an older evangelical religious view of reform dominated many Crittenton activities, this characterization shortchanges Kate Waller Barrett and her accomplishments.[4] Barrett's profession alone set her apart from most other nineteenth-century leaders of reform movements. Her seminal written work, *Some Practical Suggestions for the Conduct of a Rescue Home,* provided a standard blueprint for rescue home operation, and the adjective "practical" was certainly a watchword of Crittenton work. The NFCM became a respected institution in the social welfare field, drawing upon "expertise" as well as enthusiastic volunteers. In fact, in several instances Kate Waller Barrett and her colleagues were pacesetters who pioneered in areas that were essential to establishing what Robyn Muncy has described as the "Female Dominion." Florence Crittenton policies for dealing with unmarried mothers and their children became standard practices for women reformers engaged in social work with mothers and their children.[5]

Kate Waller Barrett achieved a national prominence few women of her time could equal. While her quest to gain expert status no doubt facilitated Crittenton work, it probably detracted from her attaining a lasting place in the public consciousness.[6] Barrett sought to avoid any association with controversy or radicalism, and she couched her comments in traditional terms, even when her message departed from generally accepted positions. She became adept at forwarding an often decidedly feminist agenda in conservative guise. She employed traditional images of home and family as a fulcrum for establishing a feminist perspective. Barrett's education, her training, and her method of reform set her apart from her evangelical predecessors and colleagues. Yet her established association with the institution of motherhood also differentiated Barrett from Jane Addams and the other single, female progressives historians have frequently studied.[7]

Few reform activities rival rescue work, and especially work with unmarried mothers, as arenas for viewing the complex relationship between middle-class reformers and their working-class clients. At the same time, the historian is on unsteady ground because the source materials are usually institution-based and it is often difficult to piece together home residents' stories. The workers themselves compiled case records, and it requires considerable speculation and extrapolation even to make educated suggestions as to the impact of Crittenton work on the inmates. The "elite domination and plebeian victimization" model fails to incorporate either the genuine humanitarianism of Crittenton workers or the ability of Florence Crittenton inmates to make their own choices.[8] Although Crittenton workers may have sometimes been unwelcome intruders into their charges' lives, interaction between "rescuers" and "rescued" took place on a number of levels. Florence Crittenton inmates were often able to avoid Crittenton institutional restraints and manipulate Crittenton regimes to meet their needs.

While conclusions regarding Crittenton inmates are tentative at best, we know a great deal about the workers' viewpoints and can trace the development of workers' attitudes through the monthly journals—the

Florence Crittenton Magazine, Girls, and the *Florence Crittenton Bulletin.* Crittenton workers designed these publications with an eye toward two different reader groups. First and foremost, the magazines' objective was to provide continuity in Crittenton work, to tie together the disparate branches of Crittendom. Articles were directed primarily at FC volunteers, the women in countless towns and cities who gave their time to Crittenton work. The magazines encouraged these women when their task seemed insurmountable and the progress slim, and fostered a sense of community for readers isolated from regular contact with their colleagues. But the magazine also served as a recruiting tool and as propaganda to convince outsiders to join the Crittenton circle. The magazines publicized the NFCM's accomplishments, highlighted the contributions of local homes, and offered commentary on issues the Crittenton organization believed were of interest and importance to readers. As a result, the magazines illustrated both Crittenton workers' self-concept and the image they sought for themselves. Examining the magazines' content provides insight into the impact that their involvement in social reform had on FC workers.

Florence Crittenton volunteers viewed their roles as wives and mothers not only as a source of their power but also as the core of their emotional well-being. They genuinely enjoyed these aspects of their lives and sought to ensure that their charges would have similar feelings. Crittenton workers were firmly convinced that efforts to separate unmarried mothers from their children—adoption, for example—deprived these mothers of one of life's most rewarding experiences. Kate Waller Barrett and her followers implemented policies that allowed unmarried mothers to keep their babies, and in fact encouraged them to do so. Crittenton workers labored to provide these mothers with the wherewithal to support themselves and their children. Ironically, when these NFCM efforts were successful, viable, single-parent families resulted. At first glance this jeopardized the traditional values Crittenton workers espoused, but the volunteers were convinced that motherhood's importance transcended all other considerations.

As Linda Gordon has recently shown, while there are certainly connections between the contemporary policy debate regarding unmarried mothers and that of the early twentieth century, the historian should guard against an ahistorical evaluation of the earlier period.[9] As they shifted their emphasis to the care of unmarried mothers, Crittenton institutions filled a real void in social welfare services. Society tended to tolerate premarital sexuality during the early years of U.S. history, but increasingly, throughout the nineteenth century, nonmarital pregnancy caused a crisis for women, and they often had no place to turn for help.[10] Appearance of this new attitude coincided with dramatic changes in behavioral patterns for young women. Working-class women in particular sought to redefine their sexual roles, and in the process they often found themselves at odds with middle-class expectations for behavior. An increase in the number of nonmarital pregnancies was one result of this clash that ironically created greater demand for the services that the middle-class Crittenton workers offered.

Historians often have judged FC efforts harshly, emphasizing the punitive nature of the Crittenton homes. Rickie Solinger has argued that all maternity homes could do was train their charges for "illicit motherhood" and "sternly fortify [them] for life as a marginal woman."[11] The National Florence Crittenton Mission embraced a much broader vision, and Crittenton women's relationship with their charges was more intricate. Kate Waller Barrett was unequivocal in her conviction that Crittenton women deserved the respect due them as mothers. Faith in motherhood's power shaped Barrett's viewpoint as she voiced her strong belief that unmarried mothers were potentially as capable as their married counterparts. Barrett's response to claims that "fallen" women should be social outcasts was a resounding no, and her answer was based on a decidedly pro-woman outlook. Barrett and her cohorts sought to protect their charges from society's attempts to ostracize them, and in fact, Crittenton women demanded fair treatment for unmarried mothers and their children. Kate Waller Barrett and her associates viewed attempts to marginalize Crittenton inmates as part of a larger societal attempt to marginalize women, and they fought both attempts.

In her seminal work *The Grounding of Modern Feminism,* Nancy Cott has argued that although the term *feminism* is inappropriate before the 1910s, the concept includes three "core components—an opposition to sex hierarchy, the idea that women's condition in society is constructed, and gender group identity."[12] Certainly, using Cott's yardstick, Kate Waller Barrett and her associates shared feminist convictions. As both Cott and Barbara Berg have shown, the apparently conservative aspects of women's traditional place in society can be a powerful tool for women seeking to establish their own agenda.[13] Kate Waller Barrett and the National Florence Crittenton Mission represent a case study of this phenomenon.

Their convictions regarding women's power led Florence Crittenton workers to embark upon a number of experiments in their institutions that were precursors to a modern feminist viewpoint. FC workers used the court system to gain child support for unmarried mothers and campaigned for legislation in this area. The homes were havens for abused and deserted women, and Crittenton workers were outspoken advocates for victims. Florence Crittenton homes provided health-care facilities designed to cater to women's unique needs, and women physicians were often the primary care givers. Florence Crittenton institutions provided day care for children of working mothers at a time when this was practically unheard of as a solution to the child-care dilemma. Under Kate Waller Barrett's direction, the NFCM made advancements in providing aid to African American women, while forming alliances with middle-class African American women involved in rescue work. Clearly, Crittenton women engaged in what Estelle Freedman has described as female institution building.[14]

Crittenton commitment often led women to examine their status and, as a result, fostered feminist and/or antimale sentiments. When they demanded a single standard of morals equally binding on men and women, when they complained about the judicial system's treatment of prostitutes, or when they turned to the courts to force men to accept responsibility for their children, Crittenton women challenged customary gender relationships. Although Crittenton workers called their institutions homes in deference to their faith in the power of home and motherhood, their institutions were female-controlled and often exclusively female in membership. The NFCM fostered independence and self-esteem for its charges and its workers.

Florence Crittenton work was difficult and often thankless, but women were willing to make sacrifices to continue these efforts for a number of reasons. First and foremost, they believed they were helping their clients. Second, they thought that women and their children had value and should receive assistance. Crittenton volunteers were outspoken in their beliefs that society too often ignored women's and children's needs, and they were determined to redress this situation. Like the club women historian Karen Blair has identified, Crittenton workers "narrowed the distance between home and public."[15] They demanded that those in power take action to aid women, and Kate Waller Barrett and the NFCM supported women's suffrage as a means for women to instigate changes. Finally, Florence Crittenton workers gained personal strength from their involvement with Crittenton homes and other activities. The Crittenton work validated perceptions of self-worth, improved self-esteem, and gave women's lives more purpose and meaning. Crittenton volunteers found their relationships with both co-workers and clients to be significant parts of their own lives.

The National Florence Crittenton Mission played an active role in the anti-white-slavery crusade of the progressive period and World War I, but unlike various other reform groups, the organization's primary concern was the prostitutes themselves. The NFCM became an advocate for immigrant women, indigent women, and delinquent girls and provided a calming voice during the white-slave controversy. While urban vice commissions and many women's organizations became almost hysterical in their fear and condemnation of the so-called white slave conspiracy, the NFCM advocated a more rational approach. A sense of shared gender motivated the Crittenton response.[16] During World War I, the organization cooperated with the Commission on Training Camp Activities' efforts to close vice districts, but FC workers never lost sight of the needs of the residents of the districts.

During the postwar period, the social work establishment devoted more attention to the problem of illegitimate children and their mothers. The NFCM played a significant role in this field. The organization's records provided a portion of the database for scientific inquiries into the problem of illegitimacy.[17] These studies confirmed what FC workers had known for a considerable period of time: fathers should support their children, and babies' health was improved when they remained with their mothers. While historians sometimes describe the FC policy of keeping mothers and their children together as punitive, Children's Bureau findings indicated that many unmarried mothers wanted desperately to keep their children and, in fact, may have chosen to enter a maternity home in order to facilitate this. The bureau found that mothers were "willing to make sacrifices" in order to keep their children with them—something Crittenton women had been saying all along.[18]

Following World War I, the NFCM sought to adapt to a changing social and political climate. Perhaps Kate Waller Barrett's pet project in the twenties, the Ivakota Farms in Virginia, best illustrated the Crittenton approach in the postwar years. The farms admitted women suffering from venereal disease and attempted the reformation of juvenile delinquents, and their long-range plans called for services to African American women as well as whites. Ivakota's methods represented a compromise, a combination of traditional Crittenton strategies with new techniques. Workers sought to inculcate self-reliance and emphasized physical fitness while not ignoring the importance of domestic skills. This combination represented a viable strategy for the 1920s.

In many ways Dr. Kate Waller Barrett and her Crittenton associates epitomized stereotypical roles for women. But they succeeded in using their traditional sphere to benefit both themselves and women of other classes. In fact, their efforts sketched out a reform agenda that, more than a century after the mission's founding, had taken on renewed significance: help for prostitutes, care for single mothers and their children, stronger laws protecting children, vocational training for mothers, changes in the legal system that allowed unmarried mothers to obtain child support, day care, and health care for women. Crittenton institutions struggled with major social problems that have continued to haunt American society. They found some solutions, and they brought compassion and understanding to their work. The mission helped to convert contemporary concepts of home and motherhood into a powerful force for women and reform. National Florence Crittenton Mission workers harnessed the power of motherhood on behalf of both their charges and themselves.

Chapter 1

The Merchant Evangelist:
Charles Nelson Crittenton

But this is a people robbed and spoiled; they are all of th m snared in
holes, and they are hid in prison houses; they are for a prey, and none
delivereth; for a spoil, and none saith, Restore!
—Isaiah 42:22

Charles Nelson Crittenton embodied the evangelical philanthropist of the
late nineteenth century so perfectly that a historian could have created
him to play that role. Crittenton traveled across the United States as a
preaching evangelist, and his sermons and writings did a great deal to
encourage a more sympathetic attitude toward the prostitute and her
problems. He opened the first Florence Crittenton mission in 1883 in order to provide a home and a second chance for prostitutes. By 1909 there
were seventy-three Florence Crittenton homes, and Charles Crittenton's
reputation as both an evangelist and philanthropist were well established.
He forged an association with the Women's Christian Temperance Union
and became a leading advocate for an end to the double standard of morals for men and women, for sex education for boys and girls, and for
more humane treatment for prostitutes and other unfortunate women.
Crittenton had indeed earned the sobriquets "Merchant Evangelist" and
"Brother of Girls."

Charles Crittenton was born in Henderson, New York, on February
20, 1833. His family was poor, and in his youth he worked for J. and D.
P. H. Chapman Company, the local general store. Like many young men
eager to make their fortunes, he went to New York City. In September

1843, he found employment as office boy for an undertaker named Dugan and learned rudimentary bookkeeping. A year later Crittenton became bookkeeper, cashier, and traveling salesperson with the W. H. Durham Company, where eventually he became a partner.[1] The partnership dissolved in 1861, and Crittenton—with the sum of sixty dollars—decided to start his own wholesale drug business. He began by taking orders and delivering goods himself, but eventually his medicine warehouse at 115–117 Fulton Street became the largest in the world. Crittenton purchased a home on Fifth Avenue and entered New York high society.[2]

Florence, his second daughter, was born in 1878, when Crittenton was forty-five years old and his other daughter, Addie, was already thirteen. Crittenton worshiped little Flossie, who reciprocated, and they spent hours together in Mount Morris Park near their home and on long walks throughout the city. The little girl would answer only to "Papa's Baby," and she would often stand on the porch, calling to passing acquaintances, "Don't you want to come in and see Papa's Baby?" An admirer explained part of Crittenton's adoration: "Rightly-named was the little girl, Florence! for a fairer flower never budded in terrestrial gardens, to bloom in full radiance and beauty in celestial fields."[3] Countless audiences would later hear Crittenton recall how he readied Florence for bed each night and sang her favorite hymn, "The Golden Harp." She usually joined in the chorus: "I want to be with Jesus / And play on the golden harp."[4]

While Crittenton was visiting in Rochester in early 1883, he received a telegram—"Flossie very ill. Scarlet fever. Come home immediately." As his first-born child, a son, had died of the disease, Crittenton recognized the seriousness of the situation and boarded a train for home. When he arrived, Florence, swollen with fever, requested a drink of water and asked her father to sing "In the Sweet Bye and Bye." She died during the song. She was four years, four months, and four days old and was buried at Woodlawn Cemetery under a tombstone that reads "Papa's Baby."[5]

The loss devastated Crittenton; he drifted aimlessly for eight months. Before Florence's death he spent long hours at his business, but following her death money making seemed to have lost its charm. He wondered why God had taken his Florence, and each day he traveled to Woodlawn Cemetery to visit the grave. Then, on October 20, 1883, while riding the elevated train to the cemetery, Crittenton heard a voice say, "She can't come to you, but you can go to her." He recalled: "Shortly after, in an upper chamber of my home, 2019 Fifth Avenue, I found Jesus precious to my soul and this was the key which unlocked the mystery of the grave. . . . Retracing my steps down stairs I realized that I was a child of God and

Charles Nelson Crittenton, National Florence Crittenton Mission founder.
Courtesy of the National Florence Crittenton Mission.

promised faithfully when called upon by anyone, to do His work, I would respond to all such calls."[6] Charles Crittenton's religious awakening placed him securely within the ranks of late-nineteenth-century evangelical Protestantism. His determination to "respond" to all calls to do God's work was a significant ramification of his religious conversion experience. Crittenton's commitment was clearly to serve God in some practical way.

Charles Crittenton began to frequent the Fulton Street noon-day prayer meetings held near his office and to testify at these and other meetings. At the close of one such gathering, attendee Smith Allen approached Crittenton and said, "Brother Crittenton, go with me to see the people in the slums." Crittenton consented and visited places he "had only dimly dreamed of as existing." They came upon two young prostitutes and Brother Allen prayed and sang "There is a Fountain Filled with Blood." Then Crittenton told them the story of little Florence, his rebellion against God, and his conversion. He said to the girls, "Neither do I condemn thee, Go and Sin no more." One weeping girl replied, "But where can I go?" Crittenton recalled that, "like lightning flashed the thought 'WHERE can she go?'" Following this experience, Crittenton devoted his life to rescuing fallen women and providing them homes. Although uncertain at first how best to aid prostitutes, Crittenton was convinced that they were a class of sinners in particular need of conversion and their reformation would benefit all of society. He decided, as a memorial to his daughter Florence, to open a home for other fathers' little girls "even more lost to them than his own Florence in Woodlawn Cemetery."[7]

Both Crittenton's early activities on behalf of prostitutes and his ideas regarding them had antecedents in U.S. history. Even before the Civil War, some American reformers had begun to express concern about the prostitute's plight, and these so-called moral reformers outlined positions that Charles Crittenton later echoed.

Even the notion of moral reform was closely tied to the predominant views of woman and her place in society. The ideal woman's sphere was generally confined to family and the home, where she was to lovingly provide a religious and moral haven. According to historian Barbara Welter, the four most important attributes of the "true woman" were piety, purity, submissiveness, and domesticity, qualities marking the parameters of women's actions in society.[8] Some antebellum women devised ways to escape the passive domestic roles society expected them to play. Reform movements provided a particularly attractive avenue for this purpose, because they did not require women to abandon totally their

Florence Crittenton. Courtesy of the National Florence Crittenton Mission.

traditional role. Campaigns for moral reform especially enabled women to remain in their accepted position and still break away from the confines of the home.[9]

The ideal of the pure, pious, submissive, and domestic woman shaped the orthodox view of sexual relations. Most people believed that women felt little sexual desire or passion; romantic love and general passivity reportedly motivated women's participation in sexual relationships. Men, on the other hand, had an "inherent need to gratify passions." While people expected women to remain pure prior to marriage and faithful afterward, many admired the male "sexual athlete."[10] Most nineteenth-century Americans accepted this double standard for sexual conduct.

Prostitution was irrevocably intertwined with the double standard, as its existence theoretically protected virtuous women from the uncontrollable sexual urges of men. Because of the prevailing assumptions that "good" women felt no sexual desire and that sexual relations, even within marriage, were only for purposes of procreation, the ideal of women's sexual frigidity may in fact have created that reality in some cases.[11] While it was relatively easy to explain why males frequented houses of prostitution, it was much more difficult to account for the prostitutes themselves. Since most middle-class Americans believed that "chastity is the natural inheritance of women," the prostitute seemed to threaten the ideal of the true woman.[12]

By the 1830s, when moral reformers attacked prostitution they also challenged the double standard. Evangelical religious conviction inspired women moral reformers to take the offensive against prostitution as a threat to the home, morality, and piety that women were bound to protect. At the same time, by assaulting the double standard, these women were striking out against their traditional position in society.[13] Women's sense of their natural place in society served as both the foundation of conservative ideas regarding women's appropriate sphere and the starting point for a considerable expansion in women's traditional role.[14]

The link women moral reformers saw between prostitution and the double standard led them to a sympathetic view of the prostitute herself. The fallen woman, although still unworthy of the society of true women, was no longer seen as a depraved harlot and hopeless sinner, but as an innocent victim of men's lasciviousness and her own eagerness to please.[15]

This change in attitude led to attempts to rescue the prostitute from her unfortunate situation. The New York Female Moral Reform Society (NYFMRS), founded in 1834, was one early effort to both end prostitution and rehabilitate prostitutes. Members of the society hoped to convert prostitutes to evangelical religion and to close the brothels. In order to rescue these women, the society's members visited jails, almshouses, and women's wards in hospitals to hold prayer meetings. They also "descended upon" the brothels themselves—often early on Sunday morning—to pray with and exhort the inmates and their customers. To combat the double standard, the society urged its members to shun association with men who visited brothels, and the society published the names of such men in its paper, the *Advocate*.[16]

The NYFMRS and similar organizations, such as the American Society for Promoting the Observance of the Seventh Commandment, relied on religious conversion and emotional appeals. The Female Moral Reform Society, the American Guardian Society, the Five Points Mission, and some other groups tried as well to establish refuges for prostitutes seeking new lives. Although reformers made some effort to prepare the "saved" women for life after prostitution, they devoted most of their energy to ensuring the permanence of the former prostitutes' religious conversions. At one of these refuges, little children came to sing:

> Were not the sinful Mary's tears
> Acceptable to heaven
> When o'er the faults of former years
> She wept and was forgiven?[17]

and reformers hoped this message would touch the former prostitutes and convince them to change their lives. The verse made the process sound deceptively simple—repent, shed tears, be forgiven—and this uncomplicated rubric guided the efforts of most rescue workers.

The founders of reform societies believed that their efforts to save prostitutes and close brothels were only stop-gap measures. They were convinced that women must unite to combat the sexual permissiveness that caused prostitution and generally agreed that the best way to accomplish this was to educate children, especially boys. They believed this was the mother's responsibility; thus the influence of women in their role as mothers began to take on an added dimension.[18]

Antebellum attempts at moral reform were rejuvenated following the Civil War when an organized and persistent social-purity movement took shape in reaction to the growth of regulated prostitution in England and America. During this period two kinds of moral reform or social-purity societies grew. Some stressed rescuing fallen women and closing houses of ill repute; others devoted their energy to preventive measures and emphasized education and child rearing. The shared belief that sexual immorality threatened society eventually helped unite these two movements.

These organizations' steps toward destroying the conspiracy of silence surrounding sexual matters and the double standard enabled later reformers, especially women, to play a more significant role in reform. Charles Crittenton's efforts mirrored these early attempts at moral reform, and perhaps his most significant contribution was the widespread success he achieved in this direction. Throughout his career, Crittenton emphasized a program of rescuing prostitutes and providing them with alternative places to live, educating women and children as to the potential danger of prostitution, and ending the double standard of morality for men and women.[19] Crittenton's career also illustrates that in the case of most prostitutes, considerably more than tears and repentance were required to achieve reformation in the eyes of reformers.

Once he decided to provide a haven for prostitutes, Crittenton searched for a suitable New York location. He and some friends finally found a building in the heart of the saloon and brothel district at 29 Bleecker Street and rented it for nine hundred dollars a year. On April 19, 1883, with Crittenton paying for most of the rental fee and operating expenses, the Florence Night Mission opened. The mission offered food, shelter, and religious comfort to prostitutes and homeless women in the neighborhood. To symbolize the work, Crittenton ordered the word "Welcome" laid in tile on the mission's front step.[20] A religious service took place at the mission every night, where only a single gas jet lit the entrance so that any woman wishing to enter unseen could do so. A picture of little Florence and a vase of white flowers were the focal points of the meeting room. The mission girls kept the vase filled, and in the words of one observer, "many a time the matron has had two or three poor little blossoms thrust into her hand by some unhappy creature who had stole in for just that purpose and then hurried away."[21] Crittenton workers took this as a sign that even women as yet unable or unwilling to enter the mission found comfort and perhaps hope.

Half an hour of singing preceded the meetings, and then the matron ushered in the "Florence Girls," the saved girls who sat across the aisle from the other women. Any men present had seats in the back. Each Florence Girl wore the mission badge and participated in the service, which continued until daybreak with more singing, preaching, and testimonials. According to an English observer of the dozen or so women present at one meeting, most of them were in rags, many were drunk, and one ate peanuts and dropped the shells on the floor. Some women made an effort to entice reformed prostitutes back to their old life. By the end of the meeting most of the women were nonetheless weeping, and

The "mother mission," 29 Bleecker Street, New York City, c. 1899.
Courtesy of the National Florence Crittenton Mission.

the matron cried, "O! Father, help the dear girls."[22] While this description does not necessarily portray miraculous conversions, it does illustrate Crittenton workers' belief in their methods.

Crittenton workers sought to widen the scope of their efforts, and to this end, Charles Crittenton organized the Florence Crittenton Rescue Band as a means of publicizing the mission and locating potential inmates. The band was strikingly similar to the groups the NYFMRS had sponsored fifty years earlier. Crittenton had cards printed and distributed throughout the neighborhood:

> Any Mother's Girl Wishing to Leave a Crooked Life
> May find Friends, Food, and Shelter and a
> HELPING HAND
> By coming just as She is to the
> Florence Night Mission.[23]

Every evening, from eleven o'clock until five or six in the morning, the small group of five to ten men and women visited cellars, dance halls, gambling houses, and opium dens, where they would talk to women and urge them to leave their "lives of sin." If a girl consented, one of the missionaries would immediately take her to the mission. Otherwise, members of the band would leave some of the printed cards, a flower, and a word of encouragement. Once the women reached the mission, they received baths, fresh clothing, and clean beds. The matron, for many years "Mother" Prindle, would take the girl in her arms and say, "We are so glad to see you dear!" The next morning there was a prayer meeting at which the matron encouraged the girl to tell her story, in the belief that this was an essential step in the reformation process. The inmates all did some sort of housework until the workers believed the girls strong enough in their faith to go out to work.[24]

Sister Charlotte was an early Florence Crittenton Rescue Band leader. The daughter of a small-town Baptist minister, Charlotte had married a man she hardly knew and gone with him to New York City. A few months later Charlotte was pregnant and learned that her new husband was a gambler and a thief. He told her that she could either remain in New York as his accomplice or return home a disgraced woman. Charlotte agreed to stay, having no other way to provide for herself. She became an expert shoplifter, began drinking to forget her troubles, and eventually turned to prostitution in order to obtain more money for her husband. One night Charlotte stumbled into the Florence Night Mission and experienced religious conversion. As a worker wrote, "Her conversion was a glorious one, and her testimonies were wonderfully used of God in bringing wanderers back to the narrow way." Besides leading the band to haunts of which they had no knowledge, Sister Charlotte was a popular and effective public speaker who raised considerable money for FC work. Crittenton told her story to audiences throughout the United States to exemplify the success rescue workers sought to achieve.[25] Charlotte's history illustrates several themes of early rescue work. Charlotte was the victim of an unscrupulous man who robbed her of her virtue and left her no alternative but a life of sin. Nevertheless, her true, womanly nature remained constant and only required an opportunity—the mission—to show itself. The result was her dazzling conversion. Sister Charlotte's story, with its theme of seduction and betrayal, resonated for many Crittenton associates.[26] Charlotte's upbringing as a minister's daughter, while certainly contributing to her naïveté, also made her susceptible to the mission's approach. The fact that Charlotte's seducer had in fact married her served as a warning to all women to guard against a similar fate. Although early Crittenton efforts undoubtedly reached only a small number of New York prostitutes, the results highlighted in the case of Sister Charlotte were sufficient to encourage Crittenton and to draw others to the work.

For six years Charles Crittenton devoted himself to the strenuous activities of running the Florence Night Mission and overseeing the Florence Crittenton Rescue Band. Then, in 1889, his health failed and his doctor ordered him to take a world cruise to recuperate. When he landed in San Francisco a year later, Crittenton planned to return to New York City to continue his rescue work, but he agreed to preach a sermon at San Francisco's Central Methodist Church. With this sermon Crittenton launched his twenty-year career as a preaching evangelist. He discussed his concern for fallen women and became involved with a faltering effort to establish a rescue home in San Francisco. Crittenton's financial backing and advice helped the home to become viable, and San Francisco supporters changed its name from Pacific Rescue Home to San Francisco Florence Crittenton Home.[27]

A short time later Crittenton went to San Jose to visit an acquaintance and while there attended several Young Men's Christian Association (YMCA) meetings. News of Crittenton's appearances spread, and because many people wanted to hear Crittenton testify, religious leaders set up a tent to hold a citywide revival. Dr. Ellen J. Smith was one of the converts, and under her direction a Florence Crittenton mission opened in San Jose on July 11, 1890. Mission workers held a street meeting every night at 7:30 P.M., followed by a gospel meeting at 7:45. Every day except Sunday there was a forty-five-minute noon meeting, and the mission also featured consecration meetings and Sunday schools. By the end of the mission's second year, 31,943 people had attended meetings, and a grateful convert wrote in tribute:

> Flowers forever live, to spread their rich perfume
> Lily, violet and rose for aye their sweetness shed
> O'er men—when dying they but cease to bloom
> Robbed only of their form—their fragrance is not dead
> Even so she lives for aye—the child whose name we bear
> Never bloomed a lovelier flower while here on earth,
> Changed by the alchemy of death she passed up there,
> Ever to stay with us—her dying gives this Mission birth.[28]

Charles Crittenton had succeeded in keeping alive his daughter's name.

In December 1890, Crittenton began a series of meetings in Sacramento. Upon surveying the situation, he and two local ministers decided the best location for a Florence Crittenton mission was in a place a saloon occupied. One of the ministers suggested that they go to Crittenton's room and pray to God to allow the Gospel to be preached there. Two days later the building was available. The mission provided lodging and meals for the indigent, as well as the usual prayer meetings. Attendance reached forty-nine thousand during 1891.[29]

The San Francisco, San Jose, and Sacramento missions began a pattern of evangelical preaching and institutional development that Crittenton sustained for almost two decades. Instead of the few days he had planned, Crittenton stayed in California for three years. While there he decided to devote his life to evangelism and to establishing rescue homes in each geographic area of the country. In his view, these two endeavors were linked, and the remainder of his life saw a congruence of the two activities.

Crittenton became known as the "Merchant Evangelist," a considerable portion of his success stemming from the fact that he had given up his business career. Wherever he visited, the local newspaper invariably featured articles that stressed his business background. "Think for a moment," one wrote, "if you, in a position to live in the lap of luxury and refinement all the days of your life, would quit your business and an actual income of $60,000 for the life of a travelling evangelist." Crittenton used this publicity to his advantage and frequently spoke of his business life in Horatio Alger–story fashion. His favorite anecdote involved an incident early in his career when he promised a druggist delivery on the same day. When Crittenton reached the express office it was closed, so he carried the heavy box of supplies two miles across town to make the delivery on time. Crittenton referred to his wife's willingness to forego certain luxuries as important to his career and called on young women in his audience to do likewise. He reflected in his autobiography that this frequent emphasis on his business accomplishments was not an attempt to "sound a trumpet" for himself but an effort to convey the lesson that "hard work, economy, and honorable dealing" would result in financial success.[30] Crittenton and his admirers believed that his economic status lent credence to his evangelical message and his claims that donations would be used efficiently and productively.

Crittenton earned a reputation as one of the leading evangelists of the period; a reporter described him as "one of the most striking personalities in the recent religious history of the country."[31] Evangelical religious leaders thought highly of him, as a southern minister's poetic testimonial indicated:

C	Courageous
R	Religious
I	Intent
T	Toilsome
T	Tenacious
E	Educated
N	Never self-hating
T	Trustworthy
O	Original
N	Never prayer-less.[32]

All of these characteristics were in keeping with the image that Crittenton cultivated. Few Americans at the time would not praise a man who possessed them, and Crittenton's ability to draw large crowds to his meetings helped ensure that his work received ample publicity, volunteers, and contributions. His name was soon inextricably entwined with the campaign to rescue prostitutes, and as a result his opinions on the subject received widespread attention.

Charles Crittenton based his evangelism on the idea of a dramatic religious experience followed by a changed life. He and people of like persuasion celebrated the anniversary of their conversions, and in fact, Crittenton knew down to the hours and minutes how long he had been "trusting Christ."[33] He wrote a special prayer designed for signing and placing in a person's Bible:

Dear Jesus, I give myself to thee. I give thee my mind to think through;
I give Thee my eyes to see through; I give Thee my hands to turn the
pages of Thy book, and to work for Thee; I give Thee my feet to run
your errands with, and I promise Thee that I shall never carry me
into a place where I have to leave Thee at the door; I give Thee all
my family and relatives; I give Thee all my possessions; I give Thee
my time and talent; I give Thee all I think of and all I do not think
of this ——— day of ———, 190-, at ——— o'clock —m.[34]

Each Crittenton meeting ended with an altar service at which those intending to lead a new life came forward and received a copy of Crittenton's prayer for their Bibles. As the prayer illustrates, Charles Crittenton believed that true Christianity required sacrifice and practical service. He was convinced that no matter how dramatic an individual's personal conversion was, work for others was needed to complete the process. Financial contributions alone were not sufficient—dedication of both "time and talent" was needed.

Crittenton's evangelical fervor shaped his view of prostitutes. The term *rescue work* itself underscored his conviction that prostitutes wished to leave their profession and were only waiting for assistance to do so. Crittenton often claimed that there were three hundred thousand fallen women in the United States and that the greatest stumbling block to their rescue was society's failure to accept the reformed prostitute. He wrote: "We are upon the ocean; three hundred thousand girls are struggling in the water; their helpless hands are stretched out for aid; their screams and cries fill the air, all about them there in life-boats safe, others in pleasure crafts are sailing by. There is plenty of room for all these girls, but no hand is held out to them; no craft stops to take them on. Perishing! Perishing! Forever Perishing."[35] Crittenton preached that God would punish Christians who refused to aid prostitutes and other sinners. Many in his audiences, particularly women, were receptive to this plea, especially to the idea that the prostitutes were "screaming" for rescue and waiting only for a helping hand to snatch them from their lives of sin.

Some evangelicals questioned whether fallen women could be saved at all. Crittenton, an expert on biblical passages dealing with this question, responded with stories of the woman at the well in Samaria, the woman at the House of Simon the Pharisee, and of course Mary Magdalene. One of his co-workers, Howard Morton, wrote a poem called "Magdalen" expressing Crittenton's own convictions, a poem that frequently appeared in FC literature:

Take her by the hand, my brothers;
Lift her from the dust;
Speak to her in loving kindness
Words of hope and trust.
In the night of sin no longer
Let her footsteps roam—
To the light of love and virtue
Lead her gently home.

Ye, with mothers, wives and sisters,
Pure and true and good,
Spurn her not, though stained, yet holy,
Is her womanhood.
Smite her not with your reproaches
Speak not of her shame—
But from scorn of men defend her
In the Saviour's name.

See her, in her woman's anguish,
Kneeling humbly there;
Every glance a cry for mercy,
Every tear a prayer.
And if manly hearts are in you,
Noble, loyal, brave,
With the shield of your protection
guard her now, and save.

Tenderly an erring sister
Back to virtue guide;
Holier work your hands can do not
In this Christmas tide.
Turn her from the path of sorrow
She hath darkly trod,
And in mercy lead the wanderer
Home to peace and God.[36]

Morton's poem illustrates an important tenet in Crittenton's philosophy: "Manly" men had a special responsibility to aid prostitutes—their "protection" was necessary for reformed prostitutes to succeed, and all "noble, loyal, brave" (truly masculine) men would defend these women. Men's reproach had contributed to the fallen woman's plight, and men had a duty to help in her redemption. Crittenton appealed to men using the same type of argument that women moral reformers had been voicing since the antebellum period: fallen women could be saved if only good Christians would reach out to them. Crittenton's plea to other men set him apart from most other moral reformers and aligned him with a burgeoning movement to accentuate and confirm men's masculinity in the light of the changing nature of society.[37]

Many rescue homes prominently displayed lilies, and rescue workers often carried them, symbolic of Mary Magdalene who had been first to visit Christ's tomb on Easter. Crittenton and his followers emphasized that, in their view, all people were sinners, and while the nature of the prostitute's sin might seem at first to be particularly damning, Crittenton people were in fact "on a dead level with her."[38] This sympathetic view of the prostitute, along with the strong conviction that every Christian (regardless of gender) had a responsibility to aid fallen women, were keystones of the Crittenton organization's philosophy.

Religious conversion was, in Crittenton's view, the first step in rescue work. At all of his public meetings he appealed to prostitutes to confess their sins and lead Christian lives, and much to the surprise of observers, many prostitutes did so. A reporter described the scene at a Crittenton meeting in Knoxville, Tennessee, where "fallen women from the lowest walks of life" came to hear Crittenton speak. According to the reporter, these women cried in response to Crittenton's appeal and were the first to come forward at the end of the service. The reporter concluded, "Nothing like this meeting has ever been held here before."[39] Crittenton was not content with a prostitute's reformation; in his view only spiritual regeneration could result in a new life.

Crittenton united a commitment to ending the double standard with his conviction that the redemption of prostitutes was possible, and he preached that both men and women should be sexually pure. Every issue of the Crittenton organization's magazine contained the pledge: "Devoted to the protection of the young, the rescue of the fallen, and the maintenance of a single standard of morals equally binding on men and women."[40] Crittenton advocated an end to the double standard on both religious and practical grounds. Women who were unwilling prostitutes would be able to testify against the men responsible and have their testimony accepted. These men, Crittenton thought, should be punished. Like many contemporaries, Crittenton and his followers believed it was healthful to exercise self-control and refrain from thinking about sex too often: an end to the double standard would thus benefit men. Finally, Crittenton favored abolition of the double standard because this would make it easier for women who had been reformed at Florence Crittenton missions and other rescue institutions to rejoin society. He often pointed out that while women would cross the room to avoid contact with a reformed prostitute, the prostitute's former patrons were probably frequent drawing-room guests.[41] Consequently, Crittenton emphasized that his missions reformed men as well as women, and he directed his efforts at both prostitutes and society as a whole.[42]

Like earlier purity reformers, Crittenton stressed the importance of both boys and girls receiving sexual information—a step Crittenton believed would go far toward ending prostitution. He wrote in *Ladies' Home Journal* that during his twenty-five years of rescue work with "tens of thousands" of "unfortunate girls," he had found that 50 percent of them "took the first step in their sad career because of lack of knowledge."[43] The responsibility for instructing children rested with parents, especially the mother. While opposed to the double standard, Crittenton and his followers still believed that women were the protectors of morality. In a period when polite society seldom, if ever, discussed sexual topics, many parents found it difficult to supply their children sexual information. Crittenton himself admitted, "I failed to realize that questions pertaining to sex are normal, fundamental and absolutely inevitable with the young." Crittenton worked to educate parents as to the importance of providing information regarding sexuality.[44]

One of the earliest and better known Florence Crittenton tracts, Mrs. Charlton Edholm's *Traffic in Girls and the Florence Crittenton Mission*, provided parents with examples of how the subject might be broached. If the mother offered an inaccurate response to a child's questions regarding where younger brothers or sisters came from, adverse effects would result when the child later learned the truth. Avoidance or ambiguity might lead the child to believe "everything connected with reproduction is 'naughty' and a feeling of contempt and horror for the organs of reproduction" could result. Instead, the mother should answer, "Darling, God gave little brother to Mamma. For a little while before he was born, while tiny legs and arms were getting strong enough to bear the cold, God let him stay in a little house right under Mamma's heart, where there could not a breath of air touch him." When the child was a little older, the parents were to discuss physiological changes that would come "to prepare them for the most sacred duties which God Almighty ever confers on human beings, those of parentage, in the creation of immortal souls." Edholm warned parents not to underestimate the role of the father in these discussions in recognition of the Crittenton philosophy that while sexual relations within marriage were natural, both men and women should be sexually pure outside of marriage.[45] While establishing a firm position on the issue of sexual purity, Edholm (and Charles Crittenton as well) did not follow some of her contemporaries in portraying sexual relations as potentially sinful. Rather, she emphasized the significant role of sexuality in the lives of both men and women. In this respect, the Crittenton organization voiced a more modern view than many reformers. In fact, approbation for healthy sexual relations within marriage tended to characterize Crittenton pronouncements on the topic.

Edholm preferred the use of the lily in teaching these lessons, since the stamen and pistils are easily seen and clearly formed. Children would sense the "simplicity, beauty, and purity of these flowers." Maple trees and pussy willows also made excellent examples, and Edholm suggested a magnifying glass to enhance the child's interest. Older children could learn from bird and fish eggs, especially fish eggs, since they are transparent. Edholm concluded, "The mother who is to her children the embodiment of purity, can reveal these truths with such sweet sacredness, and can create in the children's minds such reverence that an obscene story will seem like profanation and an impure act like sacrilege from which they would recoil in horror."[46] The WCTU distributed this tract as part of its educational campaign. Although Edholm's discussion seems quaint to modern readers, it approached this delicate subject in a way that WCTU women deemed suitable and acceptable while still conveying the basic sexual information many parents sought.

Charles Crittenton's philosophy that it was possible to save prostitutes, end the double standard, and use preventive sex education helped shape the development of all Florence Crittenton rescue work. Crittenton insisted that FC workers be professed Christians. At the sixteenth anniversary of the New York Florence Night Mission in 1899, a board member noted, "We dare to stand up and say that none but Christians shall be on our Board. It does not matter how good people are, we have quietly said to them, we can have nobody in it that does not hold up Jesus and speak for him."[47] Crittenton publications reminded readers of the role of prayer in enabling them to meet their tremendous responsibilities. At the end of a typical FC convention, a consecration service took place and the workers clasped hands and sang "Blest Be the Tie that Binds."[48] There is no doubt that for most Crittenton workers their earthly fellowship was akin to that in the Kingdom of Heaven.

Crittenton workers clearly believed that such a tie did bind them together and was in fact an integral part of their work. Florence Crittenton people thought this evangelical religious spirit was necessary both for their own strength and in order to help fallen women. F. May Gordon advised her co-workers, "The rescue worker whose very being is constantly drained physically, mentally, and spiritually needs the full equipment of the mind that was in Jesus Christ." She warned that without this workers were in danger of being like Jonah, "called to a special work" but unable to complete the assigned task.[49] Aware that some people drew away from FC work due to this outspoken Christianity, Charles Crittenton proclaimed, "We cannot lower the standard; it is Christ first, last and at all times."[50]

Indeed, Crittenton volunteers and contributors sought to rescue fallen women partly to benefit their own souls. As Crittenton wrote to a discouraged worker who wanted to resign, "What is God going to do with us if we do not do what he tells us to do, viz: 'Preach the Gospel to every creature?'"[51] When people contributed money to the Crittenton mission, Crittenton assured them that he "never forgot to first tell Jesus" about the contribution before acknowledging receipt and Crittenton was certain that Jesus had already "whispered in their ear" promising eternal life.[52] Conversely, Crittenton workers were convinced that their own relationship with God aided their efforts to assist prostitutes. Rescue worker Clara Howard described sitting next to a very repulsive woman covered with vermin and filth at a mission meeting. Due to a God-given impulse, she put her arms around the woman and kissed her. This act resulted in the woman's conversion and for Crittenton workers was another example of God's power. Crittenton workers were eager to embrace the idea that a simple act of love and/or acceptance was often all that was needed to help a fallen woman begin her reformation. At the same time, the Crittenton description of the woman as "repulsive" points to the considerable gulf workers perceived between themselves and those they sought to aid. And why wouldn't a middle-class worker find this woman's lack of personal hygiene both distasteful and deplorable? However, Clara Howard was able to repress her aversion, at least temporarily, and was rewarded for her effort. The lesson was not lost on readers of the story. Florence Crittenton workers no doubt often had to swallow deep-seated feelings of repugnance. Crittenton workers labored in close contact with women they sometimes found objectionable on a number of accounts. But Crittenton people's commitment was deep, and as Robert Crunden has explained, middle-class Crittenton workers were able to draw closer to women of other socioeconomic groups through their associations.[53] At the very least, exposure to women of other classes heightened Florence Crittenton workers' awareness of poverty and its effects.

Charles Crittenton devoted at least one night of his revival meetings in each city to the discussion of fallen women, and he used these occasions to recruit volunteers. Thousands of people in towns throughout the

United States heard the stories of little Florence, of Crittenton's conversion, and of the Crittenton mission work. They responded to Crittenton's descriptions of girls in the river heading for the falls, with rescue workers "rope in hand . . . throwing out the life buoy . . . to the struggling ones."[54] Crittenton's April 1899 revival in Spokane, Washington, was that city's largest to date, and during it, he raised more than ten thousand dollars for Spokane rescue work, along with donations of land, plumbing supplies, and lumber.[55] This result was typical of Crittenton's evangelical meetings.

Crittenton nearly always related the tale of Nellie Gilroy, orphaned at age eleven. One day a man came up to her in front of a jewelry store and asked if she would like a diamond ring and a watch and chain. Of course she answered in the affirmative. The man explained that he owned the store and if Nellie would come upstairs, she could have them. The man raped her, and since she had only fourteen months schooling, had lost her virginity, and had no means of support, she became a prostitute.

Nellie made a great deal of money and came to the Florence Night Mission every evening "in a new dress of gay-colored silk or satin, and yet with all her apparent prosperity she was far from happy, for she knew she was that object of pity and contempt—a fallen woman."[56] (Although most prostitutes failed to gain wealth from their profession, attendees at Crittenton meetings appreciated the sacrifice that a prostitute in Nellie's economic situation would have to make if she chose to give up her occupation.)[57] Nellie did not know about Christ, and although Crittenton prayed and exhorted her to reform, she believed there was no hope. Every day, even while on a ship to Europe, Charles Crittenton prayed for Nellie Gilroy.

While Crittenton was abroad, Gilroy heard some people singing hymns and went to the copy of the Psalms that Crittenton had given to her. She determined to change and told the man with whom she was living that he must leave. Nellie loved "Mr. R" and wanted to send for him again, but her faith kept her from doing so. Needing some reassurance, she sent a note to Crittenton asking him to come and, although the note did not reach him at once, Nellie persevered and kept reading her Psalms. When Crittenton arrived, Nellie's conversion took place, and she went to live at the Florence Night Mission. Eventually, Mr. R., who was after all an honorable man, repented, became a Christian, and they were married at the mission. Nellie wrote a poem that Crittenton workers often read aloud at services and included in their leaflets:

To the Wanderer
By Mrs. E—— R——

Dear one, why wander in sorrow alone?
   There's one loving heart that bids you to come
And lay your poor weary head on His breast;
   Ah, there you'll find comfort, yea peace and rest.

Oh, what have you gained since first you did roam
   From the scenes of your childhood's sweet, simple home?
Where are the pleasures, the friendships you wed?—
   Your tired heart whispers: All, all are dead.

Then why not accept the hand of a Friend
   Who offers to guide you safe to life's end?—
Then tenderly bear you to His bright home
   Where hearts ne'er grow weary, where tears are unknown.

Tell the dear Saviour you're tired of sin,
   Ask for His help a new life to begin;
He'll bless you, aid you, and give you sweet rest,
   And wash the dark past from your poor weary breast.

Another so loving, gentle and kind
   Believe me, dear wand-rer, you never'll find;
Pardon and mercy, He freely will give,
   His great love is boundless, accept it and live.

Surely such friendship you cannot well spurn,
   So why slight Him longer?—DEAR ONE RETURN,
He's patiently waiting, ope' your heart's door
   And promise to love Him and wander no more.[58]

In her poem, Nellie stressed two key elements of Crittenton work—that women were anxious to leave prostitution and were only waiting for the opportunity to do so, and that religious conversion would aid the prostitute in beginning a new life. Nellie's story supported the idea that wealth and finery could not substitute for a Christian life, and that boundless love and friendship awaited the fallen woman who would only reach out to take them. A prostitute could free herself from her "dark past" if she could only open her "heart's door" and promise to mend her ways. Nellie Gilroy's story helped create an image that was central to the success of Charles Crittenton's efforts—a picture of prostitutes as both viable and worthy candidates for redemption.

After hearing this and similar stories, members of Crittenton's audience often expressed an interest in joining the work, and he usually met with leading members of local churches and other civic leaders to organize

Florence Crittenton Purity Circles. These circles sprang up in hundreds of locations, their object to "reach out a helping hand to our less fortunate sisters, and by your sympathy and love help them to a better life."[59]

In the beginning, sympathy and love were all that Crittenton circles had to offer fallen women. Each circle meeting began with a prayer for the three hundred thousand fallen women in the United States, and it was a common practice for members to recite a newly memorized Bible verse at roll call. Various speakers, including WCTU activists, discussed purity and temperance problems, and the members sometimes pursued a regular course of reading and discussed it at the meetings.[60]

Crittenton encouraged circles to concentrate their efforts on so-called preventive work. In accordance with his faith in education as a solution to the prostitution problem, "Mother's Meetings" were a frequent circle program feature. At these sessions speakers addressed topics such as "The Necessity of Instructing Children on Questions of Vital Importance."[61] Crittenton organizers were careful to be circumspect in these presentations while making certain that the problem of prostitution received attention. Professor H. P. Van Lieu, one-time leader of FC mission work, offered to present his talk "The Slums by Flashlight" to circles. The presentation included photographs shown by "the powerful modern projection apparatus" but promised to be "chaste, and at the same time realistic."[62] Circle committees advertised the meetings, which were open to the public, and Crittenton people stressed how essential this work was to winning the battle against prostitution. Dr. Laura Morgan wrote, "It requires far less knowledge and skill to prevent disease and vice then it does to cure them when once established. A little knowledge may be sufficient to prevent an evil, but to cure the same is often beyond the power of the wisest."[63] Crittenton workers zealously applied themselves to their preventive work.

In small towns such as Wallace, Idaho, and Zanesville, Ohio, these circle meetings gave women an opportunity to discuss a topic of great interest and excitement and do their civic duty at the same time. As one circle member in a small community noted, the meetings made it possible "that our members might know something of the wickedness in the world outside our little village."[64] Rescue work itself was a preventive, as young girls who joined circles learned about the social evil firsthand. Workers claimed that "if a girl who had been thus acquainted with every phase of impurity becomes a wanton character, it is because of innate evil and absolute lack of natural refinement and goodness."[65] To this end, circles published pamphlets or newsletters and distributed them throughout the community.[66]

The distribution of literature warning girls of the pitfalls waiting for them and advertising the services available at FC missions was another circle function. Members placed literature in waiting rooms, reading rooms, and in taxi cabs and other modes of public transportation. Boston circle members had cards printed in a number of different languages for their missionary, Miss Skelton, to distribute in the Lowell mills.[67] Circles informed YMCA, YWCA, and WCTU members of the FC efforts and urged them to contact a Crittenton worker if they knew of a girl in need of assistance. A typical pamphlet explained Florence Crittenton work and also proclaimed that the facilities were open to anyone.[68] This type of activity allowed circle members to participate in the Crittenton movement without having actual contact with women of "questionable" reputations. The tales of seduction and abandonment prominent in Florence Crittenton literature led women to sympathize with fallen women and to expend considerable effort in providing them access to assistance. However, only a minority of Crittenton workers were willing to meet face to face with women whose experience and situation was so different from theirs.

In some cities, especially those without a Florence Crittenton home, a few circle members engaged in rescue work. Occasionally, circles employed a missionary whose job was to visit jails, saloons, mills, and factories where she would come in contact with girls who might be tempted to begin lives of sin. Missionaries provided temporary assistance to girls who needed it and also arranged for prostitutes wishing to begin a new life to go into Florence Crittenton homes. Some circles operated Florence Crittenton shelters as stop-gaps until workers could provide transportation or make other arrangements to facilitate a girl's entry into one of the homes. According to one historian, these shelters were the rescue workers' endeavor that provided most practical assistance to women on the streets.[69] In other areas the circles organized volunteer rescue committees to visit red-light districts, where they would sing, pray, and "weep over mother's girls"—actions circle members believed effectively demoralized the vice districts.[70] They were sure that most prostitutes wanted to leave and were only waiting for an opportunity. One rescue worker told of a girl who could not leave the brothel because she did not own a street dress. When inmates at the local Crittenton home quickly donated a complete outfit, the girl entered the home.[71] This episode again emphasized how desperate fallen women were to leave their environment and how a seemingly insignificant act of assistance could facilitate a woman's rescue. The former brothel resident was cognizant of her separation from polite society and recognized that even her attire branded her as an outcast. She did not want to risk embarrassment or censure by appearing in public without more appropriate clothing. Crittenton women were usually quick to point out incidences of their charges' charity and involvement, prima facia evidence, they believed, of fallen women's support for Crittenton efforts.

Sometimes circle workers were reticent to engage in these pursuits, but seasoned vice workers reminded them, "We must ever remember that these girls are human; they have mothers and fathers; once they were pure, once they were the joy of some home." A Crittenton rescue worker advised potential volunteers that they could never show disgust or "shrinking from filth, real and figurative" but must demonstrate their sympathy. Sister Charlotte often proclaimed that the only way to help these women was to love them. These sentiments indicate conflicting Crittenton views of prostitutes. Workers had to be dedicated in order to overcome their abhorrence of women involved in prostitution. In most cases, only a deep-seated religious conviction and genuine concern for the women victims could overcome the workers' distaste to a degree that would allow her to participate in rescue work. Even so, few FC workers could completely set aside their aversion.[72] These attitudes also explain why Crittenton people directed some of their work toward women who were not prostitutes.

So-called tenement-house work illustrated the interclass nature of rescue committee activities and aspects of committee work separate from the attempts to rescue prostitutes. Committee members visited women in poor districts and talked about religion, and they proudly reported the number of conversions made among these women each month. A long article in a Crittenton publication related the experience of a worker who went to visit a woman others had tried unsuccessfully to reach. The rescue worker knocked on the door and gained entrance by asking to see the woman's baby. According to the worker, God made the baby allow her to hold him without crying, providing an opportunity to talk with the mother. The mother said that she had married an infidel and forsaken the Lord, yet the worker reported that by her visit's end the woman was "sobbing in my arms, and seeking her Saviour's forgiveness in heartfelt penitence." The article gave no indication that the woman was too poor to care for her child, or in danger of becoming a prostitute. Neither did the worker offer the woman any practical assistance. The woman's return to Christianity was, according to the Crittenton people, enough to make this a successful case.[73] There were no reports of workers visiting well-to-do women, regardless of their marital choices or religious preferences. Florence Crittenton volunteers were convinced that their own values represented the best blueprint for women to follow. At the same time, it is evident from this account that the workers had no real leverage over the woman in question—she was living in her own apartment, not seeking monetary aid, not subject to any control on the part of the Crittenton people. She welcomed visits from the Crittenton worker, perhaps as a salve to the isolation that often accompanies the motherhood of infants and small children. Certainly, the Crittenton worker rejoiced in the success of her efforts.

Early Crittenton missions also provided assistance to girls who were not prostitutes and to their families. Boston mission case 161 provides an excellent 1896 example. A girl's father had searched for her for four months and, according to Boston workers, had placed her photo in police stations throughout the city. Police Officer Nixon located the girl in Johnson's Dance Hall and brought her to the Florence Crittenton home after midnight. Workers "restored" her to her grateful father. Although they did not take the girl's preferences into account, the workers saved the girl from jail and helped a frantic parent.[74] This scenario was replayed on countless occasions in many Crittenton homes.

The Florence Crittenton Rescue League, under the direction of Field Secretary Orrin B. Booth, strove to foster consistency and better organization in rescue work. The league's badge featured a blue enamel ribbon across a red enamel globe, symbolizing the binding together of homes and individuals involved in Florence Crittenton efforts. The motto "A little child shall lead them," found on the ribbon, obviously referred to little Florence. In the center of the pin was a white star bearing the words "Branch, N.F.C.M.," and "Florence Crittenton Rescue League" was on an outer rim of white enamel. Thus the badge featured the FC colors blue and white, plus the color red, so that the American colors were present. The badges cost fifty cents, but the NFCM numbered each one and reserved the right to recall a badge and refund the fee at any time. This was to ensure that no unscrupulous person took advantage of the Florence Crittenton name either to raise money or to snare girls looking for help.[75]

Rescue league volunteers visited girls in saloons and resorts in the hopes of recruiting home residents. Booth and other league leaders carefully screened prospective rescue workers, who had to be consecrated, have pure thoughts, and believe in the possibility of salvation for the "very lowest outcast." Rescue workers could not drink, dance, or smoke. Only strong and mature Christians could cope with rescue work, as Booth noted: "We go into the very jaws of Hell, and only those having on the whole armor of God can afford to risk almost direct contact with Satan himself and his demoniac Hosts." In asserting that the subjects of Crittenton rescue attempts rivaled Satan in wickedness, Booth revealed the Crittenton workers' estimation of their task, and it is possible to detect a certain smugness in this self-description. Crittenton workers sincerely believed that their efforts represented a direct battle with evil.[76] Workers' conviction that it was possible to save even the most hopeless sinner was an essential part of the Crittenton outlook. At the same time, the excitement and exhilaration a worker would undoubtedly feel at such a direct confrontation with the forces of darkness probably drew volunteers to the Florence Crittenton Rescue Band. In a period when evangelical protestants were committed to finding practical applications of their Christianity, rescue work was an especially appropriate pursuit.

The tactics for rescue work became more established. Booth instructed workers not to wear their fine clothing or jewelry when conducting rescue work (an indication of rescue workers' class). Once in a resort, the workers were to be kind to proprietors and employees and pretend not to notice violations of the law. According to Booth, these actions would guarantee that resort owners would continue to allow rescue workers to operate. Each worker selected a man or woman to talk with individually and wrote down the names of those they contacted on concealed pieces of paper. League members included these names in the written reports they passed on to the local missionary, who subsequently visited during the day, when fallen women had more leisure time. Booth warned workers not to patronize the girls and not to tell them that they were going straight to hell as "she probably knows it only too well." The workers were to sympathize with the girls and avoid arguments and probing questions. These tactics were designed to gain the girls' confidence and eventually to convince them to leave their old lives. Male workers visited girls alone only in "extreme circumstances" and avoided all physical contact with the possible exception of a handshake. These male workers' role was primarily to serve as escorts for the female workers and they usually occupied their time talking with men in the resorts.[77] Experienced rescue workers warned newcomers not to touch their mouths with their hands once they entered the resorts and to wash themselves and their clothing immediately upon returning home. Women workers were especially careful to turn their cheeks slightly if a fallen woman kissed them so as to avoid contact with "unspeakable" diseases.[78] Since information regarding the transmission of venereal disease was limited at best, Crittenton workers recognized that close proximity to women who frequented saloons and other night spots was risky business indeed. They refused to allow possible exposure to the diseases to prevent their rescue band activities. At the same time, workers were certainly cognizant of their own status, and an element of class pretentiousness is apparent in workers' attitudes and actions.

Usually the workers left tracts with the people they visited. One of the most popular items was the poem "Beautiful Snow":

> Once I was pure as the snow, but I fell,
> Fell like the snow-flakes from heaven to hell,
> Fell to be trampled like filth in the street,
> Fell to be scoffed, to be spit on, and beat;
> Pleading, cursing, dreading to die,
> Selling my soul to whoever would buy;
> Dealing in shame for a morsel of bread,
> Hating the living and fearing the dead.
> Merciful God! have I fallen so low?
> And yet I was once like the beautiful snow.[79]

Through the poem, the rescue league members made a personal appeal to each girl in keeping with Crittenton's view that individual conversion was the only cure for prostitution. "Beautiful Snow" speaks to the low level that fallen women occupied in the eyes of the poet. At the same time, the poem expressed the Crittenton conviction that women involved in prostitution were not beyond redemption, only in need of a prodding to change their lives. A modern observer might easily dismiss this tactic as ineffective and naïve, but frequent reports of miraculous successes confirmed workers' convictions that their methods did indeed produce results. Their faith in women's potential for change separated them from the mainstream of society.

The Boston mission reported case 33, "one of the most notorious women in Boston." After she had been arrested numerous times, the police cautioned, "That woman is doomed and damned. Do not waste a breath on her." Crittenton workers persisted, and eventually the woman agreed to go to the New York mission and into Mother Prindle's capable hands. The reformed woman wrote to Boston workers, "Tell the girls that I thought I never would get salvation, but, praise God, I have found Jesus Christ at last. I am table-girl in this Home and by the grace of God I'm going to be table-girl in Heaven."[80] This testimonial illustrates the limits of the Crittenton organization's vision: the rescued prostitute's aspiration to become a "table-girl in Heaven," while a worthy goal, was not one likely to provide a living for her during her lifetime. This woman did not envision herself seated at the heavenly table but serving, and this is perhaps a clue to expectations on the part of both workers and subjects. Nevertheless, the Crittenton volunteers persevered and undoubtedly had some beneficial effects on their charges. Case 33 conveyed to her former associates that she had achieved a great deal. Clearly, the woman in case 33 was no longer regarded as hopeless—in either her or the Crittenton people's eyes.

The story of the establishment of rescue work in Chicago illustrates the small beginnings of Crittenton efforts. In 1886 a strong WCTU contingent, including Frances Willard herself and a local female physician, Dr. Kate Bushnell, braved an undesirable part of town and rented a "dark, dingy, forbidding apartment on Fourth Avenue." With hard work, the women transformed the apartment into an inviting spot where a "poor inebriate" could get a cup of coffee while "making her daily rounds of saloons." The Crittenton volunteers were fully aware of the difference between themselves and the women who dropped by the apartment, but they were willing to brave the unsavory neighborhood and to put up with less-than-ideal conditions due to their commitment to the rescue work concept. The workers' description of the origins of WCTU/Crittenton rescue work in Chicago is telling on another account. At least in their own view, they only provided a haven, albeit a temporary one, for less-fortunate women. They did not express any expectation that these women would not go from the WCTU apartment to local saloons. According to the workers, the fact that they provided some comfort for these women was enough to label the venture a success. The women were obviously proud that they possessed the courage and determination necessary to establish a foothold in the saloon neighborhood. Certainly they risked society's censure by pursuing their work unaccompanied, at night, and in an unsavory part of town.[81]

Crittenton workers noted how their activities often reaped unexpected rewards. When Chicago workers visited several brothels in 1901, no residents chose to leave with them. A few days later, however, the workers were surprised when two of the women they had encountered in the vice district brought a young girl and turned her over to the Crittenton people. Crittenton workers were pleased that the prostitutes perceived the Crittenton establishment as a place where the girl would receive protection—no questions asked. Workers reported that the girl was "doing well" and saw the incident as an example of a successful Crittenton endeavor.[82]

As many as ten or twelve circles in a metropolitan area contributed to the support of the local home. Frequently, circles held meetings at the home and provided entertainments for the inmates such as readings, music, and refreshments. Circle activities varied with locality and the interests of the circle members. Some women sewed clothing for inmates and organized sales of embroidery and other items to raise money for the home. Circle members wrote notes to home residents during the Christmas season, often enclosing a hair ribbon or some other trinket. Initially, $12.50 paid for an inmate's stay in a Florence Crittenton home for one year. Often, money-making projects and donation drives used that sum as a goal, thus allowing the circle to sponsor a local woman's residency in an FC home.[83] Circles might contribute to the upkeep of the home's physical plant. For example, the Nelson, British Columbia, circle furnished the Nelson Room in the Spokane, Washington, home. During the summer, many circles raised money to enable home inmates to enjoy picnics and similar outings.[84] Portland, Oregon, circle members purchased jars and distributed them to women in various parts of Oregon interested in rescue work. When the women did their canning, they simply canned extra jars for the Crittenton home.[85] Thus homes relied on circles for financial support and assistance in running the home. Circle members could choose a number of avenues for involvement in rescue work.

While the early Florence Crittenton homes were combined with missions, mission work came first. However, this began to change with Charles Crittenton's association with the WCTU, probably the best-established social-purity agency. The WCTU's Social Purity Department operated some rescue homes with the same object as the Florence Night Mission, but this activity was not a top priority with the WCTU, and the homes were often poorly managed and in financial difficulty. WCTU members were most interested in preventive work, and many agreed with Jane Addams's opinion that "there is something particularly distasteful and distressing in personal acquaintance with its victims."[86]

Charles Crittenton met WCTU president Frances Willard at that organization's 1892 national convention and eventually agreed to donate five thousand dollars to open five new institutions under WCTU auspices, provided they were called Florence Crittenton homes. Under this agreement the WCTU opened institutions in Denver; Portland, Oregon; Chicago; Fargo, North Dakota; and Norfolk, Virginia.[87] The partnership was so successful that Frances Willard offered Crittenton an office in the national WCTU—the first offered to any man—informing him that "no other man has so helped with the poor dear FORGOTTEN ones."[88] Willard's stunning endorsement illuminates Charles Crittenton's established position as a rescue worker. These WCTU homes later became part of the Florence

Crittenton national organization and the operation of Crittenton homes soon became a primary FC activity. According to their constitution, the homes were "to give aid and comfort to needy, erring, and unfortunate women, in the well grounded assurance that to raise the fallen and rescue the perishing is a divinely appointed work."[89]

In keeping with Charles Crittenton's views concerning the redemption of prostitutes, religion was of the utmost importance in early Crittenton homes. An 1899 constitution demanded morning and evening services, plus three extra Bible study meetings a week. Each girl admitted to a Crittenton home received a Bible to use at all religious services and was required to memorize a Bible verse weekly. Crittenton workers encouraged their charges toward religious conversion by simple methods such as hanging a picture of the compassionate Christ in the sitting room where the girls would see it each day or displaying a picture of Florence to remind the girls of her purity and to encourage them to emulate it.[90]

Workers considered religious conversion the test of whether or not a girl was truly rescued. "Rescue from Sin by Refuge in Christ" was the motto of one home. When making reports, matrons would keep track of the number of conversions and Charles Crittenton was proud that an average of 60 percent of these converted girls "stood by their promises," and he claimed that in some homes the percentage was as high as 93 percent. One home's matron exalted, "We have the assurance that many of the names of the mother's daughters that are recorded in our books are also written in the Lamb's Book of Life."[91] Certain rooms in the homes were decorated as memorials to the loved ones of contributors, and matrons reserved these rooms for "saved" girls. Dr. C. D. Miller of Simi, California, furnished "Mary's Room" for the Washington, D.C., home. It was beautifully appointed in blue, white, and gold, with large blue satin banners lettered in gold inscribed with passages from the Bible such as "Go and sin no more." Pressures on inmates to proclaim their religious conversion were sometimes less than subtle.[92]

Girls who converted also "committed their darling babies into the Saviour's arms."[93] Many of these girls testified at local church meetings and similar gatherings despite some criticism of this practice. A worker explained, "There's more power in the sincere and earnest testimony of a saved sinner to draw others to Christ, than in any sermon that was ever preached."[94] The workers believed that the girls agreed and, as evidence, constantly quoted letters from saved girls. A former Chicago inmate wrote, "I have been anchored in this Anchorage for the past 14 years.

Its influences have done much good and my prayer this week is that many others may find this open door and the "light in the window" for them."[95] Crittenton workers labored to guarantee that this opportunity would be available for all girls.

To later observers much of what the workers accomplished in these early Crittenton homes appeared to be superficial at best, but volunteers thought they were making great strides. One home reported the story of a woman who, after a "step of faith which brought her into the Kingdom of God," agreed to contact her family. The family allowed her to return home, where, according to the matron, she made herself indispensable. The matron added, "We give this little history as it seems to be the highest ideal of rescue work."[96] During the later part of the nineteenth century, a family's community standing was tied to the reputation of female family members. The fact that this former Crittenton charge was restored to her place within the family structure was evidence enough of the efficacy of Crittenton efforts from the perspective of both the family and the girl. Although Crittenton workers' ambitions regarding their charges were clearly modest, the work made a difference in the lives of women. Perhaps more important, the Crittenton people believed their achievements warranted even greater expenditures of effort.[97]

In the ten years following his first encounter with the New York City prostitute, Charles N. Crittenton made tremendous strides in reaching his goal of providing aid and sympathy to these women. He had embarked on his career as an evangelist and had preached in cities across the country, and each Crittenton crusade bolstered the ranks of those eager to assist him in rescuing prostitutes. His sermons and writings helped form the image of prostitutes most Americans came to hold. Crittenton had established the Florence Night Mission in New York and similar institutions in California, and had forged an alliance with the WCTU that promised additional homes for the Crittenton chain. Homes were established in Shanghai, Tokyo, Marseille, and Mexico City as well.[98] Florence Crittenton Rescue bands operated in several cities, working to convince prostitutes that there were opportunities available to them. Florence Crittenton circles allowed women to actively engage in rescue work, organize educational programs, and publicize the Crittenton agenda.

Despite Crittenton's accomplishments, early rescue efforts were limited in scope. FC workers did not concern themselves with the broad social problems that often led to prostitution, only with the prostitute's repentance. Assured that the subject's soul was no longer in jeopardy, the

FC worker believed her responsibility ended. This placed early Florence Crittenton work clearly within the traditional parameters of rescue work and women's benevolence.

Charles Crittenton's endeavors tended to result in heightened enthusiasm during his revival meetings, but once Crittenton moved on, there was often an insufficient foundation for Crittenton work. As founder, chief source of financial support, and primary recruiter and fund raiser, Crittenton occupied a patriarchal role in the National Florence Crittenton Mission. He exercised leadership and control over the NFCM, and his gender, economic status, and evangelical fervor defined his role. Under Crittenton's direction, the NFCM made virtually no effort to bridge the gap that class and condition created between workers and their charges. Crittenton himself soon recognized that before the NFCM could move beyond the evangelically inspired revivalism that characterized its early years and establish itself as an important social welfare agency, a broader approach was necessary.

Chapter 2

Kate Waller Barrett:
Motherhood as a Means of Regeneration

> A partnership with God is Motherhood,
> What strength, what purity, what self control,
> What love, what wisdom, should belong to her
> Who helps God fashion an immortal soul.
> —*Florence Crittenton Magazine*, 1905

Rapid expansion of the Florence Crittenton chain followed the 1892 opening of the five Women's Christian Temperance Union Florence Crittenton homes. Because Charles Crittenton's evangelism consumed most of his time, this dramatic growth caused him to seek help with administrative tasks. He turned to Dr. Kate Waller Barrett for supervision and direction of Crittenton operations. Barrett, a transitional figure between nineteenth-century sentimental benevolence and twentieth-century professional social work, parlayed her Florence Crittenton efforts into a reputation as one of the period's most respected social-purity experts. She brought vision, fresh insight, and a decidedly female outlook to Florence Crittenton work, and the policies she established in relation to unmarried mothers served as a model for progressive reformers.

Barrett's ideas regarding the role of motherhood in society coincided with a burgeoning ideology celebrating the influence of motherhood, an ideology that became the central tenet of a considerable number of women in the late nineteenth and early twentieth century. Barrett's viewpoints epitomized many aspects of what historians have termed maternalism. As one historian has argued, maternalist women's groups figured "prominently

33

in turn-of-the-century social politics in the United States," and under Kate Waller Barrett's direction, the National Florence Crittenton Mission joined these groups. By widening the definition of family and even of motherhood itself, using a rhetoric of motherhood, and crossing class lines in the interest of families and mothers, Dr. Barrett achieved considerable success in changing women's lives for the better. The image of "mother" resonated deeply in American society—among both women and men—and Barrett capitalized on deep-seated emotional responses to convince Americans to address the plights of prostitutes and unmarried mothers. The centrality of motherhood to women's experience defined Barrett's philosophy and led her to positions that emphasized the differences between men and women (obviously men cannot experience motherhood), established the Crittenton mission squarely within the broader woman's movement, and legitimized women's public role through greater personal and political autonomy.[1]

Katherine Waller was born January 24, 1857, in Falmouth, Virginia, where her family owned several large plantations. The Wallers suffered considerable dislocation during the Civil War and for a time followed Kate's father, Colonel Withers Waller, from one Confederate camp to another. After the war and the loss of most of their wealth, the Wallers retired to Clifton Plantation, a small establishment neighboring the property of General Fitzhugh Lee. Katherine received her education at home, except for a year at a neighborhood school and two years at the Arlington Institute for Girls in Alexandria. Her background, upbringing, and education most certainly instilled the concepts of the "true woman," and Barrett gained a traditional southern view of woman's place, of propriety, and of gender relationships.

Kate married Episcopal minister Robert South Barrett on July 19, 1876. Their first parish was in the Butchertown section of Richmond, Virginia, a notorious slum area. One rainy night, shortly after the birth of the Barrett's first child, Robert South Jr., there was a knock at the door and a woman with a small baby in her arms stood outside. The Barretts asked her in, and Kate Barrett dressed the baby in some of young Robert's dry clothing and laid the baby in the crib with her own child.

While eating a meal, the woman told the story of her "fall." She was from a small town near Richmond and had accompanied a man to the city because he promised to marry her. Instead, after "ruining" her, he had deserted her. She was left with no way to support herself or her baby. As Kate looked at the two children lying side by side, she realized how different their futures would probably be, and she recognized the similarities

*Dr. Kate Waller Barrett, c. 1914. Courtesy of the National
Florence Crittenton Mission.*

between herself and the other woman: they were both country girls, and they had both fallen in love. The only difference according to Barrett was that the other woman had fallen in love with a bad man instead of a good one. Barrett felt a bond between herself and the other woman, and also a decided anger toward the unknown man who was the baby's father. She promised, "By the power of God that rules the Universe, I would spend my life in trying to wipe out some of the inequalities that were meted out to my sisters who were so helpless to help themselves."[2]

This experience differed markedly from Charles Nelson Crittenton's first encounter with the prostitutes in New York City, and Barrett's response also contrasted with Crittenton's. The woman Barrett met was not a prostitute, and Barrett viewed her as the victim of unfortunate circumstances rather than as a sinner. The shared experience of motherhood stood in bold relief in Barrett's mind, as did an awareness of women's plight. She believed the woman's dire straits reflected on her own status as a woman. One Barrett follower later explained, *"The curse is not a curse against the woman, but against the sex."*[3] This point of view played an integral part in Barrett's dealings with fallen women throughout her career. Her gender informed her viewpoint and led her to a path different from but parallel to that of Charles Crittenton. While Barrett shared Crittenton's desire to treat unfortunate women in a nonpunitive way, her compassion and vigor stemmed from her strong conviction that society's treatment of fallen women was a reflection of women's status in society. Both humanitarianism and self-interest shaped Barrett's activities as she sought to use the bond of maternalism to convince other women to join her in working to relieve the plight of fallen women.

When her husband became dean of St. Luke's Cathedral in Atlanta, Georgia, Kate Waller Barrett maintained her commitment to helping fallen women. Although the Barretts were actively involved in Atlanta society, Kate had her own agenda as well. Convinced that medical training would be of inestimable value in her efforts, Barrett attended the Women's Medical College of Georgia (often with two or three children in tow), receiving her medical degree in 1892 and the honorary degree of Doctor of Science in 1894. By this time, in addition to her duties as a clergyman's wife, Barrett was the mother of six children. To say that her medical education was a departure from the usual is an understatement. The title of doctor no doubt added to Barrett's credibility, and she strove throughout her career to establish herself as an expert in the field of rescue homes.[4]

When Barrett and some other Atlanta women planned to open a rescue home in their city, they learned the hard truth that many "respectable" citizens did not share their interest in fallen women. They hired Mrs. M. M. Wolfe of New Orleans to serve as matron, rented a house, and prepared to begin operations. When area residents complained about having the institution in their neighborhood, the ladies moved the home. This happened four times, and citizens eventually pressured the Atlanta City Council into passing an ordinance prohibiting rescue homes within the city limits.

Kate Barrett spoke before the city ministerial association, demanding that it work to repeal the act. She was the first woman to address that group, and she did so despite the opposition of several members of her husband's congregation. Barrett's speech convinced local ministers to prevail upon the city council to reverse its ruling and allow the rescue home to open. This incident illustrated a pattern in Florence Crittenton history and supports a key tenet of women's historiography. Women engaged in benevolent work often found themselves stepping outside the bounds of their traditional activities and roles in the interest of furthering their reform agendas. In most cases these women portrayed their actions not as rebellion against women's roles but as steps their reform programs mandated.[5] It is difficult to imagine that Barrett made her speech without her husband's approval; in fact, he facilitated her appearance before the ministerial association. The end result was the same, however, and Barrett often challenged the male-dominated power structure during her long career.

The Atlanta rescue home faced other problems as well. In particular, the women encountered difficulties in raising the necessary funds. Kate Barrett had read of Charles Crittenton's rescue work, and she wrote to him requesting assistance. He sent an experienced Florence Crittenton worker and a donation of five thousand dollars. The evangelist visited Atlanta in 1893 to attend the Christian Workers' Convention and to preach at St. Luke's Cathedral. On this occasion Barrett underwent a profound religious experience. Coupled with the powerful impression Crittenton made, the event led Barrett to become even more devoted to rescue work.

Barrett received an opportunity to expand her Florence Crittenton activities the next year when her husband was appointed general missioner of the Episcopal Church and the Barretts moved to Washington, D.C., site of the church's national offices. In 1895, Charles Crittenton took over the Hope and Help Mission, a WCTU-operated rescue home at 218 Third Street Northwest. Largely due to Barrett's influence, national administration of the NFCM moved from New York City to Washington, where the former Hope and Help Mission became national headquarters.

Following the early death of her husband on September 12, 1896, Barrett became general supervisor and organizer of the NFCM. Barrett was thirty-nine years old and still had young children. Although her husband left her a home in Alexandria, Virginia, and a small insurance policy that would have allowed Barrett to provide for her family, she was by then too committed to Crittenton work to abandon it. While Charles Crittenton continued his career as a preaching evangelist and recruiter, Barrett oversaw operation of the national organization. As a result of her numerous personal visits to local homes, the publication of a national magazine, her many books and pamphlets, and her administration of national headquarters, Barrett's philosophy eventually dominated the Florence Crittenton organization.

The mission exemplified women's institution building. Barrett's activities and the direction she led Florence Crittenton work expressed turn-of-the-century middle-class women's definition of vital issues. Barrett and her colleagues strove to improve conditions for other women and in the process often came to see their own situations in a new light. Barrett's sentimentalism, coupled with a nearly fanatical devotion to efficiency and practicality, presented a paradox.[6] Sometimes Barrett and her cohorts appeared schizophrenic as they sought to combine their devotion to their accustomed position with new approaches. Barrett, like other members of her generation of women reformers, including Jane Addams, used her traditional role as a springboard for reform activities and in the process she and other reformers altered women's place in American society forever. Under Kate Waller Barrett's leadership, the NFCM took on a distinctly female outlook that resulted eventually in substantial changes in mission activities and brought notions of maternalism to the forefront of Crittenton thinking.

Evangelical religion influenced Kate Waller Barrett's view of fallen women just as it did Charles N. Crittenton's. She wrote in 1897, "The only power that can save a fallen woman is the blood of Jesus Christ." Her attitude placed her firmly in agreement with members of the Episcopal Church who at the time were combining evangelicalism with social activism.[7] Thus Barrett thought that religious conversion was only the first step, not an end in itself, and she was convinced that Crittenton workers could offer more to their charges than salvation. She urged that fallen women receive both "employment and encouragement."[8] For Barrett, both objectives were integral parts of the Crittenton work. She believed Florence Crittenton institutions could equip their inmates to become productive members of society while boosting their self-esteem and sense of self worth. Unlike many of her contemporaries, for Barrett the practical considerations of making a living were a priority. Her organizational abilities, medical background, and willingness to experiment contributed immensely to the success of Florence Crittenton efforts in this direction.[9]

Barrett worked to bring order and some uniformity to the Crittenton organization. Under the auspices of the national organization, local homes received several forms of assistance as well as scrutiny. Crittenton, Barrett, and other officers spent considerable time visiting homes and making suggestions. Barrett trained field workers Ida Stewart Edgar, the Reverend Walker Lewis, and Anna Riggs to assist in the visitations of local homes and to engage in fundraising and volunteer recruitment. Their arduous work took them across the country. During one month in 1906, for example, Edgar was in Los Angeles, Lewis in Georgia, and Riggs was in Salt Lake City on her way to visit Helena, Montana, Crittenton workers.[10] Barrett coordinated field workers' efforts and kept in close contact with them via mail.

The national organization provided financial aid to local homes, and also often facilitated relationships between homes, particularly the transfer of an inmate from one home to another. The goal of these efforts was to ensure that homes across the country could, in fact, aid fallen women.[11] Crittenton people were quick to point out that while most national organizations gained their support from local groups, in the Crittenton situation, the opposite was true.

The NFCM received a charter by special act of Congress in 1893 "to aid and encourage destitute, homeless, and deprived women and men to seek reformation of character and responsibility and to reach positions of honorable self-support, especially to provide for women and young girls who have led profligate lives, or having been betrayed from the path of virtue are sincerely willing to reform."[12] At Barrett's request, Congress revised the charter in 1903 to enable the national organization to act as trustee for the property of any local home in case the local board could no longer perform that function. This gave Barrett an element of control over local property and, therefore, over local activities. The charter also provided a mechanism for Barrett, although a woman, to be in command even in situations in which the local FC work was under the direction of a man or group of men.[13] The organization considered the charter a national recognition of their role and function.

Kate Waller Barrett was especially proud of the establishment of the National Florence Crittenton Mission Training School for Christian Workers in 1898. Charles Crittenton financed the project, but Barrett guided the school's curriculum and operation. The training school prepared women for Florence Crittenton work, for other kinds of missionary duties, and for jobs in business. The emphasis on rescue work reflected Barrett's conviction that most experienced workers chose to enter a more attractive missionary field, leaving Crittenton institutions short of trained workers. Barrett touted the school as a place where "strong women of high principle" could learn to earn a living and gain financial independence. The goal of financial independence certainly flew in the face of conventional ideas of woman's place, as did the notion of a "strong woman," and Barrett joined other feminists in seeing a connection between the two.[14] Early in her career, Barrett noted her conviction that women could have, and in fact ought to have, the wherewithal for financial autonomy—a philosophy that would have a major impact on Crittenton work. Taken to its logical conclusion, Barrett's argument challenged male control.

Barrett stressed that women with training would be better able to serve Florence Crittenton interests than would other women, however well meaning. This is a major tenet of the beginning of professional social work.[15] Emphasizing that Crittenton and related efforts represented a career for women separate from male occupations was also an early example of the trend towards making social work a profession. As the *Florence Crittenton Magazine* explained succinctly in 1902, "Institutions where trained leaders are employed prove the progress made to be much greater than those where those who perform their duties have had no special training."[16] Barrett and her cohorts were leaders in establishing the notion that their efforts required skill and knowledge, not simply a desire to perform good works. Finding no suitable training program, the Crittenton organization developed its own.

Training school candidates were expected to possess the more traditional womanly traits of piety and domesticity. Consecration was an entrance requirement in keeping not only with Charles Crittenton's convictions but also with Barrett's. A prospective student had to lead a sincere Christian life; have a sympathetic attitude toward erring girls; have some education, including knowledge of the Bible; have disciplinary and executive ability; and possess a knowledge of domestic science. Students accepted into the program lived at the school and paid fifty dollars for their room, board, and tuition.[17]

The course of study and the operation of the training school underscored Barrett's vision for the National Florence Crittenton Mission. Under the supervision of May Gordon, assistant general superintendent of the NFCM and training school director, students had to accept a fairly strict regime. They wore uniforms consisting of plain blue seersucker gowns and white caps, cuffs, and aprons. The school also required that each student have a watch, preferably with a second hand, a white cannon cloth dress, a neat street suit, an outside wrap, and shoes with rubber heels. Students rose each morning at 6:00, submitted daily written reports of their work, and received visitors only after the superintendent had given permission. The school's general rules indicated that students were to eat their meals together, be "dignified and gentle" at all times, and, perhaps most tellingly, to "dwell together in peace and harmony."[18] These requirements illustrated Barrett's definition of both a satisfactory home life and a well-run institution; it is no coincidence that Florence Crittenton home schedules were similar.

The course of study included five major areas: Bible study, principles and methods of rescue work and moral reform, medical and nursing, English and commercial (vocational business), and domestic sciences. Religious services were an integral part of the school's program. Each week there was a consecration service, a Bible reading by the superintendent, and several prayer meetings, in addition to daily morning and evening services, daily services in the hospital wards and the children's department, and two Sunday services. Two prominent Washington, D.C., ministers taught history of the Bible and the life of Christ. May Gordon lectured on the Acts of the Apostles, and Barrett taught the course on women of the Bible, giving this portion of the curriculum a female perspective.[19]

The rescue work and moral reform courses featured lectures, observation, and practical work; leading Washington-area reformers often described their experiences. This area of study was devoted to expanding women's horizons and fostering a more organized approach to reform. Students learned the history of women's organizations, the rudiments of board and committee systems, and principles of state and national organization. The women practiced delivering speeches and presiding over meetings. Most women at the time had little or no experience in these areas, and Kate Waller Barrett and May Gordon hoped that, through instruction and practice, school graduates would be equipped to take the lead in moral reform movements, as opposed to filling the role of passive worker. The curriculum stressed specialization, coordination, and businesslike methods, and instructors urged students to practice "scientific charity."[20] This emphasis on women as role models and leaders as well as trained experts characterized Barrett's conception of Crittenton workers.

The students also received instruction in the proper operation of rescue homes and similar institutions, with emphasis on financial affairs.[21]

This reflected a position Barrett held for the remainder of her Crittenton work—the notion that sound organizational structure was key to Crittenton efforts and that training for women workers was necessary to ensure this. She wrote in a 1906 editorial that although Crittenton workers were peerless when it came to the spiritual side of their work, "their business training has been sorely neglected." Barrett, while recognizing that the spiritual side was undoubtedly the most important, warned, "We can have neither the time or thought to attend properly to our spiritual work if our mind is upset by unbusinesslike methods and our time taken up by unsystematic and disorganized methods of work in the home."[22] Barrett's ideas in this area continued to evolve, and eventually the notion of efficient and businesslike methods became one of the hallmarks of her leadership of the Crittenton organization.

Given Barrett's own background, the central place accorded the medical and nursing department came as no surprise. Many former prostitutes and fallen women suffered from diseases and general ill health. The Washington mission had its own hospital which provided training school students a chance to practice their skills. In addition, Crittenton institutions were beginning to deal more frequently with unmarried mothers, and pregnant women and their children required medical attention. Students learned anatomy, hygiene, and general nursing—with emphasis on obstetrical and pediatric nursing. A staff of women physicians, Drs. Ada Thomas, Anne Wilson, Phoebe Norris, and Louie Taylor, lectured on these topics.

Realizing that not all training school graduates would devote their lives to mission or rescue work, Kate Waller Barrett made certain that students received vocational business training. She believed these skills would improve FC workers' record keeping and reporting, but she also was convinced that clerical work opened opportunities to women who needed to support themselves. The English and commercial portion of the school's curriculum included courses in literature and diction, correspondence, stenography, typewriting, bookkeeping, filing and general office work. This not only prepared graduates to fill clerical positions but also provided many Crittenton workers with knowledge that would eventually aide them in developing training programs for their charges. Barrett wrote a Chicago worker, "We need young, aggressive up-to-date women, to fit our girls for the new conditions under which they must earn a living," and she was determined that the training school would provide these Crittenton leaders.[23] Barrett recognized that the economy was changing and that many women would need to find gainful employment.

At the same time, prospective Crittenton workers could not ignore domestic science, as they would be responsible for homes that sometimes housed more than fifty women. Besides, the basic assumptions were that domestic work was important for all women and that many of the school's graduates would eventually become wives and mothers. Students occupied the "student's home," an annex to the national headquarters. There they had an opportunity for practical experience, as the student home was operated along the lines that a Florence Crittenton home or other institution would be run with students having responsibility for cooking, cleaning, and management. Jessie McAuliffe taught her students how to prepare wholesome but inexpensive food and special meals for the sick and for invalids. Students learned how to mend and sew household supplies, underwear, aprons, and other necessities and how to manage a laundry for a large institution—a formidable task in Florence Crittenton homes, where the amount of laundry was prodigious.

Barrett and Gordon took special pride in the physical culture classes offered at the training school. Under Gordon's direction, students participated in physical activities three times a week and learned how to teach exercises and games in the hopes that eventually all Crittenton homes would enjoy a physical culture program. Barrett, who agreed with the growing sentiment that physical activity for women was essential to good health and mental well-being, believed that recreation was every bit as important as other aspects of a home's program.[24] She was willing to embrace new ideas and pursue any avenue that would better able Crittenton workers and inmates to adapt to a changing society.

Following completion of the Washington segment of their training, the students spent from one month to six weeks in New York City observing work at the Florence Night Mission and with the Florence Crittenton Rescue Band. During the day they visited various philanthropic institutions and took advantage of the city's many cultural opportunities. Barrett wanted to provide the students with exposure to a variety of social-work experiences, not just Florence Crittenton work. The NFCM purchased and maintained a small house in a residential area exclusively for training school students' use. The Crittenton organization made every effort to keep tuition and costs affordable for most young women, and scholarships and a "loan fund" were available. By 1906, the training school was able to report that every graduate had secured a position.

Barrett consistently noted that the school's graduates combined practical skills and training with religious conviction. Graduate Callie W.

Tarkington, who became superintendent of the Florence Crittenton home in Roanoke, Virginia, wrote, "Any woman spending six months under the influence of this Christian institution is sure to be broader in view and intellect, with a deeper consecration for the Master's service, a better understanding of where she is most needed, and what she can do for her own benefit as well as to benefit others."[25] Tarkington's recognition that her training school experience benefited *herself,* making her self-sufficient, in addition to potentially aiding others reflected Barrett's philosophy.

Indications of religious dedication and the idea of duty surfaced in the class mottoes—"What ye, stand fast in the faith, quit yourself like men, be strong" and "Let this mind be in you which was also in Jesus Christ"—and in class songs:

> Somebody must in the struggle of life
> Stand in the thickest of the fight
> Somebody must wear the royal hue
> Purity and right, "Friend, is it you?"

or

> We will work, and watch, and pray
> On the bright and narrow way.
> Leading souls from out of night
> Into God's own holy light.[26]

These songs illustrate the training school students' self-perception: capable and active, rather than passive or submissive, even to the point of adopting the behavior of men, if necessary. The school's curriculum and faculty emphasized women's role and contributions in a way that may be interpreted as feminist. From classes on women in the Bible, to the energy expended to guarantee that graduates could oversee all of the business aspects of a Crittenton institution, to the emphasis on women and children's health, Kate Waller Barrett, May Gordon, and the training school staff labored to provide students with a world view that emphasized women's importance and their capabilities. In so doing, they also created a nucleus of trained Crittenton workers who could spread these ideas throughout the organization.

Crittenton worker Orrin Booth, in a 1904 *Florence Crittenton Magazine* article, reminded his colleagues that just as civil engineers, lawyers, ministers, bookkeepers, and stenographers required special training, rescue workers would be better prepared if they had access to "a special course of training" in their field.[27] Potential students received a warning in the magazine that graduates *"must be thorough, competent and accurate:* nothing less than the *best* is accepted."[28] These attitudes are evidence of the notion that their work was a profession and a career, that it required special skills, and that those who acquired those skills deserved recognition and were entitled to respect. Religious faith was not adequate for running Crittenton homes, and workers would be "more and more selected for their systematic, practical education, administrative [*sic*] rather than for their preaching ability."[29] While historians have made note of a Crittenton training school in the 1930s, clearly earlier Crittenton efforts sought to both provide practical training in operating a social welfare institution and emphasize the necessity of professionalism in Crittenton work.[30]

As another facet of her policy to bring more uniformity and to improve communication between the disparate parts of the Crittenton network, Kate Waller Barrett initiated annual meetings of the NFCM in July 1897, at Mountain Lake Park, Maryland. These gatherings provided an opportunity for workers from various localities to exchange information and share new methods. The conferences, like all early Crittenton activities, combined religious services with practical suggestions for rescue work. Local churchmen usually led the religious meetings, and of course Charles N. Crittenton preached. Each day of the convention included morning, noon, and evening prayer services; an elaborate consecration service traditionally ended the convention.[31]

The business portion of the meeting included summaries from each home and circle of the year's activities and a Barrett presentation listing the national's accomplishments. The programs usually included speakers from the WCTU and other reform groups with similar interests. According to Barrett, the papers workers presented about home and circle operations were the annual meeting's most important feature. Following these presentations, discussion periods provided an opportunity for workers to ask questions or offer suggestions based on their experiences in a local home or circle. Some topics were "What the National does for Local Homes," the "Relationship of Homes and Circles," the "Training School and Local Homes," and "Methods for Successful Rescue Work." Workers discussed the necessity of consecration for Crittenton workers and compared notes on how their nurseries operated, as well as on fund raising and administration.[32] Reports of these sessions demonstrate that a free exchange of ideas took place, and while there was not always agreement on strategy and tactics, Crittenton workers shared their commitment to helping fallen women. The annual conference contributed to professional identification among Crittenton workers while at the same time motivating workers to renew their efforts.

Along with the training school and annual conferences, beginning in 1898 Kate Waller Barrett's effort to foster a sense of unity in the national organization included the publication of a monthly magazine. A subscription to the magazine cost only one dollar, and Barrett encouraged all interested in FC work to subscribe. The NFCM also sent complimentary copies to prominent Americans in an attempt to publicize its work. Zudie E. Leake of Atlanta, Georgia, wrote, "I anticipate the coming of my magazine with a great deal of pleasure. There is much comfort and encouragement derived from it."[33] Leake's reaction met Barrett's first goal for the magazine: that it would provide its readers with moral support as well as offer suggestions for the conduct of Crittenton work.

The *Florence Crittenton Magazine,* later renamed *Girls,* kept Crittenton workers apprised of one another's activities through a variety of articles and regular features. Each issue contained an epistle from Charles Crittenton, usually taking the form of a written sermon coupled with a description of his travels and evangelical meetings. Barrett discussed the various aspects of rescue work and her own travels and endeavors. The magazine included reports from Florence Crittenton homes and circles as well. When the magazine inaugurated the "Reports from Homes" section, editor Mrs. M. H. Gephart urged her colleagues to communicate their local home activities in an effort to have "greater unity of method," "strengthen the national association," and "inspire us all to greater effort."[34]

The histories of fallen women often appeared in the pages of the magazines, and Barrett hoped that matrons would read these articles to FC residents as a source of encouragement. Florence Crittenton officials also designed the stories to appeal to the general population of women readers; the stories contained flowery language, were sentimental to the point of being mawkish, and had easily perceived morals. Although some historians have claimed that the magazine's language and sentiment indicated women reformers' inability to face the prostitution issue directly, in fact, the Crittenton organization was simply aware of the need to avoid offending potential volunteers and contributors. The magazine's editors sought to maintain a comfort level for women across the country interested in rescue work and accustomed to the sentimental language of other women's periodicals. At the same time, Crittenton people did not wish to alarm conservative forces by calling attention to those aspects of Crittenton work that seemed to be outside the parameters of traditional woman's place.

The editors frequently serialized stories in an effort to pique readers' interest. One of the best known, "M'Liss' Child," appeared during April, May, and June 1906. It described a well-established church leader, Mrs.

Purple, who blocked the reinstatement in church of a woman with an illegitimate child unless she revealed the name of her baby's father. Mrs. Purple spoke often about good breeding and acceptable behavior and held up as examples her own two children—a son attending seminary and a daughter at home. On the day Mrs. Purple anxiously awaited her son's return upon his graduation with honors, she found out that M'Liss' child was his. The son had no knowledge of the child, but the daughter had known all along. M'Liss died, but Mrs. Purple adopted the child—and a more forgiving nature.

"M'Liss' Child" points out some key aspects of Florence Crittenton thought. The story's theme—the relationship between fallen women and others of their gender—was central to Crittenton work. M'Liss would have suffered less had she received sympathy from the one person whose acceptance should have been forthcoming, another woman. M'Liss told a group of church women attempting to discover the name of the baby's father, "You good women, you set your feet on us and you won't ever give us another chance to get up and be somebody again." Mrs. Purple told the dying M'Liss, "I'm a greater sinner than you, an' I'll work to the last day o' my life to atone-up for the way I've treated you."[35] While many contemporary stories of fallen women portrayed the man as the villain, this was not the case in "M'Liss' Child." The man in question was completely absent from the scene, and a woman is the object of blame. It took another woman, her own daughter, to show Mrs. Purple the error of her ways. The story contains no hints that there was any justifiable reason to exclude M'Liss from church membership and association with other women. Instead, "M'Liss' Child" illustrates the power women possess to lighten the burden of unmarried mothers.[36] Gender identity is a readily apparent component of the story line, as is sympathy for M'Liss. The story portrays M'Liss as brave and unselfish in refusing to divulge the name of her baby's father. At the same time, M'Liss' death is the focal point of the tale, the author apparently unable to contemplate a suitable ending that would allow M'Liss to continue on the scene. While her death was certainly designed to stimulate readers' sympathy, it also reflects the limits of early Crittenton thinking. Nevertheless, Mrs. Purple's vow to raise M'Liss' child in a loving home guarantees that M'Liss' maternal sacrifice results in her child's well-being.

During a discussion at the 1903 annual meeting, May Gordon reiterated the importance of women's sympathetic treatment of their fallen sisters: "It is a losing fight till conscience joins forces with God, interest, unselfishness, common sense, and justice, and until the Golden Rule is a practice among women."[37] Crittenton publications returned to this theme on a number of occasions, probably because it was difficult to change the behavior of most women when it came to their dealings with women who had broken one of society's most inviolate rules. The self-conscious recognition that women must stick together if they were to make progress was an essential doctrine of Crittenton philosophy, yet many women struggled to put it into effect.

Along with reports from the leadership and stories of fallen women, the magazine contained a number of suggestions for fundraising, which presented a constant challenge to local FC workers. The first FC homes relied on paid solicitors to gather donations. These fund raisers usually charged between 40 and 60 percent of what they collected as a fee, and most Florence Crittenton boards quickly sought other alternatives.[38] Given the backgrounds of the majority of Crittenton workers, it is not surprising that teas and receptions were the most common methods of raising money. The *Florence Crittenton Magazine* described silver teas; cloth socials, at which two yards of cloth represented an admission ticket; and similar functions. These events allowed interested women to meet socially and at the same time make donations. Sometimes Florence Crittenton inmates provided entertainment for these occasions, which often took place at the Florence Crittenton home. Although FC workers realized that some attended these functions out of curiosity regarding the inmates and the home, they hoped that at least a few would volunteer to help.[39]

The Washington, D.C., home distributed mite boxes patterned after the missionary work of many churches; the Work of Faith Committee placed the boxes in business establishments and passed them out to friends. Some homes held lawn fetes to collect money for summer outings.[40] Crittenton volunteers worked hard to think of novel fundraising ideas and published accounts of successful events. One popular method was a measuring party, for which circle members prepared little bags of silk or ribbons and put them in envelopes with a card that read:

> Crittenton babies send you greetings hearty
> And invite you to come to our measuring party,
> To you we send this little sack
> For use in bringing or SENDING BACK
> Two cents for every foot you are tall.
> Measure yourself on door or wall;
> An extra cent for each inch give
> And thereby show how high we live.
> There will be a program of song and speech
> And besides there will be refreshments for each.[41]

The magazine often urged Crittenton volunteers to take action in dealing with financial matters. As one article noted, "Part of the work is to *get at it*. The way to get at it, is to get at it. DO IT NOW!"[42] Similar exhortations frequently highlighted the need for funds. Despite all of these strategies and the continual work of each Crittenton home board financial committee, workers constantly worried about finding enough money to keep operating. The homes lived from hand to mouth, and many reports in the magazine indicated that in times of need some boards relied on prayer alone. Raising money required significant effort on the part of Crittenton volunteers.

The Florence Crittenton publications were quick to recognize businesses that provided financial assistance to the homes. A 1906 edition touted the "splendid line of specialties" the Walter F. Ware Company of Philadelphia distributed, including the "Rizbah collapsible Nipple" for those who "must resort to artificial feeding."[43] Another issue praised the Singer Sewing Machine Company and noted that "the Florence Crittenton workers know the value of a Singer Sewing machine, almost every Florence Crittenton Home has one."[44] The Crittenton organization hoped this publicity would encourage other companies to make donations as well as lead local home workers to seek similar associations with businesses.

The only time the national asked the local homes for contributions was during Self-Denial Week. During this week in April, usually planned to coincide with the anniversary of Florence Crittenton's death, the national officers urged each home and each inmate to give up some little luxury and donate the saved amount to the national for the benefit of Crittenton work in foreign countries. During Self-Denial Week, former Florence Crittenton girls were to write to the homes, tell of their progress, and send small donations. According to the magazine, "hundreds of letters" came to the national headquarters. Many homes gave up meat, butter, dessert, or something similar and sent the savings as their contribution. Kate Waller Barrett stressed that if FC inmates learned self-denial and donated something to the foreign missions, the girls would realize that they were not just receiving assistance but were also helping others and this would raise self-esteem.[45] The *Florence Crittenton Magazine* reported each home's Self-Denial Week schedule and praised the girls' efforts.

Kate Waller Barrett used her visits to local homes, the annual convention, and the publications as forums to discuss the foundation of her philosophy regarding women's role in society and methods for helping fallen women. Her philosophy was based on a deep reverence for the institution of motherhood, thus making Barrett part of a larger movement at the turn of the century whose goal was to elevate the status of mothers. Barrett viewed the movement as intrinsically important, but she also saw it as the avenue for women's greater influence on the direction of society. Motherhood, the movement declared, is a "peculiar gift" that can be used to justify personal and political autonomy for women.[46] Barrett's theories along these lines had several consequences for Crittenton endeavors. Home life took on a key significance for Crittenton work, and Barrett recognized that most readers of the magazine were mothers in their own right. As a result, magazine articles discussed the importance of the home and provided helpful hints for mothers. As one article exclaimed, "Home! What a hallowed name. Baby! How full of enchantment and dear to every heart. How it touches every fiber of the soul and strikes every chord of the human heart with its angelic fingers."[47]

Barrett was convinced that woman's power was dependent upon her position as mother and therefore women should recognize motherhood as an essential occupation. The *Florence Crittenton Magazine* reminded readers, "A mother must realize that child-training is her work and is quite as important as any profession." A Florence Crittenton worker noted, "The influence of faithful, godly mothers is more essential than any other element to the moral, social, and even political well being of our country."[48]

Kate Waller Barrett shared her reverence for motherhood with a growing number of other women of similar backgrounds. These women self-consciously sought to use motherhood as a way to increase their power as women. Motherhood was a uniquely female experience, a fact that had several ramifications. It was an area that did not overlap at all with the male sphere, thus leaving women free to dominate. Childbirth and child rearing were experiences women shared regardless of race, ethnicity, or class, and no one disagreed that these pursuits were important to society. Thus motherhood had the potential to challenge the boundaries between the so-called private and public spheres; and numbers of middle-class women in particular used a maternalistic rhetoric to address areas of societal concern. The National Congress of Mothers, founded in 1897, sought to institutionalize these various aspects of maternalism. Barrett was an active member of the National Congress of Mothers and assumed leadership positions in the Virginia organization. The organization devoted itself to improved conditions for women and their children in American society. These were areas that were frankly not of great interest to most men but of paramount importance to women. Due to Barrett's influence, ideas associated with motherhood were translated into policy.[49]

In keeping with the idea of the centrality of motherhood, the magazine constantly reminded mothers how indispensable they were, even in their performance of necessary housekeeping chores. The "Home Department" explained that housekeeping was of interest to everyone—"to women, because they usually have to attend to the department; to men because they suffer materially when the branch is neglected."[50] So the magazine contained information on how to select meats, how to fold the tablecloth properly, and how to improve the general atmosphere of the house: "Integrity must be the architect and tidiness the upholsterer. It must be warmed by affection and lighted with cheerfulness. Industry must be the ventilation." Of course, God's blessing was the sixth ingredient.[51] Crittenton people designed these features to bolster readers' sense of importance as well as to provide useful information. The National Congress of Mothers echoed this emphasis on the need for attention and training to household tasks. As national Vice-President Dora G. Means noted, "The unit of society is the home. It is the most sacred spot known to the human heart."[52]

Many Home Department articles highlighted the mother's role as the guardian of morality within the home, advising mother to watch the literature brought into the household and to remember that her cues guided conversation in the home and her attitudes generally set the proper tone for the entire family. The magazine's authors recognized that this placed a heavy burden on mothers, and as women suffered more from "mental and physical depression than most men do," women needed strategies for dealing with these states of mind. The magazine suggested taking walks, visiting hospitals so that their situation looked good by way of comparison, or taking hot baths.[53] In particular the Crittenton publications advised women to take solace in the real contributions they made through their ordinary duties. The magazine asked, "But as she performed the home duties, was she not gentle, kind, and bright?" According to Crittenton writers, women should not denigrate the importance of their everyday activities.[54] The magazine sought to validate the experiences of its readers—to convince them that their roles as wives and mothers were among the most important of vocations. Barrett believed this would elevate women's self-esteem and perhaps convince them to expand their influence to the world outside their own homes.

Barrett's veneration of home and motherhood greatly affected the running of Florence Crittenton institutions, and the idea that a Crittenton facility was a home was central to Barrett's philosophy. Florence Crittenton workers capitalized references to home when it referred to their institutions, as Barrett explained: "Possibly the first REAL home that such as she has ever known will be our Home, and it is a rare privilege indeed to be permitted to open up to such a one as this avenues of a truly womanly life."[55] At the Chicago Anchorage home, girls took a course in "home appreciation," and the Detroit home's annual report reminded readers, "The Florence Crittenton Home is more than an Institution,—it is a Home—more of a Home than a great many of the girls who come under its care have ever known."[56] All of these expressions indicate a deeply rooted bias most Crittenton workers shared. They had so much faith in a nurturing home life's power, they assumed it was impossible their charges could have had a proper home environment. According to the workers, some inmates needed a course even to recognize a home's value. Workers genuinely wanted to share the benefits of home life with their charges, but they struggled not to exhibit a feeling of superiority to their less fortunate sisters. One matron wrote that "the Home is so home-like. The girls certainly ought to appreciate it because it is a great deal better than most of them have."[57] Crittenton workers believed their position in their own homes was a defining feature of their roles in the larger society, and they sought to provide Crittenton inmates with a similar sense of place. It was difficult to avoid a certain smugness at having already achieved what they considered to be the pinnacle of women's success. At the same time, as Linda Kerber has noted, the concept of home also referred to a physical space—a space that by the turn of the century was more and more considered woman's domain. By calling their institutions homes, FC workers enunciated their claim to hegemony over home governance. During the early years of Barrett's leadership, the term *mission* fell into disuse and the label *home* was applied to Crittenton institutions. At the same time, more and more women occupied leadership positions when it came to local home operation.[58] While evangelical religious conviction remained an important motivation for Crittenton workers, their ideas of proper home life gained a central position.

Barrett and her followers believed that fallen women's exposure to home life was the beginning of their reformation. Crittenton workers often wrote of the refining, elevating, and redeeming attributes of home life, sometimes seeing them as nothing short of miraculous. In one case, workers had given up on a particularly recalcitrant and seemingly unreachable girl. Then one afternoon "a true, motherly, generous heart felt guided to send to our Home a jar of delicious peaches. The fruit was perfectly prepared and looked so appetizing." Soon the inmates and matron heard Mary crying uncontrollably. When asked what occasioned her change of heart, she responded, "The peaches! Oh, those peaches!" Tasting canned peaches like those her mother used to prepare reminded Mary of her own home and "swayed the seemingly stony heart."[59] Women throughout the Crittenton organization appreciated this evidence of home life's power. Most workers undoubtedly shared Barrett's conviction that every "normal girl" looked forward to "marriage and a home of her own." So the emphasis on home had as a goal something that the Crittenton workers believed their charges wanted for themselves as much as Crittenton volunteers wanted it for them.[60]

Florence Crittenton workers referred to those living in the home as the family, and this notion of family was the basis for the home's operation, especially for discipline. According to the national's suggested home constitution, "Inmates when admitted are adopted into the family and are expected to give the loving obedience of dutiful children to their parents." Since the Florence Crittenton home was to approximate as closely as possible an ordinary home, certain restrictions for admittance existed. The matron searched each girl who entered the home for opiates, liquor, firearms, and objectionable literature.[61] In some homes a doctor examined each prospective resident, since in the early years homes did not admit women suffering from venereal disease, believing these women belonged in hospitals or insane asylums due to the highly communicable nature of the maladies.[62]

Before a girl could become a permanent Florence Crittenton resident, the board of directors required her to appear before them and tell her story. According to FC workers, this made it easier for the girl to feel part of the family and the board tried to "make her understand that her past will not stand in the way of her advancement."[63] How the girls felt about this is not known for certain, but clearly potential Crittenton inmates recognized that undergoing this interrogation was necessary for their admittance and they submitted to it in order to obtain shelter. Quite possibly the question period served to satisfy the board's curiosity regarding their charges' situation. At the same time, making decisions regarding admittance placed a heavy responsibility on the board, and no doubt the members contemplated the cases they had discussed even after the meeting had ended. In 1904, the Portland board reassessed their judgment regarding a "Finnish girl" and voted to remove the designation "unworthy" from her report.[64] Crittenton workers recognized that the decisions they made might have lasting implications for the women they hoped to aid. The workers strived to guarantee that a Crittenton girl's "past" would not be a detriment to her future, and while workers realized this presented a challenge, they believed it was a reachable goal. To label a potential resident unworthy was to brand her as forever barred from joining the company of motherhood, and Crittenton workers sought to avoid taking that step.

Once the board members had inquired into a girl's background, they tried to reunite the girl with her own family. Crittenton workers hoped that after a fallen woman found God or an unmarried girl delivered her child and repented, she could go back to friends and family. This was not always possible, but it was one goal. The board members also often tried to bring about marriages between unmarried mothers and the fathers of their children. Monthly reports from local homes listed the number of weddings that had taken place in the home and workers considered this a successful solution to a case since the family would be intact and the woman would have a home of her own. Either returning to her own home or establishing a new one restored Florence Crittenton charges to their appropriate place in society.

Board members and matrons considered themselves substitute mothers to the inmates, in many ways an apt point of view. The relationship between mothers and daughters is not one of equality; it requires the mother to set limits and is not always without tension. The NFCM suggested that the matron screen all visitors and be present during their visits. The girls spent their evenings together in the parlor so that they would not sit and gossip in their rooms. Like mothers in ordinary homes, the FC workers made certain that only wholesome reading materials were available to their charges.[65] The Crittenton organization urged workers to make certain that "good" books were available in the home and that the matron lead the girls in conversation regarding their reading as a substitute for the "lewd" topics they might otherwise be tempted to pursue. Crittenton suggestions for appropriate books shed light on precisely what the workers perceived as "good." *Little Women,* for example, received unanimous endorsement. However, many workers objected to the "Pollyanna or Mary Cary types," because, in the words of one worker, those books "raise an almost impossible and unattainable standard of thought and action." According the Crittenton women, even girls living "normal lives under normal conditions" would have difficulty reaching the standards of these books; and the Crittenton girls who had definitely not led that kind of life would find them "impossible to the point of discouragement."[66] Crittenton workers' attitude is revealing in two ways. In the first place, workers were cognizant of life experiences that separated them from their charges. The use of the word "normal" is indicative of volunteers' conviction that while their own middle-class experiences ought to be considered normal, those of their charges were definitely not. On the other hand, recognizing these differences, Crittenton women tried to avoid setting impossible standards and thus discouraging their charges from trying. While confronting numerous difficulties, the March sisters of *Little Women* were able to establish themselves in acceptable home situations and were a model for Crittenton charges to follow.

The matrons and the board members were responsible for all discipline, and in many homes the inmates appeared before the board each week to hear lectures or remarks. According to discussion at one annual convention, matrons should pray with a refractory girl, use loving persuasion, "but maintain her authority and insist on obedience to the rules." Florence Crittenton workers did not resort to the use of corporal punishment.[67]

Barrett advised FC workers to make sure that the Florence Crittenton Home was as much like a home as possible. While the furniture might not be new, it should be clean and preferably of bright colors. FC boards tried to find those willing to donate pianos, as no real home was without one.[68] Workers went to great lengths to guarantee this homelike atmosphere. One described a Christmas dinner at the home with white china, snowy damask linen, the best silver, the matron dressed in white, the inmates all in black skirts and white shirtwaists, the babies in white— each with a sprig of holly. "'We' felt 'we' were just as nice as 'we' could be," she said, convinced that the Crittenton board of managers and the contributors would be proud.[69] Crittenton people thought these outward appearances of middle-class home life were a reflection of an inner change in their charges. The Crittenton worker's use of the pronoun "we" suggests her view of the relationship between herself and the inmates. This picture of Christmas dinner at a home contradicts notions that the institutions were prisonlike. The Crittenton worker reporting exhibited both pride and a sense of accomplishment, with no hint of punishment and, in fact, with a real notion of community. At the same time, the worker's comments convey the idea that it was no small feat to attain this Christmas perfection, and the worker was as much concerned with gaining approval from Crittenton benefactors as with pleasing her charges.

The matron, like every mother, was responsible for teaching the residents housekeeping skills. Kate Waller Barrett wrote, "We believe that every lady should know how to cook, wash, and iron, if she does not know anything else, and as we expect all our girls to be ladies in the highest and truest sense, they must all learn to do these things."[70] Housework was the most acceptable occupation for women, and FC workers hoped that learning how to complete domestic tasks would be the first step toward a new life. In fact, workers expressed the belief that if these girls had known how to keep house they probably would not have fallen in the first place, and workers assured one another that the inmates actually found comfort in domestic chores. According to the Portland, Oregon, home, one of their inmates had to be taught to wash dishes but "at the wash tub she said she had never been so happy and contented."[71] In reporting this girl's sentiment, the Portland worker sought to validate Crittenton methods and women's domestic endeavors as well. The historian is left to ponder the interpersonal dynamics that resulted in this report. Few people would argue that washing dishes is tremendously fulfilling. It was obviously important to Crittenton workers that the girl be happy and that she recognize the intrinsic value of housework, which was so important to middle-class women's sense of purpose and place. Quite possibly, the girl told the worker what she wanted to hear. I suspect, however, that the inmate had her own reasons for coming to the Crittenton home, and her statement suggests that she also had her own reasons for wishing to remain in the home.

The inmates learned cooking, sewing, and cleaning—skills workers found deplorably lacking among many of their charges. An FC worker warned, "It takes time and patience to teach these girls as they have never been accustomed to being disciplined, but as we know Satan finds something for idle hands to do, we cannot encourage idleness."[72] Cooking lessons began with how to operate the stove, how to make tea and coffee, and how to wash dishes correctly. The students progressed through vegetables, soups, rice and cereals, eggs, more complicated meals, bread and cakes, and, finally, the service of meals and waiting on tables. They learned to mend their own clothing, do simple sewing, and operate the laundry. Girls who did not have homes of their own could make their living as domestic servants.[73]

Whereas historians have frequently commented on the burdensome nature of the Crittenton regime of domestic work, Crittenton volunteers themselves were more sensitive to criticism that they did "too much for our charges and do not require them to do sufficient for themselves." One worker reported that "sometimes in pondering these words I have forgotten to eat and omitted to sleep," as she agonized over where the line between meaningful work and punishment lay.[74] Volunteers wanted to help inmates without making them "passive recipients of care and charity." Determining the appropriate balance remains, to this day, a troublesome social welfare challenge.

Workers noted that many of their charges were "delicate, untrained girls" who were not easily trained. Another worker reminded colleagues that "many girls come to us in ignorance of all housewifely arts." She explained that workers had to teach inmates "to sweep a floor, make a bed, dust, sew a plain seam, do their own laundry." Workers were also cognizant that both their level of instruction and inmates' chances of meaningful work were limited. One worker lamented, "We can teach them very little of the finer work women delight to do, but rather the mostly laborious tasks which fall to the lot of female servants."[75] While historians have belittled the Crittenton efforts due to exactly these limitations, many women who were neither unmarried mothers nor former prostitutes were employed as domestic servants. In fact, until 1920 domestic service represented the single largest area of female employment in this country. Noted progressive reformer Florence Kelley's first activity as a Hull House resident was to establish a training and employment bureau for domestic workers.[76] Florence Crittenton workers were keenly aware of the limitations of domestic work, did not use it as a punishment, and strived to accentuate its positive aspects. However, despite their considerable efforts in this vein, Florence Crittenton women could not eliminate the class and social lines that separated domestic servants from their employers.

Kate Waller Barrett maintained that domestic service was an honorable profession, one especially suitable for reformed fallen women. FC workers thought that at least domestic servants received some supervision, whereas factory operatives did not, and domestic workers received a set wage that was not subject to production or seasonal adjustments. While it is tempting to see the Crittenton emphasis on domestic service as self-serving, a closer examination indicates justification for the Crittenton position. As several historians have pointed out, domestic work was not rote work, a servant often made her own determination regarding what work needed to be accomplished on a given day and often enjoyed considerable autonomy and opportunity to exercise judgement.[77] Many Crittenton home programs emphasized these aspects of housekeeping.

The National Florence Crittenton Mission tried to influence its sympathizers to employ former FC inmates as maids, and the *Florence Crittenton Magazine* included testimonials to the efficiency of FC-trained servants. Middle-class women could take advantage of the opportunity to have a well-trained maid and still consider themselves philanthropists. One such employer, Mrs. G. H. G., wrote, "We like I—— and will do all we can to make her home pleasant. She is good help, has a quick step and can accomplish a good deal. . . . I think we can do good by providing homes for those who are willing to work."[78] Certainly, some Crittenton girls objected to their employer's close scrutiny and the long hours domestic service entailed. However, it was one of the few jobs that allowed un-married women to have their children with them. It is worth noting that training in domestic skills was an essential part of the curriculum at early women's colleges, in women's prisons, in schools established during this period for Native American girls—in fact, in virtually every institution for females. Consequently, while the class of most Crittenton inmates certainly determined that domestic service was a logical employment choice, their gender also destined Crittenton charges for domestic work.

Most home boards appointed guardian committees to check up on girls working outside the home, believing the girls "need frequent visits from the matron or some lady of the board, that they may feel they are not forgotten by us, but on the contrary that we are holding ourselves ready to help them in every way and count it a privilege to do so."[79] Barrett advised Crittenton boards to assure the inmate that if she did not get along in her place of employment for any reason, "she should not remain in the position, she is to come back to us, as this is her home."[80] The committee also investigated prospective employers to make sure they were Christian families. The matron of the Savannah, Georgia, home reported the success of a former inmate employed for two years and giv-ing faithful service. She added, "Such cases are incentives to others, to dignify labor and to put forth effort so as to succeed in whatever voca-tion they may choose as means of support."[81] Workers encouraged former inmates to return for visits and to continue to consider the FC establish-ment their home. One worker wrote of former inmates' visits, "How gratifying it is to see them resting at Home and availing themselves of every pleasure and benefit it affords."[82] After all, most of the women involved in Crittenton work owed their status, and in fact their self-esteem, to their position as homemaker. It stands to reason that they di-rected their charges along the same path. At the same time, Florence Crittenton records, as well as those of other groups, indicate that the majority of women who came to the homes had been in domestic ser-vice prior to their Crittenton residence. Employment as a servant often was not just the most available employment for Crittenton girls but also a logical choice.[83]

Cases involving unmarried mothers were a small percentage of in-mates in Crittenton homes during the early years (only 7 percent by 1906), but workers gave these cases a great deal of attention. Kate Waller Barrett's own involvement stemmed from her Butchertown experience. Most re-formers considered unmarried mothers in a separate class from prostitutes because professionals avoided pregnancy. Workers believed that unmarried mothers were usually the victims of a single indiscretion, but they were convinced that these women often turned to prostitution as a means of support because there were no other opportunities available. Consequently, unmarried mothers deserved consideration. In addition the plight of illegitimate children concerned many workers. Workers found that it was easier to gain sympathy and thus contributions for innocent children than for fallen women. As one worker explained, "There is something about a baby which touches the sympathetic side of every nature." This attitude was present in the Crittenton workers themselves and perhaps in part accounts for the growth of Crittenton work with unmarried mothers.[84] It certainly fit well with the Crittenton philosophy regarding the home and its position as a foundation of society.

Considering Barrett's views concerning motherhood, her attitude toward unmarried mothers and their children was predictable; she applied the biblical passage "Those whom God hath joined together, let no man put asunder" to the relationship between a mother and her baby. As a result, she urged Crittenton homes to make every possible effort to keep illegitimate children with their mothers. Although many reformers advocated adoption, primarily due to their conviction that the sinful mother was a poor influence on the innocent child, Barrett argued that both mother and child would benefit if they remained together. In a later reprinted and widely distributed speech, "Motherhood: A Means of Regeneration," Barrett told the National Conference of Charities and Corrections, "The rewards of motherhood are the most blessed hopes in every woman's life who has tasted the joys of motherhood, and why should not the poor girl who has nothing else to live for at least have that sweet consolation?"[85] Barrett believed that a fallen woman could truly reform if her child was with her; the baby provided incentive for the mother's good behavior. Further, Barrett thought there was no moral excuse for separating the two: "If a woman has the God-given endowment for motherhood, no man-made law can take it from her." According to Barrett, a wedding license did not make a woman a conscientious mother, and it was entirely possible for an unmarried mother to possess the qualities necessary for motherhood.[86] Kate Barrett's attitude represented a considerable departure from more typical perceptions of unmarried mothers, and it positioned Barrett and the Crittenton organization to alter the usual tactics for dealing with unmarried mothers and their children. Although according to one point of view the Crittenton position was one of "enforced motherhood," the situation was much more complicated.[87]

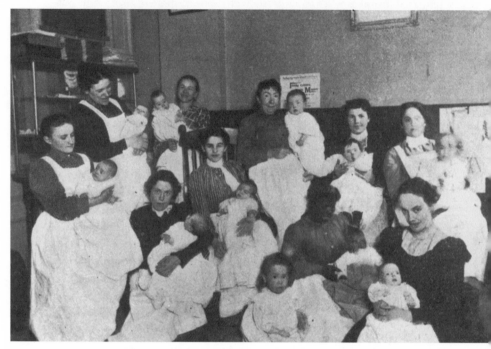

Mothers and babies in the New York City Home, c. 1900.
Courtesy of the National Florence Crittenton Mission.

While it may have been expedient to allow the girl to give up her baby, Crittenton philosophy advocated adoption only in cases in which the mother was mentally incompetent. If a girl did not keep her child, FC workers thought she was protected from the "full import of her error" and therefore might return to her old ways and "the opportunity for bringing out the best, the sterling qualities of womanhood is lost to the girl." Even if the girl gave up her baby she could never return to her former life: "Innocent girlhood, with the privileges accorded purity, is no longer to be thought of." If such a girl did not have her child, she had no consolation at all. The child also benefited from remaining with the mother because, in the eyes of FC workers, nothing could replace a mother's love. If possible, mothers in Crittenton homes nursed their children. Workers argued that this ensured the child's health, but it was also certainly designed to make certain that even the most recalcitrant mother kept her child; rarely would a woman part with her baby after nursing it.[88]

According to Crittenton people, this did not represent punishment for the unmarried mothers but provided an opportunity for the girls to receive the considerable rewards of motherhood. The Crittenton policy also recognized the emotions and preference of many of their women charges. There is some evidence that hospitals and other institutions sometimes pressured a mother to give up her child, ignoring the mother's wishes. As one worker reminded her colleagues, these mothers' "babies are as dear to these" women as "our little ones are dear to us."[89] Most Crittenton workers believed that motherhood created a bond between themselves and their charges that was preeminent. We have little evidence at our disposal regarding the attitude of unmarried mothers toward their offspring. However, Matilda Robbins's story "An Incident in Social Work (The Adoption)," which centers around a mother's trauma at the prospect of giving her baby up for adoption, provides one example. A social worker convinces Robbins's central character that she is ill equipped to keep her baby, but the mother is clearly torn and looking for options. The mother explains with considerable sadness, "I'm giving up so much. I love Jean and I'll never see her again." Crittenton institutions strived to provide an alternative to adoption, and workers acted on their belief that many unmarried mothers loved their children and did not want to lose them.[90]

Before allowing a pregnant girl admittance, most Crittenton homes requested her promise to stay at least six months after her child's birth. Frequently, a matron reported admitting a girl who claimed that she did not like children and had decided to give hers up for adoption. Prayers and quiet discussion with such a girl often led her to keep the child with results that, according to Crittenton officials, were nearly always happy. Of one such case the Peoria, Illinois, matron wrote that the girl now "prefers to keep [her baby] near her and talks to it so sweetly and baby cries when taken away from her."[91] Florence Crittenton matron Mrs. Brokow worked for five months to "overcome" one girl's "sullen determination to have nothing to do with the child after birth." At first glance an observer might conclude that the matron simply was finally able to wear down the girl's resistance. However, the final sentence of the report explained that the girl in question had not told her "mother her secret" and once that was done decided to keep the child.[92] Nonmarital pregnancy certainly presented difficult choices for women, and giving the child up for adoption was neither easy nor always the best choice for mother or child. Unmarried mothers with financial resources at their disposal had more options available to them than did their working-class counterparts. The ability to temporarily drop out of sight was a luxury that few working-class girls could afford.

Crittenton workers were cognizant of the many opportunities available to women who wished to give up their babies. The Washington, D.C., home touted its achievement in 1898 of only thirty-three mothers giving up their children.[93] Crittenton workers were pleased to report that one girl who had known a "life of comfort and ease and culture" before the birth of her child was now doing housework. She had made that sacrifice because the family would not "receive the baby at home."[94] It would have been easier for this woman to give the child up and take up her old life again, but she refused to do so. The case of the Peoria, Illinois, woman and the woman above point to a significant aspect of the plight of unmarried mothers. Nonmarital pregnancy was not only a crisis for the girl involved, it also threatened their families with embarrassment and loss of status. One of the most important Florence Crittenton contributions was to facilitate the unmarried mother's response to this crisis whether it meant admitting the situation to family or dealing with the fact that they had been disowned. Crittenton efforts ensured that girls weren't alone during what was most certainly a frightening and uncertain period in their lives. A Florence Crittenton home was better than the alternatives: illegal and dangerous abortion, infanticide, abandonment of the child, or homelessness.

Often women entered Florence Crittenton homes close to the time of delivery. Essie was admitted to the Portland, Oregon, home on January 1,

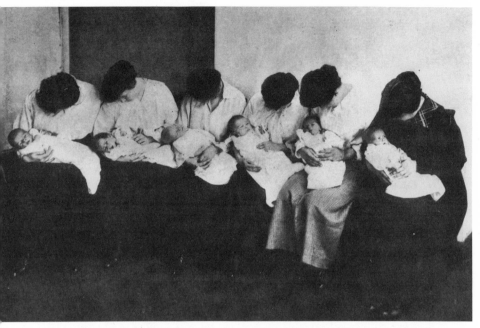

Boston home residents and their babies, c. 1916. From the Annual Report of the Florence Crittenton League of Compassion, Inc., 1916.

and her baby was born January 13; Helen was admitted on January 16, and her baby was born the next day; Clara was admitted on January 28, and the birth of her baby took place on February 14. Critics have argued that with childbirth imminent, the unmarried mothers were subject to Crittenton coercion to keep their children. The evidence indicates, however, that the mothers maintained considerable freedom of action. They could take advantage of Crittenton facilities during the immediate crisis of impending childbirth but not subject themselves to Crittenton rules and control over the long term. Grace was admitted to the Portland home on January 20 and left on February 1. Lillian refused to "comply with the Florence Crittenton rules," so went to the Salvation Army home. In the final analysis, Crittenton workers could not force their charges to either keep their babies or remain in the home. While Crittenton people firmly believed that it was in the girls' best interest to stay, the final decision rested with the inmates themselves.[95]

On the other hand there were cases in which the mother wished to keep the child but family members wanted the child given up for adoption. This situation was dramatized in the *Florence Crittenton Magazine* story "Bettie and the Baby." Bettie, a young Jewish girl, appeared at the home with a two-week-old infant. Her family wanted her to give the baby up so that she could return to work, but the girl loved her baby and refused to part with it. According to the Crittenton account, the family used bribery and threats to change Bettie's mind, but to no avail. Finally, family members relented and Bettie returned home. At eleven o'clock that same night Bettie appeared at the door of the home in "deplorable condition" and reported that the family had taken her baby. Florence Crittenton workers ignored the fact that finding one baby in New York City was nearly impossible and called upon all of their resources. They located the baby at a Catholic institution, and mother and child were reunited. Workers answered critics who argued that the baby might have been better off with an adoptive family by noting, "We are satisfied that God's plan is to keep mother and child together even if the child is born out of wedlock, and amid unfavorable circumstances. He makes it possible to surmount difficulties, opens doors of opportunity, and showers blessings upon mother and child."[96] In Bettie's case, Crittenton volunteers supported her decision to keep the baby, even though incest was involved. This insistence that it was beneficial for both mother and child that they remain together became a hallmark of Florence Crittenton work, and FC women often served as advocates for mothers seeking to retain custody of their children. Bettie needed someone to champion her rights and desire to keep her child, and Crittenton workers stepped in to help. They set aside whatever prejudices they had regarding the situation and Bettie's religious preference in order to keep mother and child together.

According to Charles Crittenton and Kate Barrett, the attitude of the girls who left the homes was the best barometer of Crittenton success. If these girls were grateful and did not forget the home, the home must be doing good work. The issues of the *Florence Crittenton Magazine* contained numerous letters from former FC girls, as did most other NFCM literature. In a typical letter a former Crittenton girl wrote, "Mr. Crittenton! How I have blessed the name ever since I came into a Florence Crittenton Home, and how many of us poor miserable creatures have found rest in these Homes he has founded for them."[97] Another girl proclaimed, "I shall never forget the kindness and encouragement given me by the dear ladies of the Board."[98]

Workers cherished evidence of gratitude. Barrett fondly recalled a girl who had done a worker's ironing while the worker was out visiting the jail.[99] The Boise, Idaho, matron wrote that one of her girls gave her "a little offering of love dear to a mother's heart," baby's first shoes. It is hard to imagine any circumstance in which coercion could have entered into a mother's decision to give her baby's shoes to the Crittenton worker, and according to the matron who received this token, "I was more than repaid for all the sacrifices I had ever made; they are not sacrifices but privilege."[100] This kind of reward assured that Florence Crittenton work came more and more to center around homes and the care of unmarried mothers and their children. The organization shifted its energies in that direction.

Within a short period following her elevation to the position of general superintendent, Kate Waller Barrett had indelibly stamped her ideas and values upon the operation and direction of the NFCM. She had already developed a reputation as leader in caring for unfortunate women. A minister in New York wrote to her about one such girl. He indicated that while there were homes in New York City, he wanted Barrett's "personal influence" for the girl in question.[101] Dr. Barrett became identified with compassionate and practical assistance for women in need of help.

Barrett had applied her considerable organizational skills to making the Crittenton institutions more efficient and more uniform in policy. She shaped the training school into a preparatory school for Crittenton workers, who received a decidedly pro-woman view of their own abilities and potential. Establishing the school brought Barrett's belief that Crittenton work required skill and training, not just evangelical conviction, to the forefront. The *Florence Crittenton Magazine* acted as a unifying force among Crittenton volunteers, and as a booster for women's contributions to society. Barrett joined other middle- and upper-class women in redefining the mother's role and seeking to expand women's influence accordingly. She tried to reach across class lines in an effort to emphasize the needs of women and children. Gender identity motivated Barrett and other Crittenton workers to adopt a more sympathetic view toward their charges. At the same time, Crittenton efforts continued to be limited, especially in the central place accorded domestic skills in the Crittenton program.

Under Barrett's direction, the National Florence Crittenton Mission came to elevate the status of motherhood and, indeed, of women to a level of significance that became the organization's most identifying characteristic. Kate Waller Barrett's overarching idea of "motherhood as a means of regeneration" became even more central as the NFCM turned a greater proportion of its attention to the plight of unmarried mothers.

Chapter 3

A Well-Run Home

In this work we should keep abreast of the times
and our watchword should be "Progress."
—Kate Waller Barrett, 1914

The National Florence Crittenton Mission's growth, accompanied by the appearance of a new national reform ethos, led the Crittenton organization to accelerate its movement in the direction in which Kate Waller Barrett had set it. The tremendous expansion of the Crittenton chain necessitated further organization and greater attention to administrative details. By 1906, there were seventy-three Florence Crittenton homes located throughout the United States, and simply keeping track of them was a complex task.[1] This dramatic growth coincided with a general change in reform attitudes that historians usually refer to as the *progressive movement*. Although by the 1970s at least one historian had concluded that because such a diverse group of people, ideas, and organizations had laid claim to or fallen under the progressive label that there was in fact no such thing as a progressive movement, there is no doubt that Barrett and other workers were part of a new wave of reform. The progressivism that influenced Barrett and thus the NFCM involved a concern for the public weal and a desire to put the Christian code to work in society. This aspect of progressivism emphasized reforms, altruism, and what one historian has termed a "new insurgent spirit." To achieve these goals, progressives often employed experts and praised efficiency.[2] Progressivism's evangelical Christian motives, adoption of reform agendas, and faith in efficiency jived with Barrett's own emerging philosophy. Barrett's ideas, and those of other women reformers, were essential to the development and definition of progressivism. In directing Florence Crittenton activities over the next two decades, Barrett combined progressive ideas with her enduring faith in the power of motherhood.[3]

It was not surprising that Barrett was interested in the new views, because she and many other progressives shared a similar background. Barrett was born and raised in a rural setting, but most of her work with Crittenton homes was in urban areas. As a physician, she was a member of a group bent upon establishing and protecting its professional status, a tendency that squared with the era's faith in knowledge and set in motion forces that legitimized claims of expertise and facilitated emerging bureaucratic processes. Barrett used her years with the NFCM to qualify her as an expert on unmarried mothers and their problems. She said, "In this work we should keep abreast of the times and our watchword should be 'Progress.'" Barrett was not, as one historian has portrayed evangelical women reformers, forced, dragging her feet, into the twentieth century. She definitely wanted to be part of a new outlook on social reform and to help define the terms of the movement.[4]

The hold of this new reform conscience on the National Florence Crittenton Mission became more pronounced following Charles Nelson Crittenton's death on November 16, 1909. Crittenton had been on an extended trip visiting Crittenton homes throughout the United States, and his death came after he had preached a sermon at the same San Francisco church where he had begun his evangelical career nineteen years earlier. The loss deprived the NFCM of its spiritual leader and was a great shock to its workers. His demise also caused a financial crisis for the organization, as he had contributed almost his entire yearly income to the work. Crittenton's will provided that about half of his three- to five-million-dollar estate go to relatives and business associates, the remainder going to the National Florence Crittenton Mission. By the time the estate was settled, Barrett, who succeeded Crittenton as national president, announced that the mission would receive about half as much as it was accustomed to each year; cutbacks and additional fund raising became crucial for the mission's survival. The NFCM greatly curtailed the training school and urged workers to send paid subscriptions for the magazine, *Girls*.[5]

Deprived of Crittenton's charismatic presence as well as his income, the NFCM sought greater recognition and a closer association with other reformers. Barrett and the organization believed that future success depended on gaining the approval and support of established progressive reformers. Endorsements from prominent progressives such as Jacob Riis, Theodore Roosevelt, and Judge Ben Lindsey were reprinted in *Girls,* but nevertheless Barrett was sometimes discouraged and frustrated.[6] Hastings H. Hart of the Russell Sage Foundation attempted to soothe her when he wrote, "The reason why social workers have not given you the assistance that you need is because they do not appreciate either the magnitude or the significance of your work."[7] To counteract this situation, Barrett urged FC workers to cooperate closely with other social workers; and she intentionally cultivated key social reformers of the period. Prominent progressives such as Jane Addams and Katharine Bement Davis did associate themselves with Crittenton activities. Addams delivered the keynote address to the 1910 Florence Crittenton annual meeting, and Davis was on the board of the Boston home. Barrett herself was a frequent speaker at the National Conference of Charities and Corrections, a gathering place for many progressive reformers. Barrett's expertise on topics such as "The Unmarried Mother and her Child" earned her the respect of her colleagues, and she frequently referred to herself and her co-workers as "social workers."[8]

Florence Crittenton workers enthusiastically adopted progressive tenets of efficiency and organization while attempting to preserve the original humanitarian and spiritual side of their efforts. A Boston worker explained, "We require a broad efficiency in every department and in every work in the Home, and we seek the same result in each girl." But another worker reminded her colleagues of their historic roots: "There is something in the spirit of Florence Crittenton Homes that makes one feel the difference, especially in that intimate interest in the girls as individuals and the spirit of family life that prevails."[9] The workers' attitudes illustrate a tension common to many progressive reform efforts—the desire for efficiency coupled with a commitment to the individual. The two values could coexist in some instances, but sometimes they were diametrically opposed and presented difficult choices.

That fact became more apparent as work with unmarried mothers accounted for an increasingly significant part of Crittenton endeavors. Many Crittenton workers realized that their attempts to save prostitutes were more costly in terms of both time and money than their results warranted. By contrast, work with unmarried mothers proved to be more rewarding and the results more easily documented.[10] Although some workers feared that the homes would become nothing more than lying-in hospitals, Barrett argued that assisting unmarried mothers filled a void in the work of existing institutions. According to Barrett, "As far as I have found them [lying-in hospitals] they are run by either women who have been themselves unsavory or women who are in business to make money." Even though a few Crittenton homes began to charge entrance fees in certain situations, none of them were profit-making enterprises, and the paying clients represented a small percentage of the inmates. The homes remained philanthropic institutions until much later in their history.[11]

This change in Crittenton emphasis reflected progressive concern with the growing number of instances of premarital pregnancy. In 1850 the rate of premarital pregnancy had been about 10 percent, while from 1880 to 1910 it was more than double that at 23 percent.[12] Illegitimacy became an issue of some import among progressive reformers, according to one historian "the most serious and vexing manifestation of a larger 'girl problem.'"[13] Kathy Peiss, Joanne Meyerwitz, Ruth Alexander, and others have pointed to changes in sexual attitude and behavior, particularly among working-class young women, as the root causes of this perceived problem. Although working women played a major role in pioneering modern courtship and recreational practices, these girls took risks when they engaged in greater sexual experimentation than previous generations. While it is easy to admire working women's efforts to create their own culture, sometimes things did not work out. Since it was difficult and even illegal to gain access to contraception and abortions, the increased rate of illegitimacy was one result of these women's greater independence. Progressives in general, and maternalists specifically, feared that the new trend threatened the hallowed duo of home and family, so they devoted more and more of their attention to grappling with the problem of illegitimacy.[14]

A nonmarital pregnancy created a serious crisis in the life of the mother. Both girls and their families were often distraught at the prospect of unmarried motherhood, and Florence Crittenton efforts filled a void for both. One mother wrote to Chicago's Florence Crittenton Anchorage, "My little girl of thirteen is a expectant mother. My pastor has told me of the Homes. For God's Sake, help."[15] A Hood River father sent several boxes of apples to the Portland, Oregon, home in an effort to express his appreciation for the home's work on his daughter's behalf.[16] When a former inmate sent a donation of two dollars, she asked that her name not be published and wrote, "I hope and pray that I may have both father and mother a long time, so that I can make up to them for all the pain and trouble I caused them."[17]

Many working-class families refused to acknowledge the problem or to provide refuge for their pregnant daughters. Pittsburgh workers reminded their colleagues that "in many cases their own homes are barred against them," illustrating the need for Crittenton intervention.[18] This was a frequent theme in Crittenton reports. Boston workers wrote of one inmate who was engaged and the man disappeared on the wedding day: "Her father cast her out from home and the time came when she could no longer hold an office position." And they wrote of another case in which the family was "well nigh broken up" by a nonmarital pregnancy.[19] The Crittenton home provided a haven in both instances. A New York worker found a young African American girl who "had run away from her southern home because of the trouble she had gotten into," and the Crittenton people provided shelter and assistance.[20] A Chicago social worker wrote to the Anchorage, "May I bring a girl to you tonight. Her father has turned her out of the house."[21] These pregnant girls had no place else to turn, and Crittenton assistance saved them from homelessness and possibly worse fates.

After the immediate crisis had passed, sometimes Crittenton workers could orchestrate a reconciliation between the girls and their families. Savannah, Georgia, Crittenton people were pleased to report that one of their inmates who "said her father was so unforgiving that she had never let him know as to her whereabouts" was reunited with her family and was making herself "indispensable." The Crittenton worker exalted, "We give this little history, as it seems to be the highest ideal of rescue work."[22] The Crittenton volunteer did not exaggerate. While this kind of case does not represent an earthshaking example of reform, the Crittenton home did provide a transitional haven for the woman in question, while also giving her family some breathing room. It was undoubtedly easier to adapt to the new mother and child than it was to have the girl living at home during her pregnancy. Crittenton workers counted on the fact that most families were unable to turn their back on the babies once the initial shock and disappointment had worn off. Certainly the Crittenton homes made a difference in the lives of the girls and their families.

The NFCM more actively addressed child health and welfare, which was also part of progressive reformers' agenda. Along with other women, FC workers recognized both the significance and the nature of child-welfare needs and problems earlier than many male progressives. These reformers viewed illegitimacy as a child-welfare problem, and unmarried mothers took on new significance to reformers during the progressive period due to the progressive concern with their children. Interest in children stemmed from the progressive belief in the perfectibility of society.[23] Where better to begin than with the children who, as *Girls* declared, were "the best asset of the nation?" From the beginning of the twentieth century, the children in Crittenton homes took on a new importance in both Crittenton thinking and literature.[24]

Workers discussed at length ways to most appropriately nurture infants and young children. FC workers wanted to place the babies on a regimen that would later enable their mothers to work and still keep the child. The workers designed their system to teach the child "to expect just its actual needs" and thus make the first steps toward self-reliance and independence. Florence Crittenton workers carefully explained that while their nursery was systematized, each child received individual care and attention. They pointed with pride to the cleanliness and comfort of their nurseries and to the cuteness, health, and cleverness of their babies.[25] The Crittenton child-care system attempted to combine efficiency and organization with the characteristics of a traditional home.

Although these notions of child rearing with their emphasis on regimentation seem far removed from current child-care practices, Florence Crittenton methods were the epitome of progressivism. Historians generally recognize the Shepherd-Towner Maternity and Infancy Act (1921) as the high-water mark of women's reform activity in relation to women and children. Under the act's auspices, progressive reformers were able to suggest child-care strategies and tactics. The manuals they prepared contained information that coincided with Crittenton practices.[26] Shepherd-Towner workers distributed cards to mothers that featured a daily routine designed to "guide their children in habit formation," a goal "that women in the Children's Bureau considered of utmost importance to the creation of a self-controlled, disciplined citizenry." Florence Crittenton workers were in the vanguard of progressive efforts on behalf of women and children.[27] Their thoughtful and organized approach to nursery administration fit nicely with progressive tenets of child care and child development.

The *Florence Crittenton Magazine* recommended that nurseries have iron beds painted white, a hair mattress covered by a white rubber sheet and then a muslin sheet, a muslin and cotton wadding protective pad, and a white blanket. Very young babies slept three to a bed; those four months or older slept two in a bed, and those over one year old had their own beds. The inmates washed the bed linen daily and turned and aired the mattresses. Many nurseries had their own kitchens where the workers and inmates could prepare special foods for the children. Each mother bathed and dressed her own baby in the morning and then went to her work in other parts of the house, returning for feedings at an appointed time. Each girl had separate toilet articles for her baby, and workers carefully marked each infant's clothes and diapers to prevent mix-ups. While the mothers worked or attended classes, the girls assigned to the nursery, under the supervision of a trained worker, cared for the children.[28]

All of this reflected progressive values, but the original Christian impulse remained strong at Crittenton institutions. Kate Waller Barrett and her followers did not hesitate to admit that according to many members of society, babies born in Florence Crittenton homes began life with a serious handicap, and they relied on Christian influence and training to prepare these children to face difficult lives. Once toddlers could talk, they learned to pray, and FC workers boasted of Crittenton children's good behavior; unlike ordinary children, they reportedly did not even cry when hungry. The workers thought that Crittenton babies had to be better behaved than their counterparts in order to compensate for the circumstances of their births. At the same time, the well-regulated Crittenton nursery regimen relied on the participation of Crittenton inmates. As one Crittenton worker explained when discussing feeding schedules, "It cannot be done unless the girls cooperate." Just as women across the country responded positively to Children's Bureau mandates regarding child care, Crittenton home residents did the same.[29]

This emphasis on child welfare also led to more open discussion of the problem of illegitimate children, traditionally considered the products of sin and therefore social outcasts. During the progressive period, reformers tended to stress the children's innocence and concentrate on ways to improve their lot. They did this not only for the children but also for the sake of society. Barrett explained that the Crittenton organization had been calling attention to the problem of the illegitimate child for thirty years in an effort to protect those children from ridicule and social maladjustment. She warned, "The name of 'bastard' which is thrown at a child by its playmates on the street has turned many a boy into a criminal with his hand against society!"[30] Barrett exerted her considerable influence and energy into ameliorating the stigma of illegitimacy.

One way Crittenton workers tried to alleviate the problems illegitimate children faced was to convince mothers to be responsible. In so doing the workers attached special importance to the child's needs. This represented a new dimension to Barrett's earlier view of motherhood as

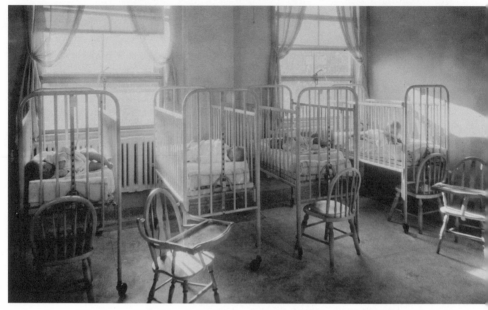

The Detroit Florence Crittenton home nursery. Courtesy of the Detroit Public Library, Burton Historical Collection.

a means of regeneration for the woman. Barrett advised home officials to remind each inmate that while she was in the Crittenton home, "she is a partner with God in perfecting a human body which will be the temple of the holy ghost" and to point out that the girl had already "been a factor in robbing her unborn child of what everyone has a right to—an honest birth and an unsullied name." It was incumbent on the mother to do everything in her power to make certain that the child was healthy and well equipped to "overcome the difficulties which lie in its pathway." According to Barrett, the young mother should be "made to feel that every thought of hers is reflected in the life of her child."[31] Crittenton people did not view this as punishment but as a validation of motherhood's preeminence. Barrett's statements in this regard illustrate the ambivalence that FC workers felt toward inmates. Crittenton women often condemned the actions of their charges' that had led to nonmarital pregnancy. While they tried to make the best of the situation, and I think were convinced that the women had the potential to be good mothers, most workers thought Crittenton mothers faced an uphill battle to overcome their situation.

While Barrett had always recognized motherhood's elevated position, she, like a number of other progressives, redefined the mother's task. The mother had to "pursue the best interests of the child" as a part of the more child-centered progressive outlook, and for this task maternal instincts were no longer sufficient: women needed education. Scientific motherhood served to elevate the mother's functions to a profession, a decidedly middle-class vision. Once a level of middle-class professionalization was reached, the task was to bring mothers of all classes up to that standard. Mothers were to spread their influence across society through their children and give their advice on any issue that concerned the family.[32] As *Girls* reminded its readers, "Everything that a man has and is he owes to his mother. From her he gets health, brain, encouragement, moral character and also his chances of success." This viewpoint empowered mothers both inside and outside of FC homes, as the National Congress of Mothers agenda indicates. Crittenton workers viewed the sacred responsibility of motherhood as a force for improving the lives of their inmates, but also for making society in general better.[33]

Since Crittenton girls bore their motherhood responsibilities in the face of society's censure, they had to sacrifice even more than other mothers if they were to achieve this ideal. Consequently, when a Crittenton mother fulfilled her obligations, Crittenton workers believed that she had performed a great service for society. The *Florence Crittenton Magazine* dedicated a poem to such self-sacrificing girls:

The bravest battle that ever was fought!
Shall I tell you where and when?
On the maps of the world you'll find it not;
'Twas fought by the mothers of men.

Nay, not with cannon or battle shot,
With sword or nobler pen;
Nay not with eloquent word or thought
From mouth of wonderful men.

But deep in the walled-up woman's heart . . .
Of woman that would not yield,
But bravely, silently bore her part . . .
Lo, there is the battle-field:

No marshaling troop, no bivouac song,
No banner to gleam and wave,
But oh, these battles, they last so long . . .
From babyhood to the grave![34]

The poem praised the long-term commitment an unmarried mother made when she decided to raise her own child, and stressed the arduous nature of the task. When comparing the unmarried mother's battle against terrific odds with the kinds of battles men fought, the poem judged the woman's battle the "bravest." Gender differences are prominent in the poem, which hints that while men engaged in battles that society noticed and acknowledged, the woman who "bravely, silently bore her part" also deserved recognition. Crittenton people strived to support the unmarried mother's effort and to aid her in practical ways. Their emphasis on maternalism placed the organization securely within the realm of similar efforts by the National Congress of Mothers and other groups who worked to make the middle-class concept of motherhood universal.

Crittenton workers actively campaigned for society's acceptance of the illegitimate child. The magazine reminded its readers that part of the illegitimate child's difficulty was due to polite society's ostracism. As Hastings Hart wrote in the *Florence Crittenton Magazine,* "Whatever blame may attach to the mother, the father, the grandparents or the community, the baby is innocent."[35] Kate Waller Barrett proclaimed, "Society can never make up to the child for that which it has been robbed," and then asked, "Is that any reason why they should further rob the child and discriminate against him?"[36] Barrett thought the term *illegitimate* was more appropriate for the parents than the child, and she sometimes used the term *anonymous child* in place of it.[37] The *Florence Crittenton Magazine* reminded workers, "There can be no hardship in appearing in public with these little waifs, even if their vociferated 'mama' or more embarrassing 'pap' gives room for speculation and blushes." This attitude placed the NFCM at odds with most of their contemporaries and established the organization as a leader in striving for a change in attitude toward these children.[38] The NFCM position represented a tacit admission that changing standards of behavior and ideas regarding sexuality had created a new situation. The children who sometimes were the result of these altered sexual norms did not deserve condemnation.

The Crittenton concern for social acceptance for illegitimate children emerges clearly in the *Florence Crittenton Magazine* story "White Lilies." The local pastor informed the story's author that pregnant and unmarried Nannie was in need of a friend. The woman, carrying an armful of white lilies to bring hope and cheer, visited Nannie. When her child was a few weeks old, the church summoned Nannie for trial, despite her benefactor's protests. The trial reminded the author of Hester Prynne's in *The Scarlet Letter,* but the woman was able to convince the church that Nannie had been "grievously sinned against by a most worthless relative." The congregation allowed Nannie to remain a church member. According to the story's author, this decision assured the child the benefits of a Christian education instead of banishment from polite society, probably to an unsavory life. The white lilies were the first step in saving the child: if other women would take similar action, illegitimate children would be spared their traditional ostracism. The lilies "brought the first ray of cheer and hope to a heart and mind desperate with feelings of disgrace and ruin."[39] Not only had the congregation's decision helped Nannie, it had saved her child from almost certain doom and had probably protected society itself from a social miscreant. Thus in the Crittenton view, aiding the children of unmarried mothers was important not only for the women and their children but also for the general community. The fact that Nannie had been the victim of incest clearly played a part in the Crittenton response. The Crittenton worker viewed Nannie as a victim even if other members of the congregation were at first unwilling to do so.

Progressive child savers were also worried about the illegitimate child's physical well-being. Mortality rates among children born out of wedlock were usually much higher than those for other children. The Russell Sage Foundation and other groups argued that this was often due to the failure of an illegitimate child's mother to do her duty and breast-feed her child. Sometimes these mothers did not wish to nurse their children, and it was acceptable to separate the mother and her illegitimate child and place the infant in a foster home. Once the child was gone, the mother could make between eight and ten dollars a week as a wet nurse. This practice not only offered the mother a means for earning her living but also provided some upper- or middle-class child with the benefits of breast feeding while not inconveniencing the child's mother.[40]

The Crittenton homes could point with pride to their established procedure of keeping mother and child together for at least six months and to accompanying higher survival rates. Workers required all prospective FC home inmates to promise to breast-feed their babies if physically possible. Workers viewed only transmissible diseases such as tuberculosis or syphilis and mental incompetence on the part of the mother as acceptable excuses for not breast feeding an infant.[41] In a typical case, Barrett told an FC home inmate that she must nurse her baby because "there is a fluid which is secreted by nature . . . that is absolutely necessary for starting that child properly in life." She explained that there was no substitute for "that medicine which God has put there." She added, "Surely you will be willing to sacrifice this little thing for the good of the child."[42] Barrett's assessment of the benefits of mother's milk was an accurate one, and Crittenton infants continued to enjoy higher survival rates than those in most other institutions. Barrett and her associates recognized the mother-child bonding that is an important part of breast feeding as well.

Eventually, most state charity organizations adopted policies similar to those of Crittenton's. In 1916, for example, Maryland made it illegal to separate a mother and child younger than six months for the purpose of placing the child in a foster home, and reformers throughout the country cited the Maryland law as a model.[43] Although it was often impractical for working women to breast-feed their children, Crittenton workers and other reformers insisted that motherhood demanded it. Some homes allowed inmates to work as wet nurses and to breast-feed their own children at the same time. Both infants received a supplemental bottle, a practice that guaranteed both children the benefits of breast feeding. It also indicated that some middle-class women were not following the advice of reformers, and that breast feeding was more common among working-class women than middle-class women.[44] Progressive women reformers became outspoken advocates of breast feeding and urged "natural" feeding on all mothers. The Children's Bureau, through programs established under Shepherd-Towner, encouraged breast feeding as the surest way to promote infant health, particularly protection from intestinal problems. Ironically, this policy tied women more closely to their children and proscribed their activities for an extended period of time.[45] In FC homes this played into the hands of workers, who were convinced that if inmates' residence was extended, there was a greater chance of the girl receiving adequate training to equip her to function outside the home environment.

Florence Crittenton workers thought that many of an illegitimate child's problems stemmed from the fact that she had no name. The *Florence Crittenton Magazine* encouraged workers to advise girls to go to court to obtain surnames other than the mother's maiden name for their children.[46] Workers attending the 1905 national conference resolved: "That this conference recommends legislation in favor of illegitimate children bearing the name of the father, and inheriting his property in cases where by admission or conclusive proof the parentage is definitely established."[47] This represented a departure from previous practices. Eventually, Barrett went so far as to contend that the mother of an illegitimate child ought to have a legal right to the exalted title Mrs., and both she and the child should have the right to bear the father's name. Although many women simply had taken the father's name to protect themselves and their children, Barrett believed establishing a legal right would remove a great handicap from illegitimate children and at the same time make life easier for the mothers. Barrett even carried a supply of gold wedding bands and made them available to any inmate who wanted one.[48] This was in direct contradiction to some progressive reformers' convictions and is an aspect of the Crittenton regime that historians have ignored. Many progressives deemed it irresponsible for workers to allow women to avoid the consequences of their actions by claiming to be married. These same reformers thought it was unethical to participate in such a rouse. The Crittenton strategy, in contrast, opened the way for unmarried mothers to return to regular society. Barrett told the National Conference of Charities and Corrections in 1910 that when reformers couldn't have the father, mother, and child, they nevertheless could have "that trinity, powerful for much good, mother, child, home."[49] Barrett's advocacy of unmarried mothers having the ability to build home lives for their children helped redefine the meaning of home and family. Even today some Americans would object to Barrett's position, but she continued to campaign for it within the social-work community. Barrett believed wholeheartedly that if Crittenton charges could be protected from censure and ostracism through simple tactics such as wearing wedding rings and using the title Mrs., they should do so, both to save their children from embarrassment and to ensure that the mothers achieved the respect their motherhood entitled them to receive.

Barrett was convinced that the unmarried mother had a right to protect herself from undue humiliation. In fact, the Crittenton practice of transferring women to homes in other geographic localities aided Crittenton girls in hiding their past. Barrett's position reflected her belief that an unmarried mother was entitled to the full status of motherhood and was perfectly capable of fulfilling her maternal responsibilities. According to Barrett, what in contemporary language would be referred to as a single-parent household was a home, and local gossip regarding a woman's marital status should not be allowed to inhibit the mother from performing her duty. Barrett was willing to risk criticism from other reformers in her belief that the power of motherhood transcended other considerations. Her attitude was an affirmation of Crittenton inmates' ability to provide stable homes for their babies and her conviction that Florence Crittenton mothers could serve as "both father and mother" to their children. This wider view of family and its definition favored women, expanded their power, and challenged traditional ideology.[50]

By 1920 the progressive child-welfare establishment had converted to Barrett's viewpoint. Following meetings in Chicago and New York, where nationally recognized leaders met to consider the issue of illegitimacy, the Children's Bureau published *Standards of Legal Protection for Children Born out of Wedlock,* the recommendations of which were for policies Barrett and her associates had been following for years: licensing hospitals receiving unmarried mothers, extension of inheritance rights, and allowing the child to use the paternal surname. Emma O. Lundburg and Katherine F. Lenroot of the Children's Bureau reported in a study of illegitimacy that "the fundamental need of childhood is maternal care, no less for children of illegitimate birth than for others."[51] While historians have labeled Crittenton policies as backward and punitive, they were in fact on the cutting edge of developments in social-welfare concerns for unmarried mothers and clearly influenced the thinking of progressive reformers recognized by historians as leaders in the social-welfare movement.[52]

The new attention to children reaped benefits as FC workers found that appealing to the public's concern for children gained substantial results. A 1910 issue of *Girls* chided readers, "While you are reading look at the dear faces on these pages—a group of little ones pleading for the home associations which you now are so fond of recollecting. . . . Are we ready to meet those little ones on the Great Day and will our skirts be clean?"[53] It was difficult for women to ignore this kind of appeal, and pictures of babies—baskets of babies, cribs full of babies, babies in every conceivable pose—began to appear in almost every Crittenton publication in

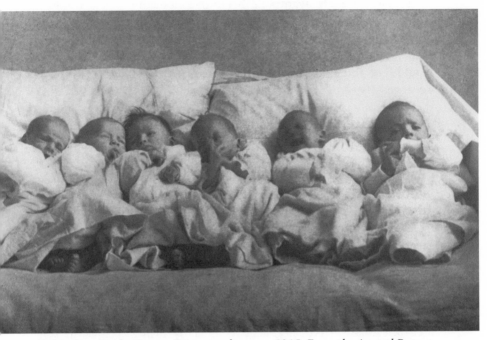

Babies born in the Boston Crittenton home, c. 1915. From the Annual Report of the Florence Crittenton League of Compassion, Inc., 1915.

an attempt to solicit support for programs and homes. Florence Crittenton workers were acutely aware of the bonds that motherhood created among women and they consciously sought to exploit those feelings.

Recognizing the potential of using the babies as attention-getters, Crittenton homes turned to an event they called a "baby show." The home would rent an empty store front and advertise the show for weeks in advance. In one of the windows workers might place a scene depicting the figure of a woman with an infant in her arms knocking for admission at a door marked Florence Crittenton Home. In the other windows there would be a crib with tiny babies in it and a number of toddlers playing on the floor. A nurse and a Crittenton worker were present to care for the children and to answer any questions. There was a conspicuously displayed box for donations, but workers preferred to emphasize the educational aspects of the "baby shows." *Girls* reported of the Washington, D.C., show, "Many a young man realized more fully something of his personal responsibility as he looked into the innocent faces of those who were through no fault of theirs deprived of their birthright."[54]

Despite the educational value, several church and women's groups objected to the display of illegitimate children. Barrett maintained that the shows were not in poor taste and that only through actually seeing the children did the hard facts of illegitimacy come across to many people. She was certain that recognition of the problem was the first step toward ending it, but she also was aware of how profitable the shows were. Barrett explained to one church group that at a recent baby show over 8,000 people had contributed money, while previously there had been only 410 contributors in all of Washington, D.C. Barrett supported the baby show because of its educational value and because "our policy in the past has been without results so far as educating the public was concerned."[55] Perhaps recent increases in numbers of nonmarital births give impetus to Barrett's viewpoint: no amount of explanation substituted for seeing the helpless infants. The window full of babies brought home the point that regardless of the marital status of their mothers, children required care and support. At the same time, the baby shows provided irrefutable evidence that it was impossible to determine the marital status of a baby's parents simply by looking at the child. Barrett risked the censure of more traditional women both in the interests of Crittenton financial solvency and as a part of her campaign to bring the issue of illegitimacy directly to the public.

Barrett was one of 215 experts on children's issues who received invitations to President Theodore Roosevelt's White House Conference on Dependent Children. Only thirty of the delegates were women, and the conference represented the first time that children's issues received such a prominent place on a president's national agenda. Barrett's inclusion among the conference attendees speaks to her established position among progressive child savers. She also addressed the conference on the topic of unmarried mothers.[56] Under Barrett's direction, Florence Crittenton homes provided considerable data and otherwise cooperated with federal agencies studying the problem of unmarried mothers and their children. The Children's Bureau proclaimed the importance of maternity homes such as the Crittenton establishments when it found that they held "the most strategic positions since a large number of mothers come to them first for assistance." As the bureau investigated this issue, it found that the policies the Crittenton organization had followed for years were in fact the desirable ones—keeping mother and child together, training the mother for domestic work, and providing follow-up services for the mothers. The bureau concluded, "Domestic service offered the readiest and frequently the only solution to their two-fold problem of obtaining situations where they could support themselves and keep their children with them."[57] This validation of their procedures provided Kate Waller Barrett and her followers impetus to continue their efforts. Clearly, the Crittenton organization played a role in creating what historian Robyn Muncy has described as a "Female Dominion," where the concerns of women and children had preeminence.[58]

At the same time, Barrett was fully aware that some progressive reformers viewed Crittenton institutions and those of other private charities as inferior to public efforts staffed by professional social workers. She complained to attendees at the National Conference of Charities and Corrections in 1908 that many public charity workers "looked down" on people who worked with private charities and considered them not as "people belonging to the same intellectual rank." The public (professional) social workers viewed their counterparts in private pursuits as "soft headed as they are soft hearted and therefore incapable of using wise discretion." Barrett urged her colleagues associated with private charities to work to change this misconception. In Dr. Barrett's view, the problem was a perceptual one, not a realistic one as several historians have recently suggested. According to Barrett, the difficulty stemmed from the fact that private charity workers did not spend as much time and effort touting their own accomplishments through a series of formal reports and similar methods. Barrett was convinced that the practices and procedures of Crittenton workers and their colleagues were every bit as professional and scientific as those in public charity efforts, but they suffered from an image problem stemming from their historical association with nine-teenth-century benevolence. Barrett set out to counteract these attitudes through a positive program of publicizing Crittenton accomplishments, and she urged other private charity workers to do the same. Barrett's ideas provide a warning to historians seeking to categorize Crittenton efforts as belonging more to the nineteenth century than the twentieth.[59] The Boston FC home annual report for 1914 said of the first Crittenton home, "It was all very simple and to modern ideas very crude. There was no attempt at classification nor scientific observation." Obviously, the Boston Crittenton workers believed that their practices were far removed from those early Crittenton efforts, and the evidence points in the same direction.[60] The National Florence Crittenton Mission boasted a pattern of increasingly sophisticated systemization that contributed to the pro-fessionalization of social work.

Due to Kate Barrett's concern for child welfare, the NFCM was one of the first institutions to demand that the government inspect child-care facilities, and that women receive appointments to the inspection bureau-cracies due to their special knowledge of child-rearing techniques. Al-though some progressives had ambivalent feelings about government intervention into philanthropic work, many like Barrett came to believe that private efforts were inadequate to maintain proper standards of care.[61] At the National Conference of Charities and Corrections in 1908, and again at the White House Conference on Dependent Children in 1909, Barrett delivered forceful speeches in favor of state supervision. Speaking as head of one of the largest chains of private institutions, Barrett astonished many when she said at the White House Conference (where this issue prompted one of the most contentious debates), "A private institution has nothing to lose and everything to gain by public investigation."[62] Barrett was convinced that public scrutiny would reveal the superiority of Crittenton methods and would help to weed out insti-tutions delivering substandard care. She believed that Crittenton meth-ods would stand up well in any such investigation.

Delegates to the 1916 National Florence Crittenton Conference voted to work for a law requiring annual licenses for lying-in facilities and child-care institutions.[63] Crittenton people hoped this kind of public examina-tion would result in more institutions patterned after the Crittenton model and would put an end to maternity hospitals that did nothing to keep the mother and child together. Barrett explained, "For a private charity receiving public money, to object to state supervision is almost *prima facie* evidence of the fact that there is something in its methods which would not commend itself to enlightened public sentiment."[64] Barrett and her followers were confident that their institutions would receive glowing endorsements from government officials and this would make it easier to raise money and would further their campaign for greater recognition. Barrett parlayed her expertise into a powerful force in this direction. When government investigators found a maternity home in Richmond, Virginia, to be substandard, they called on Barrett for assistance. According to *Girls,* she took "hold of the situation and a complete reorganization will follow."[65] By 1917 Barrett had over twenty years of experience dealing with unmarried mothers and was a recognized authority on the subject. She worked to spread Crittenton notions of proper maternity home operation and held them up as an example of scientific social work.

In keeping with her belief that child-care institutions ought to be subject to government inspection, Kate Waller Barrett also advocated that all Florence Crittenton homes be recipients of governmental funds. Barrett thought that since FC homes provided the best possible care, they had nothing to fear from inspection and they deserved government support. Like some other progressives, Barrett saw government as having the necessary financial resources to undertake support of social programs when the private sector could no longer carry the burden. As early as 1893, the federal government had provided funds for the Washington, D.C., home to care for "incorrigible or friendless girls" who came under the auspices of the Board of Charities. The government paid the home $12.50 a month per capita for these girls. In seeking federal funds, the Crittenton women confronted considerable obstacles, and their experience points to the tightrope that women reformers in the period walked as they sought to expand their activities without jeopardizing their status as "true" women. In order to obtain the funding, workers had to appear before the Senate committee in charge of the District of Columbia to present their case. In 1899 the women made an "eloquent plea" that resulted in the committee voting to double the Crittenton appropriation. The Washington, D.C. superintendent of charities, Herbert W. Lewis, reprimanded the Crittenton workers, claiming, "There was no sound reason for this appeal. This is a woman's work for women. It should be left untouched by the hand of officialdom."[66] The Crittenton dilemma was clear. When they spoke out on their own behalf, they opened themselves up to criticism. At the same time, Crittenton workers sought both attention and greater funding in order to expand their efforts. This Crittenton experience was duplicated on many occasions as women moved to expand their realm of influence from home to community.

Under Barrett's leadership, the Crittenton organization dismissed objections to their applications for public funding, and by 1912 many other homes received money from various governmental entities.[67] The 1914 annual report declared, "There is no reason why every well-conducted home should not receive an appropriation," provided of course that the home was accountable and that the money was spent on "legitimate wards of the state."[68] While increased government assistance helped to ease the homes' financial crunch, it was not entirely satisfactory because the funds were never sufficient to operate a home completely and because they depended on political considerations. Eventually, most homes turned to community chests to supplement their governmental incomes.[69]

Progressive ideas regarding education also influenced FC policy. John Dewey and other progressive educators viewed vocational education as a means of ameliorating social problems, especially those resulting from poverty. Barrett and the NFCM hoped to be part of the vocational movement and made changes in the educational component of the Crittenton program accordingly. However, as was the case with many progressive institutions, FC vocational training was sometimes based on institutional maintenance and Crittenton workers tended to exaggerate the benefits of the training the inmates received.

Crittenton workers did not abandon their ideas regarding housekeeping's significance, and Florence Crittenton girls still learned social amenities. Dr. Barrett pointed out to delegates to the 1912 convention that things like "the proper arrangement of a tray, making a good cup of tea, the proper serving of a glass of water," having good manners, and caring for house plants and flowers all were part of "training a girl into a very useful and valuable person and none of them requires any equipment."[70] Barrett and her cohorts continued to advocate training in the social amenities as an avenue for "gaining in character, dignity, and self-respect."[71] However, being able to serve a glass of water properly and care for house plants did not prepare all Crittenton girls to make an adequate living. Crittenton workers concluded that not every girl was suited for domestic service; moreover, domestic service did not prove to be the panacea that Barrett and others had intended. Chicago board members were indignant to find that one of their girls feared she was pregnant again as the result of an attack her employer had made while his wife was recuperating from childbirth. The local Aid Society had assured the board that the household was suitable, but the board believed the man was more at fault than the girl.[72] This incident illustrates both one of the hazards of domestic service as well as the Crittenton board's attitude toward their charges. It would have been common to blame the former inmate for the situation, but the Crittenton women placed the blame primarily with the man.

Some Crittenton workers began to examine the view that domestic service was the most favorable source of employment for Crittenton charges. The 1906 annual meeting included a session on "What Can Be Done to Make Domestic Service Safer and More Desirable for Young Women." Several meeting delegates in fact argued that domestic service was not "safe or desirable."[73] Crittenton literature began to comment on the number of girls who became inmates following a stint as a domestic servant, irrefutable proof that a domestic service position was not always the most advantageous for former Crittenton residents. In fact, every study of prostitution during the progressive period found that domestic servant was most often a prostitute's previous occupation.[74]

Crittenton workers also found it increasingly difficult to place girls as domestic servants. Fewer middle-class homes employed domestic help and fewer women wanted to employ Florence Crittenton girls. Workers began to admit that sometimes their former inmates did not please their employers, as Alice's case demonstrated. According to the Chicago board, "a fine family" employed Alice and the lady of the house complained that Alice stayed out two times in one week past 11:00 P.M., discouraging the lady from employing another Florence Crittenton girl. The board believed that it had done all it could for Alice and sent her on her way.[75] Domestic service had limitations as an occupation for Crittenton inmates. Workers worried that they could not assure Crittenton girls a safe environment. Clearly, Alice resented the rules her employer set for her.

In response to the recognition that inmates needed broader training, as well as the changes in Crittenton ideas regarding domestic service's safety and availability, many FC workers began to call for vocational training. As Mrs. W. Starr Gephert explained in her 1905 convention speech, "The Value of Technical and Industrial Training in Moral Reform," "We must also teach them, develop them and fit them as far as we can during the period that they are our wards for lives of future usefulness, training them to some form of self-help and self-support."[76] Crittenton people were not blind to the challenge this goal represented. Crittenton inmates battled stigma and social prejudice while seeking to make a living "without the temptation to return to the easier method of a sinful life," as one worker termed it. According to the worker's assessment, only clerks, nurses, artisans, factory operatives, or domestic servants commanded the wages necessary, and she urged Crittenton institutions to provide training in those fields.[77] The worker's list of occupations indicates the narrow parameters of women's employment in the first years of the twentieth century. Although critics have pointed to the limited nature of Crittenton vocational training, job opportunities open for women guided the organization's efforts.

The first step in many homes was to improve and formalize the usual instruction in household work. Courses became more detailed, structured, and organized. The cooking course at one home, for example, was divided into beginning and advanced classes. The beginning course consisted of ten lessons, starting with cooking methods and dish washing and progressing to simple food preparation. Girls in the advanced class learned to prepare yeast breads, pastry, cakes, meats, vegetables, and salads. The courses also included rudimentary nutritional information. To complete the course, inmates were responsible for all the menus in the home for a month. The Boston home boasted of its newly installed cooking laboratory, where ten stations allowed each girl to have her own stove, utensils, and work space.[78] Similar systematization applied to sewing classes, where girls began by learning how to position the needle and thread and by lesson twenty-one were sewing eyelets. Each inmate made an apron, skirt, drawers, chemise, shirt, jacket, and night dress and could use them as a pattern for later sewing.

The laundry course included sorting and preparing items for washing, caring for the laundry room and equipment, and starching and stain removal—with special emphasis on yellow or grimy clothing. The course outline reminded students that "in laundry work, FORETHOUGHT is as much required as actual technical knowledge."[79] One home's course outline for care of the dining room and waiting on tables was seven legal-sized pages in length, devoting over a page and a half to how to wash the dishes, including the order in which they should be done—glassware, silver, and china (cups, saucers, bread and butter dishes, sauce dishes, plates, platters, and then vegetable dishes). Four pages explained how to serve each meal.[80] Crittenton people frequently referred to these augmented homemaking classes as *domestic science courses* and often inmates kept notebooks of their work for later reference. Courses in "home management" and "household hygiene" began to appear in Crittenton curricula.[81]

These Crittenton courses reflected the general trend in education to include domestic science or home economics. Ellen Swallows Richards and others had set out to convince society that the work of women, particularly mothers, was not all that easy—an idea that certainly coincided with Crittenton viewpoints. Domestic science sought to elevate woman's work to the status of a profession, an attitude Barrett and her followers

*A domestic science class, c. 1915. From the Annual Report of the Florence
Crittenton League of Compassion, Inc., 1915.*

had embraced for years. *Girls* frequently featured photographs of the various homes' domestic science classrooms or laboratories to empha-size the sophisticated technical training the homes were providing.[82]

Crittenton ventures into other areas of vocational training were more tentative, and often informal, piecemeal, and haphazard. Usually a home began by adding basic classes in the three R's to their regimen of domes-tic work and Bible studies. In many cases, one of the workers volunteered to teach the classes. The Nashville home reported the addition of a day school for three hours each afternoon in 1905. The matron noted, "If this were seized as it should be, as preparation for battling with the world, when they again enter its strifes, much could be done in the two years."[83] While seemingly a small start, providing academic training to inmates represented a change in Florence Crittenton philosophy and was a first step to expanded educational offerings.

Home workers began to seek opportunities for girls beyond what the home could offer. When a matron believed that one of her charges showed promise, it became acceptable practice for the girl to go outside the home and take courses in stenography or typewriting.[84] If the local board mem-bers deemed a girl worthy, they might send her to NFCM headquarters for training as a worker in a Crittenton or similar institution. If a home could not afford this, the board could employ a girl as a worker in resi-dence and provide training in that way.[85]

Gradually homes began to develop programs designed to prepare inmates for specific jobs—usually nurse or clerical worker. Practical nurs-ing was a logical expansion of the traditional role of mother, and since many Crittenton homes had maternity hospitals, it was relatively easy to provide basic instruction in nursing techniques. Barrett's own train-ing was particularly suited to giving advice regarding a nursing program. Instruction generally included how to bathe patients, make hospital beds, keep a room sanitary, give basic first aid, take a temperature, take a pulse and respiration, and care for infants. Some programs included theoreti-cal instruction in simple fractions, weights and measures, and the solu-tion table, to facilitate graduates administering medication and/or pre-paring special diets. Crittenton nursing courses usually included a segment on cooking for invalids. Girls trained in these elementary nursing skills were particularly suited for employment in homes in which a fully certi-fied nurse was either unnecessary or too expensive.[86]

Several homes operated formal training programs for nurses. The Spokane, Washington, newspaper described that city's Florence Crittenton nurses' training program as "an excellent preparatory school in that branch of work."[87] Dr. Agnes Eichelburger directed a nurses' training program at Sioux City, Iowa, and Boston opened a training school in 1908. In 1909 the Boston program was expanded from six to eight months to allow for a "broader and more thorough course of instruction."[88] The Lynchburg, Virginia, home boasted to 1917 readers of *Girls* that a home resident had completed a four year nurses' training course.[89] Crittenton workers saw nursing as a profession that required training. More important, Crittenton people believed their inmates were fully capable of completing nurses' training courses and holding responsible positions in the field.

By 1912 the New York City home's schedule included two night-school classes each week in addition to classes in millinery, dress making, domestic science, and current events.[90] The Detroit home featured the only nursemaids' training school in the city. A graduate nurse and kindergartner presented lessons in the care of children, and a local physician supplemented the classes with lectures. At a time when child care performed by someone other than the mother went against the norm, the Detroit Crittenton organization was a pioneer. The Detroit home's own day nursery served as a teaching laboratory as well.[91]

Often volunteers, usually women seeking to become involved in social reform, taught the classes. Miss Phyllis Green of the American College of Physical Culture instructed the Chicago girls. In New York, Miss Kate Keenly (according to a co-worker, "a gifted young business woman, intensely interested in all that pertains to girls") taught English. Miss Owens, a shopkeeper, taught the millinery class, with practical instruction in hat making and trimming as a feature. The Chicago board hired a nurse from Alaska to instruct the girls in practical nursing and child care. In 1903 the Baltimore home employed a graduate of the Pratt Institute to teach sewing and a graduate of the Drexel Institute in Philadelphia to provide cooking instruction. According to the Baltimore board, both women were "enthusiastic and competent" and "awakened a genuine interest among the girls."[92] These early Crittenton attempts at vocational instruction relied on and highlighted women's skills, and Crittenton workers made much of the idea that women volunteers provided role models as well as instruction for the inmates.

The matron or superintendent of each home was responsible for determining which girls had potential and in what direction the workers should encourage each girl. The national organization advised the matron to make this decision after analyzing the girl's character and ability. Apparently, some inmates had little or no choice in the matter of their vocational training, while in some homes workers tried to give their charges "a chance to choose their own occupation." The Paterson, New Jersey, home boasted of a resident training to be a teacher and of another working toward a "business career." By 1913 Barrett had stated categorically, "I guarantee to any girl who is now in a disreputable life an opportunity to fit herself for any profession in life that she may desire to fill—provided that she has the ability and character that would be required of a girl from any other walk of life, who would desire to take the same training."[93]

Barrett's claim is remarkable in light of early Crittenton organization expectations for their charges. Crittenton home officials began to speak frequently about preparing their girls to earn a living. The Little Rock home was proud to note that its charges had been able to go out as "self-supporting women."[94] The Little Rock organization's announcement carried dual significance. Achievement of self-support is noteworthy, but the fact that the workers conferred the elevated title "woman" to their former inmates suggests that Crittenton people shared Barrett's conviction that a girl's past placed no limits on her future and that these women should be prepared to earn their own livings. This predominant FC attitude placed the organization in opposition to most progressives. Many reformers worked to provide mothers' pensions to single mothers. The whole idea behind mothers' pensions was that it was inappropriate for a woman to work outside the home and still raise a family. (Few states' mothers' pension programs included unmarried mothers.) Crittenton philosophy made it clear that unmarried mothers were certainly mothers, and that their ability to maintain gainful employment did not detract from their motherhood, in fact it was a necessary aspect. Historians agree that the power to support children is a key one for women.[95] Barrett made it her business to ensure that Crittenton girls possessed that power.

The emphasis on organization and training marked a pronounced intention to move away from the kind of sentimentality that elevated a jar of peaches to a redeeming agent, but at the same time Barrett hoped to ensure that Crittenton homes did not fall prey to what she dubbed "institutionalization." As she explained, "Life in most institutions is abnormal." Institutional patterns too often jeopardized the primary Crittenton goal of "life in a normal family."[96] Barrett's concern with "institutionalization" was in the mainstream of progressive thought. In the early 1900s, R. R. Reeder of the New York Orphan Asylum wrote a series of articles for *Charities* expressing ideas strikingly similar to Barrett's and describing "Institutionalism" as a "combination of rote, routine, and dead levelism."[97] These characteristics ran counter to progressive emphasis on the individual.

Barrett advised homes to fight the trend toward institutionalization through recognizing each inmate's unique characteristics and resisting the temptation to sacrifice the homelike atmosphere. She advocated tactics such as Crittenton workers sitting at the same table and eating the same food as the inmates because she believed this practice made the home more familylike; so did baking a few loaves of bread at a time, rather than adopting the more efficient method of baking all the bread at once. But given the Crittenton desire to be modern and efficient, the battle against institutionalism was sometimes a losing one. The more girls each home accommodated, the more paid workers the homes employed, and the more structured home life became, the less the home resembled a family.[98]

A few examples of home policy changes serve to illustrate this trend. In her *Some Practical Suggestions for the Conduct of a Rescue Home,* Barrett advised matrons that when a girl first arrived, "In regard to asking her name, forbear, except to ask her, 'What name did you love best for your mother to call you when you were a little girl at home?'" The workers could then call the girl by that name to "bring up recollections of the happy days when she was a pure-hearted girl, and thoughts of a beneficial character will be aroused." Once the matter of a name was settled, Barrett added that the girl's compact with the home "is sealed by bowing in prayer" and she became a Florence Crittenton girl.[99] Both this informality and opportunity for anonymity became less frequent due to requirements for more statistics and better record keeping. The Chicago board discussed a girl who gave a false name, and the members determined to contact her doctor and find her true identity.[100] The Washington, D.C., home began to use printed admission applications that asked a prospective Florence Crittenton girl her full name, address, and birth date; her father's and mother's names, address, and occupation; her brothers' and sisters' names; her marital status; her schooling and work experience; and things such as "What plan, if any, have you for your child" and "Who will assume responsibility for you and your child when you are ready to leave the Home?"[101] The greater dependence on governmental funding spurred some of this more formal record keeping, as the homes sought to provide statistical reports of their spending and accomplishments. In addition, changing philosophies regarding social work demanded complete and accurate records. The New York mission's annual report for 1912 noted that as soon as a new inmate had bathed, "then a full record is taken of her case which is afterward investigated." By 1913 a girl seeking admission to many homes would usually be subject to such a formal case investigation.[102]

Many homes adopted a uniform application form that also asked about sex instruction, age of first and later sex "offenses," the men involved, date of last menstrual period, and the father of the child—his religion, occupation, age, nationality, marital status, physical condition, and whether or not he drank. There were blanks where a worker wrote down the girl's story or the "circumstances." The interviewer also underscored which of the following traits the girl in question possessed: restless, quiet, indolent, industrious, responsible, easily influenced, obedient, selfish, gets along with others, hyper-suggestible, independent, excitable, temper tantrums, hypersensitive, reclusive, impulsive, neurotic, easily discouraged, egotistic, individualistic, inconsiderate, unappreciative, weak-willed, sluggish, lacking ambition, self-centered, sullen, or other.[103] This tendency to invade all aspects of the girl's personal life and to evaluate her was typical of the developments within Crittenton homes during the early twentieth century. It also reflected the changing nature of professional social work with its emphasis on casework.

While the early homes tried to influence the mother to keep her child as part of a gradual rehabilitative process, later homes began to demand that the girl sign a contract promising to keep the child before being admitted to the home.[104] A typical contract read, "Do you understand and agree that if you become a mother in this Home you will be required to nurse and care for your baby, or babies, and will remain in the Home and under the care and control of this Home until the child is six months old?"[105] Since in many cases a girl who desired admittance to a Crittenton home had exhausted all other alternatives, she signed the contract regardless of her true feelings on the matter. Of course, in reality Crittenton officials had no way of forcing an inmate to honor the contract. The Portland, Oregon, board voted to allow five of the inmates to leave the home "as they threatened to run away if not permitted to do so."[106] Ultimately, charges were free to leave if they wished, and clearly there were cases in which women nearing the time of delivery used the Crittenton home facilities but had no intention of submitting to the Crittenton regimen.

Crittenton homes established strict rules to govern the behavior of the girls, and these rules were formalized in sharp contrast to the more family-like discipline of earlier homes. The Chicago board voted that the matron post a list of the rules in a prominent location in each girl's room.[107] Among the characteristic rules were requirements that the girls air their beds every morning; the matron often inspected each girl's dresser drawers and closets on a daily basis. As Crittenton workers discussed homosexuality and masturbation more openly, they forbade two girls from occupying the bathroom at the same time and did away with single rooms. The girls could not talk on the upper floors of the home, went to bed at 8:30 P.M. every night, and bathed daily. They were to be "obedient and loyal to all orders" and "kind and quiet in speech." The rules even described what cleaning jobs each girl should do, down to directing that the windows, doors, and moldings should be gone over with a soft cloth and the ceilings and walls cleaned with a flannel bag tied over a broom.[108]

Homes developed reward systems for those girls who behaved well. They had so-called honor classes for girls who for six months had "made a conscientious effort to do right" and had been "truthful, reliable, and trustworthy." Members of the honor class could go out alone occasionally and had their afternoons free. Other homes rewarded good behavior with little gold pins or similar tokens. Erie, Pennsylvania, home workers allowed the girls to organize their own group, the Blue Bird Club, to work for the home. The girls conducted their own meetings and with their funds purchased items the home needed. Workers believed that this encouraged responsibility, but of course, they closely supervised the meetings. The club's principal resolution was "I strive to be dainty in speech, dress and action," an aspiration worthy of any middle-class lady. Club members elected a president, secretary, treasurer, and librarian, and the industrial, music and social committees planned programs for the group.[109] The club was obviously patterned after the women's clubs to which Crittenton workers themselves belonged. While it is arguable that Crittenton objectives had changed little from an earlier period, the methods were more structured and organized and more closely patterned on Crittenton workers' own experiences.

Punishment and discipline also became more formal. Whereas Barrett had earlier advised that the matron and her staff confer daily to discuss the characteristics of each girl and comment "kindly but firmly" on her limitations, homes began to adopt a grading system to evaluate their charges.[110] A typical one used scores of 60–70, poor; 70–80, fair; 80–90, good; and 90–100, excellent. Girls received grades in such areas of general conduct as obedience, honesty, truthfulness, perseverance, patience, contentment, politeness, orderliness, cheerfulness, promptness, peaceableness, self-reliance, and self-control. Workers graded their charges on personal habits such as writing home, influence over other girls, and care of clothing, teeth, nails, books, papers and home property. Similar grades applied to school and class work. A system of demerits often accompanied the grading. Minor offenses—doing work noisily and swearing—resulted in three demerits. More serious offenses, such as lying, taking things, sulkiness, and bad temper, warranted five demerits. Serious violations, such as willful disobedience, doing things without permission, and fighting, received twenty demerits.[111] The demerit system was indicative of dual Crittenton goals. First, they wanted inmates to follow a course of behavior acceptable in general society—obviously stealing and fighting were inappropriate behaviors. However, it was also in the best interest of the institution that there be cooperation, so sulkiness and bad temper warranted the same penalty as lying and taking things. Willful disobedience was a particularly serious offense. The demerit system reflected both societal and Crittenton notions of order and women's proper place.

Not surprisingly, many girls were unwilling to enter an institution of this type, and even Barrett admitted that often girls came to Florence Crittenton homes as a last resort. Barrett did not see this as a condemnation of the Crittenton system, but rather of the girls. She believed the girls' objections to the strict regimen prevented them "from accepting the advice and help that we are willing to give." Barrett's attitude suggested that she thought she knew better than the girls what was good for them, and that they should be glad to sacrifice their freedom and control over their lives in exchange for the benefits of the home.[112] Although Barrett unquestionably had the best interest of the inmates in mind, girls who entered a Crittenton home paid a price in lost autonomy. Even those girls who at the outset were willing to sacrifice their independence sometimes rebelled against the regimen. The Portland, Oregon, board spent considerable time discussing how to deal with Lori, who refused to go to meals, and with two other girls who "in a state of rebellion" had "thrown off their uniforms and expressed their determination to leave the home."[113] These inmates were not simply pawns in the hands of middle-class reformers but expressed their displeasure when the rules seemed too strict. In July of 1904, the Portland, Oregon, board found their home "practically deserted" and the matron absent. There was much discussion in the board meeting regarding the girls' dismissal, and according to the secretary "much disapproval."[114] The Crittenton board would have preferred making some concessions to the girls, rather than simply dismissing them. When five girls asked that they be allowed to leave the same home, workers initially refused. However, the girls threatened to run away if the board did not accede to their wishes, and the Crittenton people arranged for the girls to go home. Crittenton people were willing to alter their policies when confronted with strong opposition on the part of their charges, a fact that sheds light on the nature of the relationship between workers and home residents. The lines between the two groups were fluid, allow-

ing for adjustments on both sides. While Crittenton
siderable power to try to influence girls with few opti
homes could not operate without inmates, and the
wielded at least a certain amount of power vis-à-vis

The attitudes of Florence Crittenton workers towa
changed during this period. The scientific attitude that
of progressivism included a new realism in analyzii
Florence Crittenton workers adopted this realistic view of fallen women
readily, since years of experience with rescue work had lessened the fervor of many workers. By 1906 the *Florence Crittenton Magazine* included
reports of failure in rescuing prostitutes as well as the glowing accounts
of successes so common earlier. The Chattanooga, Tennessee, home reported, "Several girls have come to us from the police courts and houses
of ill-repute, but they evinced no genuine desire to lead better lives and
in spite of all persuasions have gone back to their old lives of sin."[115] A
Bismarck, North Dakota, worker told of a girl who had said she wanted
to lead a different life, "but she was not able to hold out in her resolutions, and left in two days, probably to go back to her old life."[116] The
Boston superintendent admitted that during 1918, eleven inmates were
discharged before they delivered their babies.[117] In several instances workers described recalcitrant inmates as "incorrigible," a label that could
include everything from refusing to follow Crittenton rules to open rebellion. (Social workers often applied the adjective *incorrigible* to problem girls.) Inmate response to discipline also played a role in how board
members reacted to misbehavior. When the Portland board called Maude,
Earl, and Louise to "give an explanation for their conduct," they allowed
Louise to stay in the home since she seemed "overcome with contrition."
On the other hand, Maude indicated that she did not think she was "fit-
ted for the work," and Earl was "excited and resentful in her spirit." The
board asked both Maude and Earl to leave the home.[118] Sometimes notwithstanding all the workers' precautions, inmates engaged in conduct
that workers found unacceptable. On the other hand, Crittenton residents
sometimes chose behaviors that caused them to risk dismissal. Quite
possibly, Maude, Earl, and their colleagues behaved the way they did as
a strategy for obtaining dismissal.

Workers began to discuss openly alcoholism and drug addiction and
to admit that they were ill equipped to cope with these problems. The
Chicago home could not accept a morphine addict because it had no bars
on the windows nor door locks, and there were fears that she would sneak
out and take the drug.[119] The Denver home president requested prayers

...irty-nine-year-old Jennie Turner, "who struggled to overcome and ...ed . . . against drink, morphine, shame, her poor weak will yielded, and she is still a wanderer from the Father's House."[120] Substance abuse problems were difficult ones even in the early twentieth century, and Crittenton people recognized that they sometimes lacked both the facilities and the methods to deal with these problems.

Homes began to admit publicly that disciplinary and behavioral problems existed. The Boston superintendent reported, "I remember a large part of two days, hour after hour spent in trying to bring stubborn wills that had never been conquered, into subjection to Him."[121] After what some members felt was a scandalous display at a fund-raising tea, the Chicago board banned dancing in the home. One member thought that dancing was a "connecting link with the underworld," and the majority voted in agreement with her.[122] The same board took steps to stop girls from flirting at the upstairs windows after three girls had done so and "two rough looking men rang the bell and when admitted demanded to see the girls who had called them in." The shocked matron threatened to call the police, and the men left. The matron referred this problem to the board who acted to prevent any reoccurrence. A board member wrote to the people who brought May ——— to the home and told them to find her another place. The board sent one girl to the Home for the Friendless (apparently an institution the girls liked less than the Florence Crittenton home) and instructed the "ringleader," Helen ———, to make arrangements elsewhere for herself and her child.[123]

On another occasion the matron reported to the board that Marie and Kate had purchased liquor from a nearby shopkeeper. The board notified the police, who promised to keep an eye on the man and arrest him if he repeated the offense.[124] When Edna attacked another inmate with a safety pin, the Portland board decided that a medical examination was in order to determine whether or not Edna was mentally ill. Her presence in the home was causing the matron "much anxiety and worry."[125] Maud refused to wear her uniform and to eat with the family, and the Portland women asked her to leave.[126] The Detroit home noted that they refused to place inmates in positions if the board could not recommend them, and as a result several girls had left the home to "seek work for themselves."[127] Crittenton workers found these behaviors worrisome and reporting them represented a departure from past practice. These incidents again suggest that Crittenton inmates maintained control over their own actions as well and resisted Crittenton efforts to define their behavior.

The Chicago Florence Crittenton Anchorage. Courtesy of the National Florence Crittenton Mission.

Sometimes the board and matron were not able to deal with disciplinary problems themselves. In July 1913, the Chicago board discussed what to do about stealing in the home. Someone had stolen eighteen dollars from Sylvia in June, and in July another twenty-four dollars and some clothing were missing. The board secretary searched and questioned each girl individually, with no success. The board members hoped that the guilty girl would confess, and they joined in "earnest prayer" to that end. No girl came forward, and, indeed, two months later someone stole the matron's watch and rings. The board decided to have a police officer stay in the home for a week on the assumption that some girl in the home had an outside accomplice.[128] When the Portland, Oregon, matron could not control Helen, she summoned the police for assistance.[129] These Crittenton workers required the services of police officers to maintain order and discipline in their homes, and these incidents indicate the changing nature of Crittenton efforts. They also highlight a more realistic approach. Crittenton workers confronted the difficult nature of their task and did not pretend that prayers and kindness could solve all inmates' difficulties.

Barrett warned workers, "Never congratulate yourself upon not having bad girls in the Home unless you have been able to see them grow from bad girls into good girls. Remember that Florence Crittenton Homes are for bad girls just as much as they are for good girls." Heeding Barrett's advice was not always easy for Crittenton people.[130] Expulsion for not wearing the uniform and for flirting from the second story window suggests that some Crittenton workers had little tolerance for disobedience. This scenario led one historian to describe the Crittenton setting as featuring "more control than love." At the same time, the inmates had their own agendas, which obviously sometimes included resistance to Crittenton authority. Residents were often able to gain accommodation to their viewpoints through challenging workers' authority.[131]

Crittenton workers continued to make a concerted effort to provide their charges support and shelter during a time of emotional stress and trauma. During the early twentieth century there was a noted improvement in physical plants of Crittenton homes, as many moved to larger houses better able to accommodate the residents. Crittenton boards took great care in providing facilities that boasted yards and sunny, open spaces, and workers tried to make the inmates' rooms as bright and cheery as possible. Barrett reminded them, "Remember how much time you spent decorating your own daughter's room, don't these women deserve the same?"[132] Many workers took this notion of family responsibility to heart and expended considerable time and effort in decorating the homes.

In a similar vein, workers tried to provide residents with little tokens of encouragement and homes were grateful when circles gave residents something new to wear or some little trinket. From the workers' perspective, these things seemed to "satisfy the desire and restore happiness."[133] Workers did not expect their charges to give up everything and to live a life devoid of pleasure, and this attitude represented both a more realistic and more sympathetic side of Crittenton work—one many historians have ignored.

Most homes featured Christmas celebrations, and the care, planning, and pride in these events point to the familial relationship that existed. Boards tried to the best of their abilities to make certain that the inmates at the very least enjoyed a tree and a special meal. The Boston matron described Christmas in 1918, when Mrs. Jacob Frederick Brown sent a check for fifty dollars and each girl received a beautiful shirt waist and two pairs of stockings and each baby two warm garments. Mrs. Francis S. Cobb and some of her friends sent each inmate a "beautiful sewing box with all the necessary fittings," and the home staff gave each girl a silver thimble. Miss Lotta Crabtree had Christmas dinner at the home and left crepe de chine shirt waists for the girls and "exquisite" garments for each baby. Mrs. Anna Gage and Mr. Preston provided new Victrola records that "added much to the day's pleasure."[134] There was much more to Crittenton work than the desire to control inmates' lives.

Crittenton workers were aware that life in a Crittenton home meant a dramatic change from the "incident and excitement" many Crittenton inmates were accustomed to enjoying.[135] The workers attempted to present alternatives to the life-style that they hoped their charges had given up forever. They sponsored nightly entertainments and often recruited young women from various church and social groups to help with these evening programs. The magazine urged that "the successful young woman, especially if she be self-made and self-supporting is a constant object lesson and a stimulus to these broken young lives that have proved so sadly unsuccessful."[136] Whether or not these Crittenton attempts at providing role models for their charges succeeded is not easily documented, but their motivation was undoubtedly to encourage the Crittenton inmates and to underscore the possibility of an independent, self-supported life-style.

Attempts to make home existence more pleasant abound in the Crittenton literature, and the workers' desire to bring happiness to the inmates is often very touching. The Brookline, Massachusetts, circle donated money to send inmates to a vacation rest home on the Merrimac River.[137] In Boston, workers filled the back yard with a deep bed of sand

and planted ferns, flowers, and vines all around the grounds and installed garden seats. All summer long workers and inmates enjoyed "going to the beach." The superintendent reported, "It is impossible to estimate the benefit to the health of the girls by this happy out-door life, and the pleasure and fun were well worth the expenditure. The laughter and joyful shouts during the before-breakfast games of 'bean-bags' struck the right note for the long busy day."[138] Certainly, this picture of life in a Florence Crittenton home illustrates its most pleasant aspects and shows a side of the Crittenton work that was decidedly non-institutional and definitely not the "unfailingly grim" existence one historian described.[139] The Crittenton workers who reported these activities were genuinely pleased at the inmates' positive reactions. In contrast to the situation in 1904, when board members found the Portland home deserted, board members visiting the home in 1907 interviewed the residents and found "everyone was happy and contented."[140] Even with its negative aspects, life in a Crittenton home was often more desirable than alternatives available for unmarried mothers and their children. Crittenton workers certainly made an effort to guarantee that this was the case.

The years following Charles Crittenton's death saw the NFCM seek a closer association with the progressive movement. Crittenton workers adopted progressive tenets to their organization when they placed greater emphasis on work with unmarried mothers and their children. Crittenton efforts on behalf of illegitimate children were well within the framework of progressive concerns. When Kate Waller Barrett and her associates campaigned for government inspection and funding of child-welfare agencies, they were leaders in what became a key progressive demand. As the institutions embraced vocational education, they sought to increase their inmates' ability to support themselves and their children. Barrett and the other Florence Crittenton women were constantly striving to retain the homelike aspects of Crittenton institutions, while at the same time serving more women and instituting more sophisticated methods.

The tension between efforts to make inmates' stay happier and efforts to enforce Crittenton rules point to the complexities of Crittenton workers' relationship with their charges. As workers themselves grappled with seemingly conflicting views of their charges, and as they tried to help Crittenton inmates adjust to the changing nature of society, they found themselves expanding both their vision of Florence Crittenton work and their attitudes toward relationships among women.

Chapter 4

Helping Hands:
Women's Florence Crittenton Work

> Hands which lift up and never pull down.
> Hands which cover faults, rather than uncover.
> Hands that toil for others rather than for self.
> Hands which bear, rather than smite.
> Hands that bind up.
> —*Florence Crittenton Magazine*, 1906

The motives driving the growing army of NFCM workers help define the Florence Crittenton contribution to reform. Dr. Kate Waller Barrett's ideas regarding the elevated status of motherhood shaped Florence Crittenton policies and practices and certainly informed Crittenton relationships with other women. At the same time, in the view of some historians the workers, as well as those engaged in similar activities, were middle-class women who meddled in and manipulated working-class lives in an effort to bring about a well-ordered society. While conceding that the desire for social control motivated some aspects of Crittenton work, I have identified and stressed the presence of a genuine regard for the well-being of others as the primary incentive for most Crittenton activities. The Boston Florence Crittenton organization's formal name—the Florence Crittenton League of Compassion—was a reflection of workers' attitudes toward their Crittenton involvement. When Detroit matron Mary Heartwell told co-workers that "her heart ached" for the girls who entered the home, she expressed a sentiment other workers probably shared.[1] As workers sought to translate their concern for their charges into action, they often reevaluated their relationship with their clients, as well as their own positions as women in American society. Informed by their own experiences, Florence Crittenton women established programs and policies that tacitly challenged the standard interpretation of women's sphere as being limited to domestic concerns and elevated motherhood to new heights.[2]

Crittenton work was neither glamorous nor popular, because most people outside of the organization found the idea of associating with typical FC clients repugnant. Barrett reported that in the first years women would draw their skirts away when she and other rescue workers passed, for fear of contamination.[3] The Augusta, Georgia, matron remembered, "Everyone stared at me when I went out. I would hear them whisper, 'There goes the matron of that Florence Crittenton Home.'"[4] Volunteers often encountered strong opposition to the establishment of homes in local neighborhoods, and these objections sometimes included personal attacks. Los Angeles workers reported with pride and considerable defiance that they had placed a copper box in the cornerstone of their new building. The container held a copy of the temporary injunction that area residents had obtained after claiming the Crittenton home would decrease neighborhood property values.[5] Despite this opposition, the workers had persevered and completed construction of their new building. Barrett and other workers were sensitive to these condemnations, and although the *Florence Crittenton Magazine* urged critics to suggest alternative strategies and to make constructive suggestions, this request apparently had little effect. Crittenton people remained on the defensive, constantly seeking to justify their actions.[6]

Florence Crittenton work was often difficult, always time-consuming, and sometimes thankless; all aspects required commitment and dedication. Workers frequently commented on how tiring and even debilitating the work was and on the considerable physical and emotional toll it took. One remarked, "No one but those connected with a Florence Crittenton Home can realize the discouragements and seeming disappointments."[7] Another worker noted, "There is something particularly distasteful and distressing in personal acquaintance with the victims, a distaste and distress that sometimes leads to actual nervous collapse."[8] Grace Topping, a longtime Crittenton worker, spoke of her determination to continue the work even though she sometimes felt disappointment that she spent considerable effort with no results. There is an element of negativity in these comments, as well as a clear indication that workers themselves often had serious reservations concerning their daily, face-to-face dealings with women whose actions violated society's most basic rules. Crittenton workers could not avoid a certain repugnance for their charges in some cases. However, the fact that Crittenton workers overcame their objections illustrates the level of both mental and physical commitment Crittenton involvement required. Yes, the workers were cognizant of vast differences in class and behavior that sometimes appeared insurmountable, but they refused to give up, they refused to allow their own prejudices to prevent them from continuing their efforts. This is not to say that Crittenton workers totally put aside class differences, any more than they could forget completely that their charges had engaged in behavior that most workers thought was both unthinkable and reprehensible.

Rising to the challenge, a cadre of women devoted their lives to Crittenton endeavors. A pattern emerged in which women's volunteer work evolved into full-time, paid employment. Kate Waller Barrett's career had followed this course. So did that of Mrs. J. C. LeVey, for many years treasurer at the Charleston, South Carolina, home, who was widowed and left with a small son and a limited income. The national organization enlisted her services as one of the field secretaries, thus enabling her to continue in work that she found fulfilling and at the same time provide for her child. Others, such as Grace Nieman, Margaret Luther, and Grace Topping, were unmarried women who filled a number of positions in the Crittenton organization during their careers.[9] Mary Heartwell founded the Detroit home in 1897 and served as its superintendent for twenty-five years.[10] Sarah Malone, an active Crittenton worker among African Americans for more than twenty years—first in Topeka, Kansas, and later on the national level—was able to report, "It is simply a calling and I am not a bit more tired now than I was when I started."[11] Malone's sentiments resonated among Crittenton women. Despite all of their own inhibitions, society's censure, and the continuing struggle for results, Crittenton workers persevered and formed long-lasting relationships among themselves in the process.

Many of these workers assumed the position of matron in Florence Crittenton homes. The matron needed to possess a number of virtues, as well as practical skills. A Spokane board member wrote to a prospective matron in 1911 that the board wanted a matron who was a trained obstetrical nurse, who could be sympathetic but at the same time "sufficiently stern to enforce the rules." She had to be able to gain the girls' confidence while "at the same time not unduly prying into their affairs." She had to know how an institution such as the Crittenton home "should be managed" but needed to delegate the actual work to others. The matron needed to be prepared to supervise and train girls in the areas of nursing, sewing, laundry work, and all areas of general housekeeping. In exchange the board was prepared to pay fifty dollars a month, plus room, board, and laundry.[12] Obviously, the Spokane home was looking for a matron who possessed considerable skills and talents. During the early years of the twentieth century, Crittenton organizations strived for even greater professionalism in their workers. When the Washington, D.C., home appointed Miss McAuliffe as superintendent in 1906, officials proudly announced that she had passed the New York Civil Service Examination and had "held a responsible position in Bedford Reformatory." Reformers considered Bedford a model institution, and the Crittenton organization sought trained social workers for its positions.[13]

While some historians have emphasized the benevolent and voluntary aspects of Crittenton work, from the beginning most matrons were paid employees. As early as 1899, the National Florence Crittenton Mission reported that nationwide the organization employed 125 salaried workers. In fact, it was not unusual for salaries to constitute half of a home's monthly budget. Mary Heartwell, Sarah Malone, Margaret Luther, Grace Topping, and others made Crittenton work their careers.[14] The *Florence Crittenton Magazine* reminded readers that while the organization's salaries were not large, workers lived in comfortable homes and received board and laundry as well. Few occupations for women could offer more in terms of actual remuneration or, certainly, the fulfillment that comes from performing meaningful work. Crittenton workers filled responsible positions while enjoying safe and comfortable living quarters.[15] Matrons considered themselves "workers," and Crittenton boards recognized that matrons were professionals, possessing skills and knowledge that warranted payment.

Matrons were in closest contact with the girls and subject to considerable pressure from several directions, making this job's taxing nature a constant source of concern for the organization. In 1896 the Boston home lost two matrons because both "found the work too severe for their strength," and in 1904 a similar situation forced the home to close temporarily. Frequent reports that workers were "resting," "recovering their strength," "broken down," or suffering from illness that required a respite from Crittenton work highlighted the physical and psychological burdens the matrons bore.[16]

The Crittenton organization attempted to ameliorate this problem in a number of ways. The Los Angeles women planned a home for tired Crittenton workers that featured a beautiful mountain view; and the Los Angeles women promised their colleagues around the country that they would find "the latch string out and a warm welcome."[17] Barrett built a summer cottage at Cape Henry for workers to escape the Washington, D.C., heat and established a cottage at Ossening Heights, New York, for

Matron at the door of a Florence Crittenton home. Courtesy of the National Florence Crittenton Mission.

New York City workers.[18] The Phoenix, Arizona, matron was delighted when, after she had been "almost worn out" from nine summers in Phoenix, the local board rewarded her with a trip to the national WCTU convention in Los Angeles and five dollars spending money for an excursion of her choice.[19] *Girls* reported that the New Haven, Connecticut, home sponsored an October social hour for members of local philanthropic organizations. All of the attendees were invited to bring pictures of their summer vacations to share. *Girls* editorialized that other homes should follow suit, since the gathering was a "delightful" way not only to broaden Crittenton associations with others in the social work field but also to "brighten the lives of our workers."[20] Despite these concerted efforts to prevent what modern observers call "burn-out," that phenomenon plagued the Crittenton organization just as it does helping professions today; and Crittenton people constantly searched for ways to alleviate stress.

Similar opportunities for relief were usually not available to the volunteer Crittenton board members, who were usually middle-class wives who devoted years to FC efforts. Cornelia Russell Rockwell was a typical board member. A Nashville native, she married in 1873 when she was only fourteen years old (her new husband was thirty-six). Cleveland Rockwell was a prominent civil engineer, surveyor, and landscape painter. Cornelia Rockwell, the mother of two daughters, was instrumental in founding the Portland Florence Crittenton rescue home. Oregon governor George Chamberlain appointed Rockwell to supervise the home finances when the state took over its operation, and in 1911 she became board president. This work was incredibly time-consuming as the boards usually met once a week and board members were constantly on call to take care of one emergency or another. Crittenton boards had responsibility for admission, discipline, supervision of staff, and the day-to-day operation of the homes. Although in some localities men were ostensibly in charge of the financial side of home operations, these male roles were usually merely honorary or symbolic, and women in fact dealt with these aspects of home administration. A Spokane, Washington, newspaper article described the division of work as the men taking responsibility for the financial decisions and the women dealing with the "reform" aspect.[21] However, when the Boston Florence Crittenton organization was incorporated in the state of Massachusetts in June 1898, the articles of incorporation listed only women as officers and members of the board. As the transition from Charles Crittenton's leadership to the Kate Waller Barrett presidency symbolized, women took complete control of most Florence Crittenton organizations early in the twentieth century.[22]

Barrett recommended that each home include committees for purchasing, admission, house, devotions, education, nursery, hospital, clothing, and entertainment. The list illustrates the wide array of board functions. A well-organized and efficient board was undoubtedly essential to a home's success, and the board members often felt overwhelmed as they attempted to perform their duties. Board members had to assume heavy responsibilities, sometimes for the first time in their lives. The Portland board struggled over decisions such as whether to purchase some pigs and chickens and whether to install a telephone in the home. The Chicago board voted in 1903 to pay the treasurer a small percentage on each check written, "the work being so much to take care of all the checks."[23] Home operations required considerable managerial and organizational skill, and women board members devoted vast amounts of energy to keeping the homes running smoothly.

At a typical board meeting, the Portland, Oregon, women selected a delegation to discuss Crittenton work with the governor, planned to organize with neighbors to petition for a light at the intersection near the home, and heard a report from the home's physician urging the establishment of an isolation room for women and children suffering from contagious diseases. Mrs. Wood agreed to serve as a committee of one to approach a local sand company for a donation of sand for use in the home's play area for children. When residents of the Chicago home complained that one of the babies, James, was so mischievous that he was disrupting the home, board member Mrs. Kline even took James to her house for several days. The Portland board voted to drop Mrs. Bailey from their group and replace her with a "working member." It was obvious that there was no room on the board for women not willing to devote considerable time to the Crittenton causes.[24]

All of this was strenuous enough during good times, and a great burden in bad times. Any emergency could require quick action on the part of the board members. When Portland home babies became ill with dysentery, the board voted to put up a tent in the yard to accommodate the home's residents while the entire house was disinfected with lye.[25] Board members invested considerable emotional reserves into attempting to provide assistance to inmates. A board might engage in a lengthy discussion of the "mental, physical, and moral" condition of inmates and debate possible solutions to various problems residents encountered.[26] Inmates' plights were heartbreaking, and sometimes board members had no concrete recommendations to offer. At times, board members could not but feel helpless in the face of these burdens and, as one historian has pointed out, been patently aware of their powerlessness in a male-dominated society.[27] Crittenton charges were often women without family or financial resources, and the board could not alter that situation.

Many women board members were unaccustomed to supervising others, particularly those of the same social class such as most matrons. Often board members found themselves in the role of intermediary between the matron and the inmates, and several Crittenton organization conference sessions dealt with the relationship between matrons and boards. When Chicago home inmates complained about their matron, the board confronted her with the complaints. The matron offered to resign in the face of this criticism, leaving the board in the unenviable position of having to choose between the matron and the girls. In this instance, inmates exercised considerable influence on their own behalf. They were both willing and able to bring their dissatisfaction to the board members. For their part, the board women took the inmate concerns seriously enough to act upon them and voiced the girls' position so strongly that the matron tendered her resignation. Even if the matron's departure appeared to be the best solution, the board was then left with the problem of recruiting a replacement and keeping the home running in the interim.[28]

The boards also navigated a tricky course in their relationships with the national organization, and several boards became exasperated when Barrett and other national officers intervened in local affairs. Boston board chair Mrs. N. H. Bardwell threatened to resign over a dispute involving field worker Dr. Frederick Sturgis's refusal to deliver a speech without taking up a collection. Barrett attempted to assuage the ill feelings, and although Bardwell agreed to continue on the board, the relationship remained strained. Chicago board members sought to sever their NFCM ties over a disagreement with Barrett.[29] Florence Crittenton board members felt pulled in several directions, but they managed to keep homes operating despite formidable odds.

Members of Crittenton circles also made significant contributions to the Crittenton effort. Some circles included several hundred members, while others were as small as a dozen or so, but all circles provided key services for homes. In certain localities prospective members submitted to an investigation of their backgrounds and final acceptance required majority approval by the membership. The circle provided an occasion for socializing but also an opportunity for women to learn and utilize organizational and parliamentary skills, as the obvious care that went into the preparation of the groups' constitution and bylaws illustrated. Emma

A. Fox's *Parliamentary Usage for Women's Clubs* became the authority for questions of parliamentary procedure, and circle members followed a proscribed order of business and plan for committee organization. Circle members engaged in fundraising activities, planned social events for the homes, and provided support for the boards.[30]

Circle members and Crittenton volunteers were not always upper- and middle-class women. Alice Manning was a member of the Chicago Kings' Daughters circle that met at the Chicago home each Tuesday evening. According to Manning, the members tried to make these evenings as "pleasant and unconsciously helpful" as was possible for "very tired young girls with eight hours of office both behind and before them." The members were employed as bookkeepers and stenographers.[31] The Parkersburg, West Virginia, circle was composed primarily of unmarried women, many of whom were "breadwinners," including several teachers, stenographers, and clerks.[32] Like their middle-class counterparts, these working women found something in the Crittenton work that attracted them to it despite its considerable demands. While historians tend to concentrate on the class relationships between women reformers and their clients, any examples of women of different classes cooperating in reform activities are certainly noteworthy. The occupations of these Crittenton volunteers—most were clerical workers—reflect the changing nature of women's employment. These women's willingness to give their precious spare time to Crittenton activities provides evidence of the importance they attached to aiding other women.

Lasting friendships and deep personal relationships were one compensation for Crittenton work. The bonds that formed among board and circle members played a significant role in the lives of many Crittenton women. Upon returning from a long illness, Cornelia Rockwell, then serving as the Portland, Oregon, board secretary, wrote in her minute book, "The secretary was very much touched and grateful for the reception, the loving and prayerful words of her dear friends and co-workers after her long absence. The sweet spirit which governs them in their work of charity cheered and comforted their co-worker more than she can ever express."[33] Rockwell's expression of appreciation for her Crittenton associates was heartfelt and should not be ignored in assessing the impact of Florence Crittenton activities on the workers themselves. The camaraderie that developed was often Crittenton workers' main reward, and the shared sense of dedication and even self-sacrifice was an integral part of the Crittenton experience. They were, as one historian has described women reformers in this period, "protestant nuns," and the image this conjures of community and commitment applies to the Crittenton situation.[34] Certainly, a feeling of usefulness was a vital part of volunteers' experience, and workers firmly believed their efforts were necessary.[35]

Crittenton activists frequently commented that their colleagues were people of high caliber, and this helped validate each volunteer's own activities. Barrett made this point in a moving fashion when she recounted for *Girls* readers a trip to visit homes in the Midwest. She recalled "the faces of the many noble men and faithful women whose hands we have clasped," "the flower of Christian civilization" who had given "the best years of their lives." Barrett concluded, "Surely no organization in the United States is richer in the class of workers that have rallied to its standards."[36] This shared sense of belonging to a movement with other high-minded individuals attracted many women to Crittenton work.

Their conviction that they were in fact having a positive effect on the lives of others nurtured the workers' continued willingness to volunteer. The Boston annual report for 1914 noted that "anyone facing motherhood out of wedlock needs someone to save her from abject despair and return her to society with a new vision." Crittenton workers everywhere agreed that their work was needed desperately.[37] Workers recognized that their charges dealt with great adversity. One FC woman challenged readers to "parallel the hard task" of the young unmarried mother who struggled to provide for her child in the face of economic difficulties and the stigma attached to her predicament.[38] Charles Crittenton reminded workers that sometimes their charges would be shunned by members of the community "not worthy to touch the hem of her garment." In Crittenton's view, the best counterattack was to surround the girls with "strong, self-reliant Christian women who can make her understand that these things are possible."[39] The responsibility Crittenton people attached to their own efforts was weighty, indeed.

Crittenton workers respected those girls who succeeded in overcoming these seemingly insurmountable obstacles, and at the same time the workers believed their own efforts played a vital role in facilitating the girls' successes. Practically every Florence Crittenton report included glowing accounts of the organization's impact on its clients. A girl wrote to the Denver home, "I can never tell you how much I appreciate the Home I was given when I was in trouble and no other door was open to me. The love that was shown to me and to my baby has proved to me that there is much in the love of Christ."[40] Phoenix matron Ellen M. Broadbook was thrilled when a chance encounter with a former Crittenton inmate demonstrated the efficacy of Crittenton work. Visitor Broadbook asked "a neatly dressed lady" for directions to the Los Angeles Florence Crittenton home. When the lady learned of Broadbook's identity, she exclaimed, "Now I see why the Lord let me miss the other two cars; it was that I might meet you." She went on to explain, in confidential tones, that she was a former Crittenton girl herself and asked to be remembered to Mrs. Bisbee, the Los Angeles matron. Broadbook recounted, "I could scarcely wait until I had properly introduced myself to the dear co-worker before telling her the glad news."[41] Crittenton workers rightfully rejoiced in these affirmations of their work, and these testimonials spurred the volunteers to greater efforts. The fact that Broadbook had been unable to identify the girl as a former Crittenton inmate and in fact described her as a "lady" is a telling comment, certainly different from earlier workers' claims that they were able to identify a fallen woman by looking at her.

A sense of identification with their charges as women prompted many women to undertake Crittenton work despite the effort involved and the lack of prestige and status associated with FC activities. The notion that Crittenton work was primarily women's work and was women's special responsibility became increasingly pronounced in Crittenton literature. When a New York night court worker cried, "Oh God! They are my sisters," other Crittenton workers shared her emotion.[42] The magazine often included stories along the lines of "The Tragedies of Human Lives," which described an anonymous woman found dead in Central Park. The magazine chided readers, "How much it might have meant if some friendly hand had been outstretched to save her, someone to give her words of comfort and hope."[43] Workers came to believe that the fate of other women rested in Crittenton people's willingness and ability to act, and that Crittenton work was often the determining factor in these women's very survival. Robert Cumbler has argued, and Crittenton experience reinforces, that exposure to women from different backgrounds led middle-class reformers to a greater identification with these women and to at least a cross-class understanding if not an elimination of class and social delineations.[44]

This greater emphasis on the idea of Crittenton endeavors as "women's work for women" caused a subtle alteration in workers' views regarding gender and its relationship to Crittenton efforts. Workers came to believe that women had a mandate to pursue rescue work—that sisterhood required it. An 1899 issue of the *Florence Crittenton Magazine* included the poem "Woman's Sphere":

They talk about a woman's sphere
As though it had a limit;
There's not a place on earth or heaven
There's not a task to mankind given
There's not a blessing nor a woe,
There's not a whisper, yes or no,
There's not a life or death or birth,
That has a feather's weight or worth
Without a woman in it.[45]

Fourteen years later *Girls* proclaimed, "Woman has always contributed to progress and in every line of advancement she has assisted and encouraged, even at great cost."[46] Crittenton workers came to believe that it was part of their mission to be "a factor in the movement that has for its aim the creation of a broader sphere for women," and FC volunteers consciously tried to achieve this goal.[47] Crittenton women perceived a direct relationship between their own status and that of their charges. *Girls* explained, "Women will not be soiled by trying to help their fallen sisters to rise. They can only be glorified as they realize their responsibility, and use their power to protect and elevate their sex."[48] Workers sought to emphasize bonds that tied them to their charges and in so doing to secure their own positions.

Barrett and her associates were cognizant of society's efforts to prescribe women's roles, and they sought to combat these attitudes wherever possible. Barrett lashed out at what she perceived to be the unfairness in social relationships when she complained in 1914 that the "daughter of a strong, virile, successful man is supposed to be satisfied with the inane existence that is the fate of the daughters of the most successful men."[49] While Barrett made certain that her own existence was anything but inane, she recognized that she had limited powers to assist her peers. Barrett and her compatriots did attempt, whenever an opportunity arose, to support women seeking to expand their horizons. One such case involved E—— A——, who according to Crittenton workers had been ambitious despite the fact that "her people were not in sympathy with her ambitions." E—— A—— had entered a hospital training program for nurses and had been working very hard. She had attempted suicide, and the Crittenton people placed considerable blame on the lack of encouragement E—— A—— received from her family. The Florence Crittenton home took E—— A—— in and provided a restful and supportive environment for her recuperation. She was able to return to her training, and Crittenton home workers were happy that they had been able to coun-

teract the discouragement that came from E—— A——'s own home.[50]
The Crittenton people found E—— A——'s ambition laudable and sought
to aid her in furthering it, despite objections from the girl's family.

On the other hand, Crittenton people's response to A—— C—— was
more ambivalent. She was arrested for disorderly conduct when it came
to light that she had been masquerading as a man. A—— C—— had
disguised her true identity for over a year in order to engage in her trade
as an undertaker. While Crittenton volunteers tended to be sympathetic
to women's desire for meaningful employment, the first thing they did
was provide A—— C—— a dress and return her to her own home. The
Crittenton women could identify with E—— A—— and her goal of becoming a nurse, but not with A—— C——'s ruse to hide her gender and
pursue a traditionally male occupation. At the same time, the Crittenton
workers did not believe that A—— C—— deserved to be incarcerated
for her attempt at making a living, and they were quick to take on her
case.[51] Crittenton workers, along with women in general, struggled to
fashion a definition of appropriate work.

Crittenton workers candidly assessed the class differences between
themselves and their charges, and they recognized that these differences
were an impediment both to recruiting volunteers and to providing real
assistance to the Crittenton girls. According to *Girls,* when women built
up barriers between one another this "lack of sex fealty" damaged the
status of all women.[52] Barrett warned workers in her 1912 annual letter
to remember that if Crittenton people did not aid women in need, a lost
woman at the "Bar of Justice" might claim, "I am what I am because you
failed to do your duty." *Girls* reminded workers that they should "establish a personal relationship with all and every one" of their charges,
regardless of the differences in social background.[53]

Workers were cognizant of the class issue throughout their history,
and they sought to downplay differences and accentuate the community
of interest they shared with their charges. However, there were two areas of pronounced separation. Women who inhabited Florence Crittenton
homes had, in many cases, violated one of society's most stringent rules
of behavior for women. Sexual relationships outside of marriage were
unimaginable to most of the women who engaged in Florence Crittenton
work. Even as they strived to be sympathetic, it was difficult to not har-
bor a level of blame and disapproval. As workers came more and more
to recognize that the traditional explanations of seduction and abandonment were not realistic, their ambivalence increased. In addition, there

was frequently a difference in the socioeconomic status of workers and inmates. While unmarried motherhood was not strictly a lower-class phenomenon, upper- and middle-class women often had access to resources that could shield them from the societal censure that accompanied unmarried motherhood. Rescue worker Dr. C. S. Carr pointed out, "Between those who are seeking help and the ones who are the objects of this work, there yawns a wide chasm—very difficult to cross."[54] Carr's reminder serves to illustrate Crittenton workers' awareness that they needed to put forth considerable effort to overcome their own prejudices. This was especially true as workers came to recognize that their charges had often made choices that had led to their predicament.

Despite this recognition, it was often easier to verbalize the notion of sisterhood than to act upon it, and workers frequently reminded one another what an essential tenet sisterhood was. Barrett wrote, "Remember we are working for women, all women, and if we really are faithful to our profession we will find that there is no place where we can rightfully repeat, or even think an unkind thing about any other woman, it matters not what her position in life may be." Workers then struggled to implement the idea of sisterhood and in the process redefined Crittenton work. As they assaulted barriers their charges needed to overcome, the Crittenton workers were clearly reminded of their own dissatisfactions with their traditional womanly role.[55]

Barrett's support of woman suffrage was one ramification of this dissatisfaction. Barrett served as vice-president of the Virginia Equal Suffrage League, spoke at public pro-suffrage forums, and testified in favor of votes for women before a Virginia legislative committee conducting hearings on the question. The National Florence Crittenton Mission position reflects what some historians describe as "social feminism." Crittenton women did not plead for suffrage based solely on arguments of equality but coveted suffrage as a tool for furthering the Crittenton program of improving conditions for women and children.[56] Crittenton publications' pro-suffrage position became more pronounced over time. As early as 1901, the *Florence Crittenton Magazine* urged woman readers to become politically aware and interested, since politics had an impact on two areas of vital concern—their children and the economy. It became apparent to Crittenton workers that the ballot could be a powerful weapon in furthering their agenda. Seattle worker Mr. Hitter reported on Washington state's vice crusade at the 1912 FC convention. He claimed that without woman suffrage "the victory could not have been won," and Crittenton people embraced that message. *Girls* informed readers that states in which women could vote were making faster progress toward improved legal recourse for women seeking child support and toward other social reforms.[57]

By 1917 the National Florence Crittenton Mission was avowedly pro-suffrage. *Girls* reprinted Lida Keck Wiggins's poem "Woman's Rights":

> Woman has a right to stand
> waiting 'till man begs her hand;
>   Has a right when wooed and wed
>   To keep his house and bake his bread.
>
>   Has exclusive right to be
> Mother to his progeny.
>   Has a right his ills to tend,
>   And his worn out clothes to mend.
>
>   Has a right to read and sew
> In his firelight's ruddy glow.
>   Has a right to go to church,
>   Though he leaves her in the lurch.
>
>   Has a right their child to give
> Rules by which to nobly live.
>   Has a right a house to own,
>   And 'neath taxes great to groan.
>
>   Has a right, if man should shirk
> Or grow ill, to do his work;
>   Has a right to toil all day
>   At one-half her husband's pay!
>
>   Has a right if law's defied,
> For her error to be tried;
>   Has a right should counsel fail,
>   To be fined or sent to jail.
>
>   Has a right to haggard grow,
> Losing health and beauty's glow.
>   Has a right to grieve and cry,
>   Has a perfect right to die!
>
>   But, when man puts on his coat
> And goes out to cast his vote,
>   Woman can't go with him then.
> She is not a citizen![58]

A Columbus, Ohio, Florence Crittenton worker stated the case for suffrage in a powerful way when she described a visit she and a co-worker made to the city prosecutor's office to urge that he prosecute a man who, according to two girls sheltered at the Crittenton home, was planning to

force them into prostitution. The Crittenton women received only "eva-
sive, noncommittal replies" from the official in question and realized that
the prosecutor had ridiculed them and put them off. When they left his
office, one worker told her companion, "Now I am a suffragist. I'll never
go to the authorities again in such a matter until I have a vote which will,
at least make them listen to me with a due regard for the possibilities
which lie behind that vote." The editors of *Girls* could not resist com-
menting, "Every woman who has tried to accomplish results in social
service realizes, as no one else can, the truth in Ellen Key's words, when
she says that such attempts are, without the ballot, 'like endeavoring to
walk in deep mire.'"[59] Crittenton women believed that they had a right
to the vote and that their social welfare efforts demanded it. The fact that
the magazine quoted Ellen Key in a favorable way is noteworthy. Key was
regarded as a "tremendous radical," to the point that most suffragists in
America distanced themselves from her. However, as the title of her book
Renaissance of Motherhood (1914) suggests, Key celebrated the influence
of mothers. She championed unwed mothers, argued for state support
of unmarried mothers, and even advocated "free" motherhood, or motherhood outside of marriage. While most Crittenton workers were not
willing to go that far, they appreciated Key's viewpoint regarding the
preeminence of motherhood in both women's lives and as a valuable
contribution to society.[60]

Their conviction that women had the right to play a central role in
reform and their dedication to the ideal of sisterhood led Crittenton
women to adopt enlightened programs directed toward working women.
Similar convictions motivated them to establish different priorities for
reform and to put these into practice in the operation of Crittenton homes.
The result was a group of institutions that responded, perhaps more than
most others, to women's needs. As the Crittenton organization developed,
the breadth of its efforts on behalf of women grew and the organization
instituted policies that had a dramatic impact on women's lives and addressed issues that remain of vital importance to women. This aspect of
the NFCM's history has not received the attention of historians.

Kate Waller Barrett and other Florence Crittenton workers sought to
make real the ideal of sisterhood between themselves and women of other
classes. The Crittenton organization labored to provide assistance to poor
and homeless women. The New York mission reported a Christmas dinner for homeless women during which they dispensed with "all institutional forms and ceremonies." The women could sit where they wanted
and eat when they wanted, and the Crittenton workers provided paper

napkins so that each woman could wrap up food to take with them. One woman remarked to a worker regarding how long it had been since she had sat down to a table. Many of the guests commented on how much they enjoyed the meal, but the Crittenton women agreed that the "greatest pleasure of this memorable occasion belonged to the contributors." These Crittenton women sacrificed part of their own Christmas Day to provide their less fortunate sisters with Christmas dinner. While the Crittenton observer could not resist noting the class differences, she concluded, "No lady gowned in silk, bedecked in diamonds, entertained in a drawing room, ever showed more appreciation or courtesy to her hostess." While dripping with class bias, the Crittenton woman thought her comment was a great compliment to the dinner guests.[61] Many Crittenton workers undoubtedly expected gratitude from the women who benefited from Crittenton activities.

Barrett and the national organization advocated sympathy and good treatment for shop girls and other employed women. The *Florence Crittenton Magazine* urged its readers to "remember the nervous strain, the long hours, the small salary, the obligation to dress well, and then pause and consider how your life has affected her. Did your love overflow toward this pure, brave girl, who was obliged to leave home and join the mighty army?" Barrett asked women to boycott establishments that did not pay retail clerks adequate salaries and/or provide appropriate treatment, even if they had to pay a little more for the items purchased. Barrett was convinced that even these small acts would serve to encourage shop girls and others to continue to work at respectable jobs and avoid the temptation to turn to "lives of sin." Her suggestions were typical of Barrett's general approach in that a call for concrete economic action was accompanied by kind and sentimental words. Barrett's agenda also illustrates her recognition of women's place in society. She provided some positive action for women who were able to directly confront the situation and those who could only act in a more circumscribed way. Barrett sought to capitalize on women's role as consumers, and her position aligned her with Florence Kelley and other progressives who sought similar actions encouraging cross-class cooperation and/or understanding.[62]

Crittenton organizations began to sponsor activities and provide facilities specifically designed for working women. The Florence Home for Working Girls in New York City offered a "Christian atmosphere" at a relatively low cost. San Jose operated a reading room, provided lodging, and featured a restaurant with affordable prices that catered to working women's needs. Fostoria, Ohio, sponsored a reading room for the many mill workers in the area, and the Detroit home owned a house for working girls. The Barberton, Ohio, circle organized evening classes in arithmetic, grammar, and sewing for the benefit of working women, particularly those from immigrant backgrounds. In many cities the Florence Crittenton organization made a special effort to assist working women by investigating and then providing lists of legitimate employment agencies. The workers placed brochures containing the information written in several languages in factories and mills. Crittenton homes provided shelter for women facing the economic crisis of unemployment.[63] The Crittenton organization campaigned against "meager wages" that were "insufficient" for subsistence and in the FC view resulted in "dangerous temptations."[64] Once again, these activities placed workers in alliance with a number of other women progressives, especially settlement house residents, who campaigned for higher wages for working women.

Florence Crittenton workers gave more direct aid to working women as well. The police arrested J—— C—— for stealing three eggs from her employer. The girl's defense was that she was extremely hungry, since the employer had not paid her for her work. The employer offered to call the matter square, which would have meant the cost of the eggs was equivalent to four month's salary, about fifty dollars. Crittenton worker Margaret Luther took J—— C—— to the Crittenton home, secured her wages, and found her a new job. In this instance, Luther served as an advocate for a working woman who probably would otherwise have been a victim. Luther recognized that J—— C—— lacked power in dealing with her employer, and that the employer was exploiting J—— C——. Luther did not blame J—— C—— for acting as she did. On another occasion Crittenton women went to the aid of "three foreign girls" who experienced difficulty collecting their wages. FC women convinced the employer to pay the wages.[65] Both of these cases feature victims who confronted obstacles due to both class and gender, and Crittenton women were committed to combating both kinds of barriers.

Crittenton people paid particular attention to the plight of domestic workers. Although home statistics indicated that many Crittenton inmates had been employed as domestic servants, Crittenton workers wanted to send their charges to work as domestics because that employment allowed women to keep their children with them. Another aspect of the dichotomy that often characterized workers' relationship with inmates was that, without servants, middle-class Crittenton workers would not have had the time to devote to philanthropic work. This may have been one motive for the emphasis on domestic service. Crittenton volunteers decried the ill treatment of domestic servants and, in fact, the *Florence Crittenton Magazine* objected to the use of the term *domestic servant* because *servant* carried "odious" connotations and might cause girls to seek less-wholesome employment. The article concluded that the shortage of domestic labor was a direct result of women employers degrading the servant girl and urged readers to rectify the situation.[66]

Crittenton people thought that one way to address this problem was to deemphasize the class differences between domestic workers and their employers, while at the same time elevating the status of domestic work. The Florence Crittenton practice of requiring workers to wear uniforms was a specific attempt to achieve this goal. The matron's uniform was all white and included an apron and cap; other workers wore blue dresses with white caps and aprons; and an inmate who was promoted to head of her department received a striped gingham uniform, white apron, and white cap. Workers hoped the uniforms would set an example for inmates who would later earn their livelihood in domestic employment. Barrett explained that the cap and apron were badges of authority in the Crittenton home, and, therefore, when Crittenton girls obtained employment as domestics, they would not view the uniform as a symbol of inferiority. She wrote, "Soldiers, sailors and policemen are all proud of their uniforms; why should not the pretty, becoming, serviceable cap and apron be looked upon with pride."[67] Barrett made little progress in guaranteeing domestic service workers the same respect police officers and military men received, but she continued to work in that direction.

Barrett often discussed the obligations of women employers to their domestic employees, particularly their responsibility to instruct and advise. A *Florence Crittenton Magazine* article thus admonished women to refrain from firing inferior maids, but rather to teach them. One entire session at the 1906 Convention dealt with the question, "What can be done to make domestic service safer and more desirable?" In the view of most Crittenton workers, the key objective was to eliminate the "impassable depth fixed between the maid and the Christian mistress."[68] Barrett was realistic enough to recognize that this was much easier to preach than to practice and that domestic service was sometimes less than alluring for Crittenton girls. She wrote, "Having been reared in the South with plenty of servants, I have often wondered how heaven could be heaven if everybody had to wait on themselves, and on the other hand, I certainly never could see how it could be heaven if you had to do the waiting on."[69] Barrett certainly spoke for many of her colleagues, and her remarks highlighted the Crittenton dilemma regarding domestic service: Barrett and her associates were not interested in abandoning the privileges their own class status accorded them. Barrett's statement carries racial overtones, since during her southern girlhood the "servants" in question would have been African Americans.

Speaking at the 1906 national convention, Barrett told participants that professionalization of domestic work through the activities of domestic-science training schools would increase the status of that occupation. Barrett recognized that even greater training was not enough to "bridge the gap between the drawing room and the kitchen," and Barrett admitted that she was "not seer enough to tell" her colleagues precisely how this could be accomplished.[70] Barrett and her cohorts were well aware that since they yearned for productive and interesting work for themselves, Crittenton charges probably had similar aspirations.

Barrett was convinced, however, that the alternatives for single mothers had little to recommend them. Furthermore, in seeking to elevate domestic service to a position of greater esteem, Barrett and her Crittenton colleagues attempted to rationalize their policy of encouraging inmates to pursue employment in this area while at the same time validating their own primary occupation—housewife/mother. Most of the Crittenton workers realized that their status depended upon the recognition of the essential contributions of mothers and homemakers, and they sought to instill this notion in their charges.

Florence Crittenton women faced enormous difficulties as they attempted to prepare girls for domestic work. The Boston matron noted that some of the girls who came "do not know how to do anything well. . . . it requires constant vigilance." A Los Angeles worker wrote, "You perhaps do not realize that we have had girls who did not know how, or *never* had threaded a needle. What do you think of that?"[71] In their view, the workers faced insurmountable odds as they tried to teach pregnant and unmarried women, who could not even do basic housework, enough skills to support themselves and their children.

Crittenton women's ideas of sisterhood led them in other directions besides their efforts to be more sympathetic to working women, to provide these women support, and to make domestic service more attractive. Workers embarked upon a controversial campaign to require fathers of illegitimate children to pay support. This campaign stemmed from the longtime Crittenton commitment to ending the double standard, but involved a new outlook. Whereas the original contention had been that the standard should be purity for all as a reflection of Charles Crittenton's religious beliefs, later attacks on the double standard revolved around questions of equity and fairness. Crittenton workers turned from the strategy of appealing to men's sense of morality to urging equal treatment as women's right. While Boise, Idaho, matron Anna D. Barrett wrote in June 1900, "Thank God the time is coming when there will be one standard both for men and women when we stand equal before God to be judged by our life's record," Kate Waller Barrett proclaimed seven years later, "I have often felt that the time would never come when women could have the same opportunity for rehabilitation that men have, until her own sex demands it for her, and is willing to labor to bring it about for her."[72] This more strident position was evident in the poem "The Two Sinners":

> There was a man, it was said one time,
> Who went astray in his youthful prime.
> Can the brain keep cool and the heart keep quiet
> When the blood is a river that is running riot?
> And boys will be boys, the old folks say,
> And the man is better who's had his day.
>
> The sinner reformed, and the preacher told
> Of the prodigal son who came back to the fold.
> And the Christian people threw open the door,
> With a warmer welcome than ever before.
> Wealth and honor were at his command,
> And a spotless woman gave him her hand.
> And the world strewed their pathway with blossoms abloom,
> Crying, "God bless ladye, and God bless groom!"
>
> There was a maiden who went astray
> In the golden of her life's young day.
> She had more passion and heart than head,
> And she followed blindly where blind Love led.
> And Love unchecked is a dangerous guide
> To wander at will by a fair girl's side.
>
> The woman repented and turned from sin,
> But no door was open to let her in.
> The preacher prayed that she might be forgiven,
> But told her to look for mercy—in Heaven
> For this is the law of the earth we know,
> That the woman is stoned, while the man may go.
> A brave man wedded her, after all;
> But the world said frowning, "We shall not call."[73]

The poem not only objected to the unequal treatment of men and women but also indicated that everyone shared a responsibility for that inequality. Barrett blamed the discrepancy between society's attitude toward men and women on the fact that "this is the man's world, with man-made laws governing it."[74] Barrett's comment reveals resentment regarding her lack of power, and the underlying message was that if women attained more of a voice in social decision making, there would be an accompanying change in the climate for women.

Crittenton and other women explicitly objected to the idea that men engaged in "sewing wild oats" out of necessity. Dr. Adelaide Abbott, superintendent of purity for the Suffolk County and Boston WCTU, warned her Crittenton audience, "If you believe it is necessary for some one's daughter to be sacrificed on this shameless altar of 'physical necessity,' if you believe this condition must continue, then again I ask whose daughter?"[75] On many occasions Barrett recalled accompanying her son Robert to a Florence Crittenton baby show. When he asked where the fathers were, she responded, "God only knows," and the message that the father ought to at least share culpability was patently clear. While FC workers did not argue that no sin had been committed, they believed both parties should suffer equally for their indiscretion. Barrett told her followers that although she did not advocate that women join men in avoiding any consequence of promiscuity, she thought men should be "made to step down where she stands and to take his place beside her."[76] Crittenton demands that men share in the responsibility of parenthood represent a noteworthy evolution in FC thinking. Soon Crittenton workers sought to apply their revised ideas to actual situations.

Crittenton women had no patience with men who took advantage of women with physical or mental handicaps. According to *Girls,* such men "deserved a prison sentence," and Crittenton workers campaigned for stiff penalties for these offenders. In a telling comment, the magazine noted that women with disabilities should be "free to come and go at will" and deserved protection even if they could not protect themselves.[77] The magazine's statement represented an indictment of any man who threatened these women's freedom.

As a way of forcing recognition of the male role in the plight of unmarried mothers who were not disabled, and partly because of their established interest in protecting the futures of illegitimate children, workers devoted more and more time to identifying, locating, and gaining some financial support from the fathers of these children. The workers became more aggressive in their efforts to encourage marriages. When a Crittenton worker said, "I am glad to say that only one of the men was forced to marry the girl, whom he had betrayed, in the presence of the sheriff," she implied that workers would not have hesitated to enlist the sheriff's services in other cases.[78] At the same time workers began to realize that marriage was not always the best resolution. The New Haven, Connecticut, home even reported the story of one of their charges whom a young man "was anxious to marry." She decided against it after concluding that he was not worthy of her; the workers applauded her decision. Their support for this girl indicated both a recognition of the girl's value and agreement with her contention that no marriage was better than marrying an unsuitable candidate.[79] Again, this represents a giant leap from earlier Crittenton doctrine, which viewed marriage as the epitome of successful FC efforts. Crittenton workers believed that an unmarried mother was fully capable of creating a home for her baby and might only be hindered in achieving that goal if she married an "unworthy" man.

When marriage was neither an appropriate nor desirable outcome, workers still wanted to ensure support for the child and gain retribution from the man involved. At the 1906 annual conference a session informed workers about "Truant Fathers and How they May be Reached."[80] Many Crittenton home boards designated one of their members to determine the father of each child and secure from him some form of child support. The Erie, Pennsylvania, home, for example, appointed one of the officers of the admission committee to investigate and prosecute the father of each child born in the home. An Erie board member explained, "By these results we bring one standard of morals for both sexes."[81] Men were to suffer at least some consequences for their actions, and Crittenton workers went so far as to argue that this was true even if the woman involved was not a virgin. The *Florence Crittenton Magazine* attacked as a "pernicious doctrine" the belief that if a woman had already "committed the unpardonable sin," the accused man was innocent of the "major part" of the offense.[82] The doctrine made a pure life very difficult for reformed girls, but it was also detrimental to men, who used it to rationalize unforgivable behavior. The idea of fairness again emerged as Crittenton workers believed that the woman bore a disparate share of the blame. This is yet another position that separated the Crittenton workers from most officials and progressive reformers. This attitude represents a major development in Crittenton thinking and marks the beginning of a modern, pro-woman viewpoint as Crittenton workers claimed that women who had, for whatever reason, engaged in nonmarital sexual activity were not irrevocably branded.

The workers pursued "truant" fathers with almost fanatical diligence. At the initial interview with the girls, board members made every effort to ascertain whether a court case against the male was feasible. This policy involved a change in Florence Crittenton procedure as the girls obviously had to identify the alleged father before the board could take any action. Sometimes the girls were reticent about pressing the matter in court, but the boards strongly favored legal proceedings—especially if they meant the girl and her child would gain at least an element of financial security. Boards provided legal counsel and support for women seeking these damages in court. In this regard, the Chicago home board secretary relished Jeannette's case. The man involved was a prize fighter whom the authorities arrested and incarcerated in county jail. He "begged" Jeannette to get him out because he was losing ten pounds a day and he feared he would lose his ability to fight. Jeannette refused and the workers praised her decision on the grounds that the man was only getting what he deserved.[83] While many inmates declined court proceedings on account of the publicity involved, Crittenton workers viewed public scrutiny as a small price to pay for both improving the financial situation of mother and baby and making certain that the father accepted responsibility for his actions.

Often Crittenton workers' involvement in these cases lasted for some time, the workers acting as the girl's advocate throughout the process, with the board members advising girls as to testimony and providing encouragement during the trial. The man in Amelia's case at first denied any relationship, although the authorities arrested him on charges of rape and bastardy. He finally offered to pay three hundred dollars, but the Chicago Crittenton home board minutes reported that "we" refused. The board secretary described the trial: "His wife, lawyer and most of his relations were in the Criminal Court on Monday morning. Amelia had her dates all right and although frightened to death she did not hesitate once." The board secretary informed the man's attorney that Amelia would settle for one thousand dollars, half immediately and half secured on real estate to be paid within five years.[84] Without the coaching and encouragement of the Crittenton board members, Amelia probably would never have gone to court. It must have been intimidating to confront the father of her child and his wife in court. Clearly the process of preparing for the trial and the trial itself provided an opportunity for the Crittenton workers to fight against male domination and to facilitate a similar effort on the part of the woman herself. When Crittenton women and their charges successfully prosecuted a putative father, the women gained concrete evidence of their own power and autonomy.

Boston workers went a step further. Recognizing how difficult it was for someone in Amelia's position to testify, the Boston organization campaigned for a special women's court, presided over and directed by a group of women.[85] Boston Crittenton women were convinced that a women run court would establish an environment that was both more sympathetic and more equitable. Their demand for a women's court was an expression of women's dissatisfaction with their treatment in male-controlled courtrooms.

Most Crittenton workers agreed with Hastings Hart that while sometimes these court cases were unpleasant, the prosecution of offenders was a "duty to the community."[86] In fact, Crittenton workers embraced Hart's viewpoint with a vengeance and battled tenaciously to identify and prosecute guilty men. In 1912 the Fargo, North Dakota, home investigated forty-one of these fathers with the result that, in the superintendent's words, "many of the fathers of these children have been shown their responsibility of Fatherhood."[87] The Boston general secretary was pleased to report in 1915 that the Crittenton people had prosecuted successfully more court cases than ever before. Workers referred to these judicial proceedings as bringing justice to "offenders." Men may have found it more convenient to admit to possible paternity than to face a court case and the zealous board women, and the FC expression carries hints of antimale sentiment.[88] Crittenton workers also campaigned for changes in laws that made it easier to prosecute these men, and they supported judges and prosecutors who actively pursued the cases. Doubtless, few public officials were in a position to argue with Crittenton demands in this area, despite the official's personal opinions. However, Florence Crittenton women worried that men in positions of authority did not take them seriously, and *Girls* was quick to point out that in localities where women had the franchise much stricter laws had been enacted.[89]

While the major goal of these efforts was to insure financial support for women and children, there is a decidedly antimale tinge to this aspect of Crittenton work. FC women were unabashedly pleased when they were able to force men to recognize their offense and pay for it as well. Current efforts to collect child support from recalcitrant fathers echo these earlier Crittenton activities to some degree, and undoubtedly Florence Crittenton workers sought to require that men share both the blame and responsibility for children born outside of wedlock. Crittenton workers were cognizant of the fact that economic well-being was a necessary prerequisite to women establishing successful single-parent families and achieving personal independence.

Crittenton people made positive changes in their institutions in response to their dedication to helping women and treating women's issues as priorities. As historians have argued, women were usually the first to recognize the needs of women and children.[90] Thus it is not surprising that the NFCM was at the forefront of efforts to obtain adequate health care for women. The mission responded to what they viewed as insufficient attention from the medical community in the fields of obstetrics and gynecology. Crittenton groups were aware that obstetrics and gynecology required special and sympathetic care and they turned to their own hospital facilities in search of these attributes. It is clear from Crittenton writings that many women involved in Crittenton work objected to their own treatment in regular hospitals, so they designed Crittenton hospitals to be responsive to women's needs. Crittenton hospitals augmented their patient care with state-of-the-art technology and the most up-to-date treatments available. The Spokane, Washington, board of physicians pronounced the home's obstetrical wards "splendid."[91] The Sioux City, Iowa, home featured the only incubator in the state, and the Detroit organization boasted a large hospital with a free dispensary for working-class families. This combination of modern facilities, sympathetic care, and an atmosphere that was conducive to women exercising control over their own treatment caused many women to select Crittenton hospitals over other alternatives and probably speeded the transition from home births to hospital births in some locations. These paying patients helped to supplement Crittenton income and of course Crittenton inmates received all of the Crittenton hospital benefits as well.[92] This aspect of Crittenton work reflected a growing concern among many women's groups about women's health issues.

No doubt Florence Crittenton home medical staffs also attracted women patients, since they employed female physicians whenever possible. This reliance on women doctors was due not only to the conviction that it was "pre-eminently woman's work to care for and succor her unfortunate sisters" but also to the Crittenton belief that women physicians were more sympathetic to unmarried mothers than their male counterparts.[93] By all accounts, the women doctors spent more time with their patients and were less likely to resort to forceps or similar procedures designed to speed the birth process. Women patients maintained greater control over their own health care when women physicians attended them.[94] For their part, Crittenton people preferred women physicians, as they worried about the propriety of male physicians entering and leaving the home at all hours, and some FC workers thought male physicians advocated adoption and abortion more frequently than females. Maternalism played a role in this area, as in most other areas of Crittenton endeavor. Since Crittenton charges were "away from their parents and friends who cannot be advised with in case of emergency," the female physician could play the role of both mother and doctor. Crittenton workers believed they could trust women physicians not to "make public anything objectionable to the Home" which might come to their attention. Finally, Crittenton people appreciated the difficulties many women physicians encountered in attempting to practice in other hospitals and saw this as another facet of women's inferior status. In Crittenton homes women physicians were the workers' first choice, and some boards even voted not to admit male physicians' patients to their homes.[95] Crittenton women were self-conscious in their support of women in the medical profession. Walsh has pointed out that without opportunities provided through charity work and the assistance of organizations such as the Florence Crittenton homes, female physicians could not have even begun to establish themselves in the medical community.

Numbers of women physicians—Kate Waller Barrett among them, of course—found Crittenton work to be fulfilling and an appropriate use of their skills. A *Florence Crittenton Magazine* article, "The Opportunity of the Christian Physician to Aid Unfortunate Girls," discussed the unique circumstances that rescue work presented woman doctors. Women physicians were in a position to provide expert advice regarding matters of hygiene and cleanliness in the home, and they were also able to counsel the inmates regarding their pregnancies. As Dr. Ada Thomas reminded her colleagues, "This is not only an opportunity but a gracious privilege."[96]

Crittenton organizations hoped to extend the benefits of improved obstetrical care beyond the actual homes and hospitals. Crittenton nursing programs had, of course, long emphasized this aspect of nurses' training. The Boston home proudly reported that graduates of its nurses' training program would be "helpful towards better obstetrics in their communities," and others nurses' training programs met the same objective.[97] Women involved in FC work viewed women's health care as both a priority and a field in which they had the power to make a difference. Consequently, they implemented programs to address this issue. Perhaps no other part of Crittenton work was as blatantly feminist as the determination to provide women with the best available health care in a nurturing setting. When they designed their own hospitals and set standards for care, Crittenton workers took control over an important aspect of their own lives. Only recently, have women again begun to address this key area, and the Crittenton example of making a conscious decision to provide the best possible care is relevant.

Crittenton workers' concern for their less-fortunate sisters, unlike that of many of their contemporaries, often extended to black women as well as white. While historians typically described Crittenton homes as being segregated, the Crittenton record in race relations was not so clear.[98] Racial prejudice was endemic during the period under discussion, and Crittenton workers shared predominant white perceptions of African Americans. Chicago workers were obviously upset about the case of a young girl from a small town in Michigan who ran away from home and ended up in Chicago. She did not have much money and asked a man on the street to direct her to an inexpensive boarding house. The man "took her to a colored den on D Street." That night the police raided the establishment and took the girl to jail. The FC worker was appalled to find her "locked in with a great, burly negress" and arranged her release and transportation home.[99]

When Charles Nelson Crittenton wrote of a 1901 experience preaching at the "colored" Methodist Episcopal church in Alexandria, Virginia, his account echoed stereotypical images of African Americans: "It is a great pleasure to speak to these dear people who are so childlike and simple in their trust of God." A few years later, Mrs. Starr Gephert told her colleagues at the 1905 annual conference that the solution to the race issue in the United States rested on the success of vocational training experiments such as those at Hampton and Tuskegee Institutes. As was true for many other white Americans, Booker T. Washington's philosophy of accommodation did not threaten the comfort zone of Gephert and her Crittenton colleagues.[100]

Yet another example of stereotypically prejudiced perceptions within the Crittenton organization arose at the 1906 annual convention, when Mrs. Frances of New York urged her co-workers to adopt toward their servants the same attitude expressed by Virginia's Governor Wise, who told of servants "handed down from generation to generation and treated almost as one of the family." As a result, she said, the servants "loved their masters." This description of southern slavery did not coincide with the African American viewpoint, was self-serving at best, and ignored moral objections to the institution of slavery.[101]

Barrett reflected the ambivalence of Crittenton workers to the race issue. She had been raised in the South, her family had owned slaves, and, in fact, she had received a slave for a birthday present as a young girl. She later admitted, "I looked upon them as mine by 'divine right' and many were the lessons of cruelty and lack of appreciation of the rights of others cultivated in one." Barrett recognized that she had not treated the slave as "one of the family." However, her ideas regarding the effect of slavery on African Americans reflected some careful thought. She contended that the fact the slaves did not rebel despite their treatment—and even after the war most did not leave the Waller plantation—illustrated the slaves' "loss of independence and self-respect." (She believed the same logic applied to white-slave victims who had no desire to escape their situation.) Barrett's recognition of the power of paternalism to control victims was echoed in recent historical analyses of slavery.[102] Nevertheless, Barrett's southern roots and training meant that she struggled to overcome the attitude that African Americans were not equal to whites. The majority of white Americans clung to the conviction that African Americans were satisfied with their status, and the period under discussion coincides with the actual institutionalization of Jim Crow practices in the South. The historian must guard against an ahistorical evaluation of Crittenton attitudes and motivations.

Within this context, the NFCM made pathbreaking overtures to the African American community. While homes in the South were restricted to white women (by both custom and law), the NFCM tried to respond to the needs of African American women. Southern homes often arranged for African American girls to find shelter in northern Crittenton establishments. While this practice certainly reflected racist attitudes in the South, during the period under discussion it also represented a considerable departure for the southern women who arranged for the transfers, the northern women who provided accommodations, and the African Americans who entered integrated northern homes. The Crittenton organization reasoned that it was preferable to provide help for African American women somewhere rather than to simply ignore their plight. This NFCM practice is noteworthy. While many white Americans believed that African American women did not require the services of rescue homes because they were incapable of meeting white standards of sexual behavior and therefore were not candidates for rescue efforts, Florence Crittenton workers refused to embrace this perception of black women. Crittenton workers also discounted another white viewpoint— that African American women did not need maternity homes because black families readily accepted unmarried mothers and their children.

In a period when most white women in the United States had absolutely no social interaction with African American women, the NFCM attempted to involve black women in the Crittenton campaign. Following a request from black Nashville residents, Barrett directed field secretary Mrs. Hazzard to meet with members of the African American community at the Nashville home and plan for work with "the colored girls of Tennessee."[103] The Crittenton organization risked censure when they

131

invited local African Americans to the Nashville home, and many Americans would have looked askance at the prospect of including African Americans in the planning process of social welfare work. Florence Crittenton workers treated African Americans as being capable of engaging in rescue work, and the mission sought to facilitate that process.

Due to Charles Crittenton's early efforts and to Barrett's continuation of them, the national operated a "Colored Mission" in Alexandria, Virginia. All of the workers at this establishment were African Americans, and the mission included a kindergarten, vocational training courses in the evening, and other charitable work. Mrs. Johnson, described by the *Florence Crittenton Magazine* as "one of the most competent cooks in Alexandria, besides being an educated Christian woman," facilitated a sewing society and mothers' classes at the Alexandria mission.[104] The magazine's description combines a backhanded compliment regarding Johnson's accomplishment in an accepted profession for black women with one of the greatest compliments the Crittenton women could bestow. Johnson's course offerings certainly fit the Crittenton formula for success and indicate that middle-class black women sought to inculcate their ideas regarding motherhood into women from other classes in much the same way middle-class white women did.

However, while white women risked social ostracism and vocal criticism when they engaged in rescue work and work with unmarried mothers, African American women confronted even greater challenges. Fighting sexual exploitation was inextricably tied to attempts to end racial subjugation. At the same time, African American women also had to combat the prejudices of African American men. W. E. B. Du Bois's seminal study of African American families concluded that "the black women's sexual immorality was the 'greatest single plague spot' in the reputation of African Americans."[105] Black women fought the double standard of morals as a part of seeking equality, just as white women did. But African American women had to confront white men, black men, and white women as well. Black women reformers wanted to attack the problem of illegitimacy in order to protest the myth of black women's promiscuity and protect their own reputations, while offering help to other black women.

Consequently, some African American women believed they had a mandate to engage in rescue work and work with unmarried mothers. The Crittenton home for African American women in Topeka, Kansas, illustrates this and also points to the differences between the NFCM and most other women's organizations of the period. Sarah Malone founded the Topeka home and was its driving force for more than two decades.

Malone, whose photograph reveals a proud and determined countenance, was a dark-skinned woman—at a time when most of the better-known African American reformers of the day were notably light-skinned.[106] Although the Topeka home sometimes provided a refuge for black inmates from parts of the country where Crittenton homes were closed to them, for the most part the "Topeka Home (Colored)," founded in 1904, served local African American women. Malone and other local black women organized their home and after operating it a few years, sought affiliation with the National Florence Crittenton Mission. The NFCM accepted the home for membership and paid off its mortgage to establish the home on a firm financial foundation. Home operation remained in the hands of Malone and her associates. The Kansas Federation of Colored Women's Clubs made the home one of its service projects.[107] Both the institution and the physical space were under the control of African American women—a rare occurrence.

Sarah Malone, a tireless worker, operated the Topeka home in much the same way as other homes in the Crittenton family. She reported with pleasure during 1910 that four home inmates had been "married and established Homes of their own." The next year the home's report to the national noted that they were keeping chickens for eggs and sale, and that they also raised fruit.[108] According to the worker, the girls were "carefully trained and taught different branches of industries," and by 1919 inmates received training in cooking, decorating, and catering. Just as was the case at other Crittenton institutions, workers tried to make certain that inmates would not be reliant on charity but would be "self-supporting and self-respecting."[109] This suggests programs that were similar to those of Crittenton homes throughout the United States, and like other Crittenton establishments, the Topeka home was a member of the community chest.[110]

While African American women involved in reform movements complained that white women refused to address them using "Mrs." and slighted them in other ways, Crittenton workers always accorded African American colleagues their courtesy titles. Sarah Malone attended annual Crittenton meetings and spoke at them, and her remarks were included in the conference reports. The Topeka home received coverage in *Girls*. Barrett noted that Malone and the Topeka home had done "admirable work," and in recognition she appointed Malone field secretary of colored work for the NFCM in 1919.[111]

However, Sarah Malone knew that race informed her relationship with the NFCM and with other Crittenton workers. In an effort to reassure

Sarah Malone, president of the Topeka, Kansas, home. Courtesy of the Kansas State Historical Society, Topeka.

her would-be colleagues that Crittenton work among African Americans did not threaten whites, Malone told the 1919 annual meeting audience that her "people were just getting awake" regarding FC work, noting that "when our standard is lifted both races will be benefited." Malone shared this idea of uplift with other African American club women, who as a group did not challenge the status quo of race relations.[112]

Sarah Malone recognized that her charges suffered under a double handicap of gender and race. She recounted the case of one girl who said, "How can I be anything, my mother was nothing, my father was nothing, how can I be anything?" Malone was determined that the girl have opportunities that would allow her to overcome racial prejudice.[113] Topeka home reports demonstrate this determination. The home's motto, "We as a race must care for our girls, when she falls we must take her by the hand and say, sister arise," illustrates both racial pride and a dedication to uplift. It also shows that the class differences that were common between inmates and workers in white homes were present in Topeka as well.[114]

The Topeka home also provided an opportunity for black physicians to obtain internship situations, thus filling a vital role in the African American community. During the 1920s, another African American home associated with the Crittenton chain opened in Kansas City, becoming "a leading provider for Negro unmarried mothers in the country."[115]

Northern homes were integrated; the earliest accounts of the Florence Night Mission explained that women of "whatever caste, creed, or colour" were admitted to the mission. The Chicago board noted, "We have never drawn the color line," and the Crittenton organization was "open to all colors" as early as the 1890s. Boston workers reported in 1896 that a "colored" girl was drawn to their institution by the word "home." Although she was not in need of the usual Crittenton services, the workers found that she only had thirty cents in her handkerchief, and they quickly provided her a place to stay. Pictorial evidence indicates that black women were inmates in homes in New York City; Detroit; Trenton, New Jersey; Boston; and Fargo, North Dakota; and integration was in fact the norm in homes outside the Deep South.[116] In 1912 the Los Angeles home provided care for forty-six women. Of these, seven were "Spanish" and three "Colored." This coincided with the numbers in the general population.[117] In fact, Miss Mary E. Heartwell, the perennial Detroit matron, was moved to engage in Crittenton work through her experience with a "colored girl." When Heartwell was employed at the Detroit Women's Hospital Open Door, an early effort to provide obstetrical care to indigent mothers, she worried about an African American woman who left the facility

The Topeka, Kansas, "Colored" Florence Crittenton home. Courtesy of the National Florence Crittenton Mission.

with her baby. The mother spent weeks trying to obtain care for her child but could not because she did not have the required twenty-five-dollar cash downpayment for child-care services. Seeking an alternative for women in similar straits, Heartwell turned to the Florence Crittenton mission and established an integrated institution to accomplish those ends.[118]

While most Crittenton work was apparently directed toward white women, Barrett and the NFCM made some strides in providing services to African Americans. The organization's willingness to respond to needs expressed by African Americans themselves and to employ black workers was atypical in the period before World War I. The NFCM accepted the Topeka and Kansas City African American–run homes on the same terms as other homes in the chain, and the organization went on record as opposing racial prejudice. *Girls,* in its report on the Southern Sociological Congress in Nashville in 1912, noted, "It promises well for the Southland to see so many of her sons and daughters so wide awake, so alive to the interest and welfare and the needs of their homeland, and so unprejudiced and willing to avail themselves of every opportunity to better conditions, to uplift humanity, without respect to race or color."[119] The NFCM record of providing services for African American women was certainly not up to contemporary standards, but Crittenton efforts surpassed those of most other white reformers of the period.

Aid to poor, homeless, destitute, and troubled women and children became another significant facet of Crittenton activity, stemming from workers' belief that poverty threatened families and that an impoverished home environment might result in immorality and delinquency. Poor and working-class families often teetered on the brink of disaster, any shift in the delicate balance having the potential to cause family disintegration. The mother's absence due to illness or childbirth, temporary unemployment, or a domestic squabble could spell crisis for a poor family, so Crittenton programs attempted to avert these catastrophes. Crittenton interactions with poor families illustrated the complexities of workers' relationships with their clients as well as the difficulties Crittenton people faced when they attempted to translate their ideas of sisterhood into actual practice.

Most Crittenton homes offered room and board to their former inmates' babies, and eventually homes made this service available to other women. Crittenton workers viewed the practice of boarding working women's children as an opportunity to provide the youngsters with the kind of environment that middle-class children enjoyed. Workers made certain that the children received adequate nutrition, proper training and discipline, and loving supervision without breaking up the family. A young Detroit couple found their family situation precarious when the mother and her twenty month old son both contracted whooping cough. When the mother regained sufficient strength she went to work in a laundry for $12.50 a week and paid $2.50 a week to board her son at the Crittenton home. When her father could not care for her, the Portland home took over guardianship of an eleven-year-old girl following the death of her mother.[120] In each case, the Crittenton intervention prevented the working-class parents from losing custody of their children.

Boarding children at the Crittenton home did expose the working mothers to interference in their child-raising practices. Sometimes this was beneficial and perhaps warranted. The Chicago board, for example, urged Frankie's mother to pay her bill so that "Frankie could have a cure for his spinal trouble." Due to the board's insistence, Frankie's mother made the payment and the child received his treatment. Of course the board could have paid for the treatment, but members hoped to instill a sense of responsibility in Frankie's mother.[121] Frankie no doubt benefited from the board's actions. Nevertheless, the board imposed its notions of satisfactory motherhood on Frankie's mother.

Thanks to uncertainties in the workplace, working mothers were often behind in their payments. Sometimes the boards granted extensions when they thought the mother was genuinely trying to fulfill her obligations. On other occasions board members believed the mother was not making a sufficient effort and they acted accordingly. The decision rested solely with the board, and its members seldom consulted the mothers involved. The Chicago board consented to give Baby Brown's grandmother time on the baby's board after she pleaded with them, and the board excused Fredda from her baby's payment for one month because the mother was ill.[122] However, when Effie owed sixty dollars for Myron's board, the Chicago home reported that she cared little for the child. The members decided that Mrs. Von Kettler should get the city detectives to "spot the girl and see if we can secure evidence that she is not living the right life" and then use that evidence to have the child committed to the Chicago home. In a similar case, Maud did not return to her baby after finding employment despite appeals from the matron. The board urged Maud to give up her child because a lady wanted it, but Maud declined. The board took legal steps to obtain custody of the child when Maud "refused to leave the life she had started in."[123] Crittenton workers were anxious to help when they believed the woman was trying to give her child a proper upbringing, but when they judged that this effort was lacking, board members thought the child would be better off elsewhere.

In most instances workers made every effort to assist parents and allowed several transgressions before depriving parents of their children. A Detroit couple had a history of unemployment and poverty and on one occasion had left their two offspring at Children's Free Hospital for seven months without communicating with the hospital regarding the children's well-being or their own whereabouts. Eight months later, social workers again reported the parents were neglecting the children, and the Michigan Children's Home Society obtained a boarding home for the juveniles. Despite these incidents, when the mother became pregnant again and needed a place to board the children, the Florence Crittenton home provided that service. The parents' employment continued to be sporadic, and the father was often away from home for extended periods of time. Following a report that the parents had boarded the children in a place where they suffered abuse, the FC home took the baby for adoption.[124] Crittenton workers wanted to keep families together, but were well aware that it was not always either possible or in the best interest of the children involved to do so. On the other hand, in this case the mother involved used the Crittenton home for her own purposes for a considerable length of time without submitting to FC control.

Sometimes the Crittenton and other social workers' view of the family situation did not coincide with that of the woman involved. Workers continually reported that the husband in one household was abusive and failed to support his family. When the wife became ill and entered the hospital, workers took the three children to the Florence Crittenton home and the father was to pay eight dollars a week for their room and board. Upon her release from the hospital, the woman reclaimed her children and returned home, despite workers' insistence that she make some other arrangement. The woman maintained that her husband was not abusive and that she wanted to return to her own home. She did so, much to the chagrin of the Crittenton people.[125] The woman involved resisted efforts to convince her to leave her husband, a response that continues to be commonplace among victims of abuse. However, the decision belonged to the woman, and despite efforts workers made to change her mind, in the final analysis the woman's wishes won out.

The nature of the problems their clients faced often almost overwhelmed Crittenton workers, and with good reason. Workers purchased a wagon and team of horses as a means for one man to make a living to support his family. The wagon was stolen and the family had to sell the horses in order to eat. Left again with no livelihood, the woman came to the Florence Crittenton home to deliver her baby and the baby died.[126]

In another particularly worrisome case a thirty-eight-year-old mother and Gladys, the eldest of her ten children, were both inmates at the Crittenton home. Apparently, a boarder in the family home was responsible for Gladys's pregnancy, so when her mother returned home, workers were hesitant about allowing Gladys to accompany her. When the mother claimed she needed Gladys to help with the other children and the housework, the Crittenton people decided that perhaps Gladys would be a good influence on her mother and her siblings. Finally, Gladys returned to the Crittenton home and entered a nurses' training program. The home provided child care for her baby.[127] The Crittenton workers made concessions to accommodate the needs of their clients and continued to work with their charges as long as they thought they could provide assistance. At the same time, workers' own ideas about proper family life informed their actions.

These cases indicate that Crittenton workers were compassionate and understanding, despite the disparities between their own lives and those of the women they sought to help. Some Crittenton workers' desire to help other women surpassed the expectations of even their co-workers. L—— C—— was unmarried, gave birth to a stillborn child, and disposed of the evidence in a vacant lot only to have a doctor discover it. The authorities charged L—— C—— with failing to report the birth of a child. During the investigation she stayed at the FC home, and eventually the court placed her in the home, where she received training and later a job.[128] The Wilkes-Barre, Pennsylvania, shelter reported a similar case involving Russian immigrant Rosie ——, charged with concealing the death of a child. The Crittenton people found attorney Mary L. Trescott to defend Rosie and ultimately obtain her release. Trescott agreed to serve as a special probation officer for a period of three years during which time Rosie would live in the Florence Crittenton home.[129] Crittenton workers thought that both L—— C—— and Rosie were victims, not people guilty of criminal acts, and the Crittenton intercession saved the women from jail while offering them a supportive environment for their recoveries. While workers placed great store in the institution of motherhood, their first consideration was for the mother herself. They recognized the desperation some women experienced upon the birth of a child, and they were sympathetic even in cases where many would have viewed the women in question as criminals. This attitude separated Crittenton people from many other social workers, and even today it would be no easy task to locate people willing to serve as advocates for these women.

Crittenton workers strived to aid victims of incest, certainly a particularly disturbing issue for the FC women. Workers referred to the cases of two incest victims as "a tale too bad to print," thus defining the Crittenton attitude toward this problem.[130] Despite their reticence to discuss the topic, cases of incest required Crittenton women to use the court system to assist victims. In 1899 Los Angeles matron Mrs. Bisbee appeared on behalf of a girl who ran away from her foster father, a man who "subjected her to all sort of indignities." Although the man tried to retain control, the judge awarded custody to the Florence Crittenton home.[131] In 1917 workers went further. Fargo volunteers were pleased to inform *Girls* readers that a male relative guilty of "atrocious abuse" was sent to the penitentiary due to an "energetic" Crittenton worker. The Fargo women described themselves as "fighting almost a single handed battle against this form of atrocity and others like it in North Dakota."[132] Incest victims found advocates at the Crittenton institutions when they could find them no where else. When Crittenton workers spoke out against incest, they challenged the sexual hegemony of men.

Florence Crittenton homes sponsored some of the earliest day-care facilities for working families in the United States—another example of a pioneering Crittenton response to a vital social problem.[133] Their commitment to day care clearly indicated the greater understanding that workers were beginning to develop for the challenges working mothers faced. It was a dramatic enough departure that the Detroit home felt compelled to describe its novel day nursery: "Here children are left in the morning under competent care while the mother goes to her day's work. In the evening she calls and takes them home with her." Since there were only 206 such nurseries in the country in 1905, Florence Crittenton institutions were indeed breaking new ground.[134] Crittenton organizations charged a nominal fee for this service, but only if the mother was able to pay. Detroit workers believed the nursery saved "the utter destruction of many a home," and workers also realized that knowing their children were well cared for and comfortable eased the minds of working-class mothers.[135] Many homes recognized that this service was especially valuable to women who were deserted, to families undergoing financial crisis, and to "mothers temporarily under stress of circumstances until they can once again gather their little family together in their own home."[136] Through the nurseries, workers could both preserve the institutions they revered— homes—and at the same time ease working-class women's burdens.

Workers recognized the fragile nature of many working-class homes' economic existence, and the day nursery was a godsend for many families with money troubles. When FC workers heard about a husband who failed to make support payments during divorce proceedings, social workers

A Florence Crittenton nursery, c. 1914. The NFCM was a pioneer in day care. Courtesy of the National Florence Crittenton Mission.

intervened on the wife's behalf and took the husband to court, at the same time attempting to bring about a reconciliation. During this period the wife gave birth to another child in the Crittenton home, and the FC workers cared for the baby while the couple tried to iron out their differences. When debts plagued another family, the Crittenton day nursery cared for the five children until the family regained its economic footing.[137] Often had it not been for Crittenton intervention, mothers would have been compelled to part with their children. By 1904 the Portland, Oregon, home had enrolled one hundred children in its nursery and kindergarten, and other homes' day-care facilities had grown accordingly.[138]

The Crittenton home was also an early haven for women victims of abuse, desertion, and homelessness; women who had no place else to go were certain to find shelter and protection at the home. Deserted wives accounted for 65 percent of the population of the Spokane, Washington, home in 1910. While many of these so-called deserted wives would probably be described as "separated" in contemporary terminology, their need for help remained the same.[139]

The Detroit home reported the case of a family with seven children between the ages of seven months and thirteen, and a father who drank and verbally and physically abused his wife and children. The boys sold newspapers and the father took their earnings in order to purchase liquor. When he deserted them in 1910, the family found refuge at the Florence Crittenton home. The mother found herself homeless and in need of shelter on several occasions in 1911 and 1912, and the Crittenton home was always available. In another situation, after a mother swore out a warrant for nonsupport against her husband, the Crittenton home cared for the children during the interim judicial process.[140] During one month in 1910, the New York mother mission provided food for 536 homeless women and temporary shelter for 52 of them.[141] As in the case of the day nurseries, this aspect of Crittenton work filled a void in social services available for women.

Workers remained sympathetic even when their charges failed to live up to Crittenton expectations. One forty-three-year-old Detroit woman had been a Florence Crittenton inmate when she was a young unmarried mother. The Children's Aid Society investigator reported that the woman's children were dirty and underfed and that the ten-year-old daughter "ran wild," notwithstanding all the home training the woman received during her Crittenton stay. Despite this report, when her husband deserted her, the woman again turned to the Florence Crittenton home, where she received shelter for herself and her family.[142]

Sometimes the Crittenton involvement was a long-term one and ended in disappointment, as in the case of a African American Detroit family with a history of domestic difficulties and other problems. The wife had been a contortionist with Ringling Brothers' Circus. No doubt both her race and her occupational association with the circus made the woman suspect in social workers' eyes. However, she left her husband to escape his cruelty and sought shelter with her baby at the Florence Crittenton home. Following her reconciliation with her husband, the Detroit Children's Aid Society placed the child in the FC home so that he could receive better care and protection from the father. In the following years the family experienced poverty, unemployment, and separations. The husband deserted, and the wife, "ill and destitute," again found refuge at the Crittenton home. Divorce proceedings began and FC workers urged that the woman be committed to Eloise Insane Asylum and the child placed for adoption. The police court ordered a mental examination and found the woman was "mentally abnormal but not insane—she cannot control herself along the lines of decent conduct." The woman spent three months in Eloise. A year later, still destitute, she returned to Eloise and workers put her children up for adoption. In the workers' view, the woman was an unfit mother in spite of all their efforts. Possibly the mother had exhausted any other possibilities and determined that her own confinement at Eloise would at least guarantee her children's well-being.[143] While the workers were no doubt convinced that they had exerted considerable effort on the woman's behalf, it is apparent that both her race and life-style may have affected their response.

As another offshoot of their work on behalf of women, homes tried to assist young girls in need of advice, counsel, or temporary shelter and companionship. Often the authorities referred to Crittenton care girls who were not in immediate danger of getting into trouble and who were free to leave the home at any time. Most did once they secured employment. Crittenton homes served as an alternative to jails in a number of instances and were certainly preferable to the workhouse or reformatory, particularly in cases involving intemperance and similar offenses. Matron Lola Zell of Peoria recounted the story of a thirteen-year-old girl taken in "an intoxicated condition, surrounded by dissolute companions." The girl was destined for a reformatory, but the home agreed to keep her and "give her every opportunity."[144] The Crittenton people assisted M—— H——, whom the police accused of intoxication in the public streets. Since she was a first offender, the judge had the Crittenton worker take charge instead of committing M—— H—— to a workhouse or levying a fine. M—— H—— reportedly was grateful, and following a period as an inmate in the home, she returned to her own life.[145] The Boston home described its role as giving these girls time to "catch their breath" and "think it over."[146] In this way the Crittenton people provided a real service to countless women who only needed a place to reconnoiter, but who would have found themselves incarcerated without the Crittenton alternative. The Jackson, Mississippi, juvenile court judge reported that, because of the "Crittenton work," he had only sent one girl to reform school during 1918.[147]

Crittenton workers were especially interested in providing this kind of opportunity to young girls, since along with other progressive juvenile reformers, they believed the delinquent child was less at fault than were her environment and probably her family situation. Detroit workers aided a thirteen-year-old girl community workers described as "incorrigible." The girl apparently did not get along with her stepmother, so she left home several times, and the Florence Crittenton home provided her a haven.[148] Some social workers would have recommended a reform school for the runaway, but workers sympathized with the girl in this case.

The Michigan Crittenton organization described one of its goals as the care of young women not "as yet entirely wayward nor profligate, but where morals may be in danger owing to circumstances."[149] Many judges were pleased to commit girls to the charge of a Crittenton home rather then sending them to jail. Often a close but unofficial relationship developed between Crittenton workers and the court system. The chief of police or another official would request that the Crittenton home take charge of a particular girl, and the FC workers were happy to oblige. In 1913 the New York workers reported that a number of "colored girls under 16" were sent to them directly from the Children's Court "as the means of caring for this class is so limited."[150] According to one estimate, by 1914 a quarter of the girls in Florence Crittenton homes were referred by the courts. In a state such as North Dakota, where there was no juvenile court system, the Fargo home played an active role in this area. The superintendent advocated "training and not punishment" for first-time offenders. This discretion on the part of the judicial system and the homes gave workers considerable power over girls but also protected them from the harsher aspects of the criminal justice system.[151] The Crittenton viewpoint was that the home was a "privilege" in comparison to reform school. From the perspective of the girl, both represented a constraint on liberty and no one consulted her as to her preference.

Judges actually sentenced girls to FC homes in some instances. Juvenile Court Judge Ben Lindsey appointed Denver's home matron, Mrs. Cotton, as a probation officer in his court. Judges in other parts of the country made similar appointments. As probation officer, Cotton had authority over girls who appeared before Lindsey. Often such a girl had committed no crime, but Lindsey and the Crittenton officials believed that she was liable to do so because of her environment or known associates. Crittenton workers and progressive judges believed it was their duty to step in and take control of a girl before she broke the law. According to longtime Crittenton worker Grace Topping, one chief of police confided to her that he had his "eye on twenty girls who needed protection."[152] Since they were guilty of no crime, these girls could not be sent to reform school, but the police chief and Topping feared that the girls would soon become victims of unscrupulous men. This situation was ideally suited for Crittenton intervention. This scenario did not take into account the wishes of the girls involved, who quite possibly sought excitement and independence through their actions. Since they had not broken any law, this meddling is difficult to justify.

One of Lindsey's letters to such a girl revealed the kind of problems these girls had and the way that Lindsey and the Crittenton home workers acted to save them from future mistakes. Lindsey had placed Blanche Stalling under Cotton's supervision in response to complaints by Blanche's sister and others. Blanche smuggled to Lindsey a note seeking release and claiming that her mother was ill. Lindsey wrote to the girl suggesting that perhaps she did not understand the purpose of her stay at the Crittenton home. He reminded her that "you were not conducting yourself in a manner that would lead us to believe that you were trying to do right." Lindsey went on to point out that Blanche's surreptitious methods in writing to him seemed to confirm that judgment, and he concluded that although he sympathized with the girl's desire to visit her mother, he would not allow it until she proved herself. He chided Blanche for writing the letter in the first place without consulting Cotton, "a good and kind woman, who has given her life to the uplifting of fallen girls." According to Lindsey, he and Cotton were "trying to make a good woman of you."[153] (One is tempted to add "in spite of yourself.") Crittenton workers' attitude that they knew what was best for young girls was a prevailing one and typified progressive approaches to juvenile problems. Young girls usually had less control over their situations than older women. This was particularly true of African American girls. The Topeka home workers were "glad that it has been made possible to have a home to lift

up and place them in the right path of life with a white family."[154] Whether
or not the young African American girls shared their gladness is not clear,
and these girls had to cope with interference from both middle-class black
women and white women.

Sometimes Crittenton action actually resulted in the separation of
family members in order to protect children and their welfare. Crittenton
workers removed Ethel, a seventeen-year-old African American girl they
described as "illiterate and immoral," and thirteen-year-old Grace, who
had argued with her stepmother, from their homes. The FC people feared
these girls were in danger of becoming delinquent if they remained with
their families.[155]

In large cities the Crittenton mission began to devote a great deal of
effort to working with juvenile and other courts. Whereas FC workers
had initially concentrated on rescuing prostitutes, they now tried to assist any woman in trouble, whatever the nature of her difficulty. Margaret Luther was in charge of this facet of mission work in New York City
and was present in night court each evening wearing a ribbon bearing
the words "Florence Crittenton Home, Can I help you?" Between the
hours of nine at night and three in the morning, Luther was available to
take charge of any girl and provide her shelter and, eventually, employment.[156] Crittenton workers hoped this method would prevent potentially
dangerous situations for these girls.

Florence Crittenton workers' self-perceptions and their attitudes toward their charges as "sisters" led the National Florence Crittenton
Mission to offer many and diverse services for women and children. For
the most part, historians have ignored this variety in Crittenton endeavors. The workers consciously attempted to transcend class differences
between themselves and their charges. While this goal was not achieved
entirely, Crittenton "women's work for women" did take pioneering and
influential forms.

National Florence Crittenton Mission efforts in the field of health care
for women, particularly obstetrics and gynecology, represented an early
step in women's quest to control their own health. Crittenton homes provided shelter and refuge for women victims of sexual abuse and incest,
at a time when few other options were available. The homes helped
women facing economic crisis due to separation from spouses, unemployment, and gender discrimination in the workplace. Crittenton insistence
that fathers provide support for their children pitted workers against a
male-dominated court system and a patriarchal society. Day-care facilities were the result of new attitudes regarding women and work, and

Crittenton institutions were on the cutting edge of this development. At a time when few institutions allowed blacks, many Crittenton homes accepted African Americans, and African American women were active participants in Crittenton endeavors in Topeka, and to a lesser degree, elsewhere.

All of these programs represented an expansion of earlier Florence Crittenton efforts to save prostitutes. These activities represented challenges to male hegemony and illustrated a woman-centered approach to social welfare issues. As such, Crittenton endeavors have significant contemporary resonance and are critical aspects of the National Florence Crittenton Mission's role as a pioneer in social welfare work. However, popular opinion soon led the NFCM to return its attention to more traditional rescue work.

Chapter 5

The National Florence Crittenton
Mission and "White Slavery"

We have neglected to protect the innocence and virtue of children;
we have failed to help unfortunate women; we have disregarded
the presence in our cities of this hideous monster vice. We have
blamed the individual girl and thought her vicious and bad. We
have not laid the blame where it belongs—upon ourselves.
—Maud Miner, 1916

"Hear ye! Hear ye! How much will ye give for a human being—body and soul?"
"What is the soul worth?"
"Nothing," cried the auctioneer, "I throw that in with the sale of the body."
That is the value they place upon the soul of a girl when she is auctioned off
to the highest bidder for a house of ill repute.
—Clifford G. Roe, 1909

In the years leading up to World War I, Americans became alarmed at
what they feared was the widespread sale of souls into prostitution. At
no time before or since has so much been written about the subject or
have so many campaigned so actively against it.[1] This obsession reflected
many of the progressive traits that influenced the National Florence
Crittenton Mission's home operations, particularly the idea that reformers
could manipulate and control society's behavior. Middle-class progressives thought they could impose their moral standards on the rest of
America through education. Certainly prostitution represented an affront
to progressive values, and consequently many progressives viewed it as
one of the most serious problems of urban social control. As was the case

with other reforms, the vice crusade served to accentuate the differences middle-class reformers perceived between themselves and other groups. Gender, too, was obviously a defining issue.[2]

As a result of the heightened interest in prostitution, the NFCM found itself in the mainstream of a progressive reform campaign. *Girls* reported with pride that other reformers were studying Crittenton work and consulting the NFCM as the agency that "can throw more light upon the life, character, and conditions of the victims of the Social Evil than any other."[3] This attention prompted many Crittenton workers to reassess their views of rescue work, an area of endeavor many had shunned as unproductive and an inefficient use of resources. Few FC workers could resist the temptation to be involved at last in a popular activity, and Kate Waller Barrett particularly enjoyed her new-found status as an expert. *Girls* exalted:

> To a great many persons no doubt the history of the white slave
> traffic is comparatively a new subject, but all of us who have been in
> this wyork [*sic*] know that more than twenty years ago our beloved
> Mr. Crittenton called attention to the fact that girls were being held
> in such slavery. At that time, however, good people did not hesitate
> to say "Crittenton is insane." Since then this monster evil has grown
> and flourished, devastating many homes, taking from the family
> circle many of its fairest daughters until at last the people are waking
> up to the necessity of action.[4]

Both self-satisfaction and vindication characterized the Florence Crittenton response to the new interest in prostitution.

This heightened concern over prostitution had antecedents in both the British and American purity movements of the late nineteenth century, when reformers had warned the public about the dire consequences of prostitution and venereal disease. Reformers on both sides of the Atlantic experimented with legislation and regulation designed to control prostitution. The St. Louis Social Evil Ordinance regulated prostitutes, and from 1870 to 1874, St. Louis operated a system of inspection of prostitutes coupled with the quarantine of those found to have venereal disease. Physicians and city health officials favored this solution to the problem, but religious leaders opposed the ordinance on the grounds that, rather than diminishing prostitution, it simply provided official government recognition of vice. Eventually, doctors and public health authorities could not combat the wrath of the religious community and the experiment failed.[5]

Opponents of the St. Louis law used many of the same arguments that Josephine Butler offered against the English Contagious Disease Acts. These acts allowed a policeman to stop any woman on the street and require her to submit to a physical examination for venereal disease. Butler led agitation against the acts for sixteen years, and Parliament repealed them in 1886.[6] Both episodes point to the public's unwillingness to countenance regulation of prostitution as a solution.

About the same time, William Stead, editor of the *Pall Mall Gazette,* made revelations that shocked the British public. Stead had heard rumors regarding the sale of women for immoral purposes, and he set out to test their validity. He and his collaborators visited London brothels and took copious notes; Stead even arranged to purchase a virgin from a London procurer and then turned the unfortunate girl over to a philanthropic organization. On July 6, 1885, Stead published an exposé entitled "The Maiden Tribute in Modern Babylon" wherein he voiced his concern for the young victims of vice. Over 150,000 people gathered in Hyde Park on August 22, 1885, to hear Stead and others describe the plight of white-slavery victims and to demand legislative action to protect innocent children.[7]

Stead's campaign received little attention in the United States. According to one reformer, Americans did little more than ask, "Can these things be true?"[8] Charles Crittenton, however, followed Stead's activities closely, and at his suggestion, Charlton Edholm included "The Maiden Tribute in Modern Babylon" in her widely circulated book, *The Traffic in Girls and the Florence Crittenton Mission.*[9] While Crittenton succeeded in raising awareness and social conscience, he was unable to make prostitution a central issue for most Americans.

A number of progressive impulses coalesced to bring the prostitution issue to prominence. As part of the progressive penchant for realism and for gathering evidence to define problems, vice reformers explored prostitution in great detail. This emphasis on knowledge—along with a certain amount of curiosity—motivated reformers to publicize every sordid fact they uncovered. Several cities appointed vice commissions to gather as much information regarding prostitution as possible, and for the first time, upstanding Americans read about and discussed topics such as the psychology of the relationship of a prostitute and her pimp and the various modes of operation that prostitutes used. Reformers learned that prostitutes plied their trade in many places and under different circumstances. One commission investigated 142 houses of ill repute and found that 20 were fifty-cent houses, 80 charged each customer a dollar, 6 were two-dollar houses, and 24 charged five dollars per visit. The "tenement call houses"—where the madam called a woman and arranged a meeting after the patron made his selection from a group of photographs accompanied by descriptions, measurements, and a price list—appalled vice investigators.[10] Vice commission employees reported that many hotels featured a rebate system to encourage prostitutes' patronage: the woman received a kickback on the room rent in addition to a commission on any wine or beer her customer ordered.[11] Perhaps most shocking were the punch cards madams used to keep track of each prostitute's wages. Every hole punched in a woman's card represented a customer, and investigators exhibited one card that contained thirty holes for a single day's work.[12] According to one historian, these vice commission reports came to include one billion pages of documentation.[13] This kind of detailed and explicit evidence was a far cry from early Crittenton tracts, which generalized on matters "too horrible to repeat."

These discoveries seemed particularly outrageous in light of the widespread belief that many prostitutes had not voluntarily chosen their careers. Reformers estimated that house of prostitution inmates' professional lives averaged five years, so that brothels required sixty thousand women each year to maintain their "inventory."[14] Rumors of a far-reaching trade in women ran rampant, its victims allegedly innocent and unsuspecting females tricked into a life of shame. A plethora of literature described the operation of this trade and resulted in a state of near hysteria; women feared procurers would snatch them if they ventured out alone.

Vice crusaders described the most common procurement schemes in great detail to warn potential victims. Promises of marriage attracted many women to procurers. Often the panderer would go to a small town in the guise of the son of a prominent city banker in need of a rest from bustling city life. A "pure girl" would fall in love with him and thus seal her fate. Another successful method was for the procurer to advertise for workers, promising attractive wages. He would take the women who responded to the city, where he ruined them. A proven ploy was for the panderer to play the part of a theatrical agent casting a new play or revue. Paul Sinclair, a reformed procurer, confessed, "I posed as a theatrical manager that summer and caught many an unwary, stage-struck girl."[15] Some stories circulated dealing with the forceful abduction of women, but most responsible reformers discounted them. *Girls* published stories along these lines that were reminiscent of earlier Crittenton tracts. Progressives came to call these machinations the White Slave Conspiracy, a term attributed to Clifford Roe, an Illinois assistant state attorney general and ardent antiprostitution advocate.[16]

New information about the harmful effects of sexually transmitted disease also spurred the progressive's antiprostitution campaign. Scientists discovered the causes of syphilis and gonorrhea and gained refined ideas about their transmission. In addition, they became better informed regarding the dangers the diseases posed to innocent victims, such as the wives and children of men who contracted the diseases from their contacts with prostitutes. Physicians and health-care professionals concluded that these diseases were a more serious threat to the public health than they had heretofore suspected.[17] Doctors hoped to combat these illnesses through public education, but most middle-class Americans were reticent to discuss the matter. Consequently, many physicians came to believe that only a change in sexual behavior could control venereal disease and, as a result, formed alliances with reformers of the Crittenton persuasion.[18]

In her book *A New Conscience and an Ancient Evil,* Jane Addams explained why "white slavery" was such an apt term for the business of procuring women for immoral purposes. Besides the obvious comparison regarding the sale of human beings, Addams believed that she and other anti-vice crusaders were "new abolitionists." Like the original abolitionists, they faced unpopularity and campaigned actively despite the wish of most Americans that the subject not be broached.[19] Crittenton workers knew only too well what Addams was talking about, as they had confronted these barriers since the beginning of their movement.

Anti-vice crusaders and social hygiene advocates alike believed that it was vital to end white slavery and to save women from prostitution. Jane Addams thus compared rescue homes to the stations of the underground railroad that daring abolitionists had operated before the Civil War.[20] Florence Crittenton work thus finally received the kind of recognition that Kate Waller Barrett had long demanded. Crittenton workers now viewed Charles Crittenton's efforts on behalf of prostitutes as nothing short of prophetic, and *Girls* noted that those who had thought him "fanatical" "have long since been compelled to change their opinion."[21]

The traditional Florence Crittenton appeals on behalf of fallen women took on a new significance in the light of the white slave revelations, and local homes played upon public concern to gain support. Many Crittenton organizations offered the vice commission reports as evidence of the great need for FC organizations, and once again Crittenton literature was filled with stories of women betrayed into prostitution and of rescue attempts. The Boston Crittenton organization began to publish a newsletter, *The Protector,* to keep patrons up-to-date on efforts in that city.[22] The Florence Crittenton League of Virginia printed and distributed a leaflet, *Where White Slaves are Recruited,* which asked, "What can a girl do if she is led astray and is desirous of retracing her steps and making good? There is nothing but the suicide grave or a house of sin unless she comes across an organization like the Florence Crittenton League of Virginia."[23] These publications served to spotlight the Crittenton organization's essential role in efforts to curtail white slavery.

Crittenton workers returned their attention to professional prostitutes, and *Girls* contained vivid reports of this work. In St. Louis even a trained nurse reported upon visiting a local vice district, "I have stood over the dissecting and operating table and yet never felt like fainting before but this is so much worse than anything that I have ever seen."[24] Elizabeth Howard, the Harrisburg, Pennsylvania, matron and her colleagues visited over 30 houses of ill repute during a four-month period and rescued 28 girls and 7 children.[25] During 1912, New York City Crittenton volunteers talked to 1,238 girls, visited 210 dance halls and cafés, and made 620 hospital and prison calls.[26] The anti-vice crusade became so central to Florence Crittenton work that all of the delegates to the 1912 national convention in Chicago visited the red-light district where Kate Waller Barrett presided over a prayer meeting. The magazine described the unforgettable scene of Barrett "as she stood in the glare of the lights of the saloon on the corner, and talked straight into the hearts of the young men who stood facing her on the pavement."[27] This could easily have been an account of one of the Florence Crittenton Rescue Band's nightly forays during the 1890s. The Louisville, Kentucky, Crittenton group hired photographers to take pictures of clients leaving houses of prostitution. The photographs were published in local newspapers, reminiscent of New York Female Moral Reform Society practices almost a century earlier.[28] Charles Crittenton informed readers of the *Florence Crittenton Magazine* that when the Crittenton circle members in Bainbridge, Georgia, visited that city's red-light district, their prayers and presence resulted in the whole district becoming "demoralized."[29]

What set Crittenton activities apart from those of the majority of progressive-era reform groups who targeted prostitution was that the Crittenton organization continued to emphasize their concern for the women trapped in lives of vice. *Girls* touted Charles N. Crittenton as someone interested not in punishing offenders but in helping "victims."[30] The Crittenton organization was a minority voice. As Barbara Meil Hobson has pointed out, most of the progressive anti-vice reforms had the greatest impact on lower-class women who were the most visible and vulnerable participants in the prostitution system.[31] Because of their gender, the female prostitutes were much less powerful than their male customers and pimps. A 1905 *Florence Crittenton Magazine* editorial describing a red-light district raid in Philadelphia complained, "Throughout the entire course of action, one cannot fail to be impressed with the double standard—one for men and one for women." The men paid fines and went about their business, while the women were kept in jail.[32] Margaret Luther described plain-clothes police in New York who entrapped women pressured by pimps who were "waiting to beat them" if they didn't make sufficient money.[33] Crittenton workers hoped to soften the impact of new antiprostitution laws on women. According to Judith Walkowitz, prostitution served as a paradigm for the female condition, leading reformers to a powerful "identification" with prostitutes. Many Crittenton workers recognized that while they operated in a more genteel society than prostitutes, the power relationship between men and women was repeated, and the Crittenton workers sought to alter that power relationship for both prostitutes and themselves.

Margaret Luther of the New York City Crittenton home devoted her time to saving potential white-slavery victims. In order to protect innocent girls, she visited movie theaters and other places procurers frequented. Emile D. Stonehill described a typical incident in a *Girls* article entitled "A Midnight Rescue and a Narrow Escape." Luther had observed a girl who had stayed out too late with an escort, who attempted to convince his target that, since it would be embarrassing to return home at that hour, she should spend the night in a hotel. In the morning the girl could tell her parents that she had stayed with a friend, but of course the man planned to sell the girl into prostitution. As Stonehill recounted, "When you try to save a pretty night-moth from the flame around which it is hovering to its doom you have no time to lose, and it was with a suddenness and energy which completely surprised the man that the sister appeared on the scene crying, 'Don't go with him, child!'" Luther's quick action brought the girl to her senses, and she "returned to the protection of her mother's arms."[34] Of course, it is certainly possible that the girl in question was enjoying herself and knew exactly what awaited her in the hotel room. Luther's interference may have disappointed the couple, but probably did relieve the girl's mother, while providing an illustration of heroic Crittenton action that *Girls* readers appreciated. Margaret Luther did not concern herself with the issue of the girl's individual freedom of action.

Luther expanded her night court activities to include sending telegrams to arrested girls' parents informing them of their daughters' predicaments. A typical message read: "Mr George ———, Asbury Park, New Jersey, ——— your daughter has been arrested. Come to the Night Court tonight at eight o'clock, 125 6th Ave., N.Y.C." Luther kept an eye on the girl until her family could arrive to assist her.[35] This kind of story definitely appealed to audiences and no doubt led to contributions to Crittenton work. The organization pointed to this and similar efforts in other communities as evidence of the NFCM's ability to take concrete steps to combat white slavery.

Because the National Florence Crittenton Mission could boast of more than twenty years experience dealing with prostitution and its victims, many progressive vice reformers turned to the mission for expert advice. James Bronson Reynolds, Clifford Roe's designee to investigate the white-slave traffic in New York City, used Florence Crittenton records of six thousand cases as part of his investigation.[36] Prominent vice reformer George Kneeland described the New York FC home as one of two in the city that "touch the problem of the prostitute and commercialized vice more closely than any others."[37] *Girls* claimed that no other group had done as much work among prostitutes as had the Crittenton organization.[38] Crittenton workers were sought after to attend white-slave conferences and impart some of their knowledge to the uninitiated. Barrett traveled over twelve thousand miles during 1912, discussing Crittenton work at more than 265 public meetings—many on college campuses; and the World Purity Federation named her to the post of superintendent of rescue work.[39] She served as chair of the Committee for the Abolition of the White Slave Traffic of the National Council of Women and discussed Clifford Roe's latest book on vice commissions to the National Conference of Charities and Corrections.[40] *Girls* claimed, "Our President, Dr. Kate Waller Barrett, is without a doubt, the best informed woman in America on all subjects pertaining to this traffic."[41]

The great interest in rescue work enabled the Florence Crittenton organization to enjoy tremendous growth. In Detroit, for example, the local home launched a citywide campaign and planned to recruit between sixteen hundred and two thousand precinct and ward leaders to raise money. Each precinct would have a committee to investigate "plague spots" in its area and enlist the help of the entire group in closing them.[42] During 1912, Crittenton homes received $230,777 in donations and $50,000 in public aid; the NFCM claimed it owned real estate valued at $942,000. More than twenty thousand women received Florence Crittenton assistance in 1912, causing *Girls* to proclaim, "Thus you see it is the organized, legalized Christian Institution which watches over, protects and rescues girls from that awful white slave traffic, which is said to be greater than the black slave traffic before the war."[43] This Florence Crittenton success was due in large part to the compatibility of the FC philosophy and the policies that progressive vice reformers supported: sex education, an end to the double standard of morals, concern for women and children, and a recognition of the economic causes of prostitution.

Jane Addams, William Stead, Prince Morrow, and other anti-vice crusaders agreed that the majority of white slavery would disappear if young girls received explicit sex education. As one reformer noted, "Though it may be difficult and delicate and often unpleasant work it is becoming absolutely essential *that the young of both sexes be instructed in the purpose and problems and perils of sex,* including information as to the awful penalty nature imposes in the form of social diseases, such as syphilis and gonorrhea."[44] The NFCM, in keeping with Charles Crittenton's early advocacy, supported sex education, and its magazine contained articles designed to convince readers of its value. The Crittenton people combined their customary sentimental appeals with advocacy of education as a means of combating the social evil, as in the poem "No One Told Her":

> She was just in the bloom of life's morning
> She was happy, and free and fair;
> And a glance in her bright eyes would tell you
> Of nothing but innocence there.
>
> She was waiting for someone to tell her
> As she stood with reluctant feet,
> On the banks of the wonderful river
> Where childhood and womanhood meet.
>
> She waited, but still no one told her
> The secret of life so sublime
> And she held not the safeguard of knowledge
> In life's beautiful morning time.
>
> The flower, so sweetly unfolding,
> Was crushed by a rough hand one day,
> And the jewel, so sacred, so precious,
> Was stolen and taken away.[45]

The fallen woman in this poem was reluctant to engage in sexual activity and was, according to the poet, "waiting" for someone to provide her with the education she needed. "No One Told Her" placed the blame for wasting this "flower" upon those individuals who should have provided essential information to the girl.

Delegates to the 1910 Florence Crittenton convention passed a resolution recommending that school boards throughout the country provide for "sex physiology" classes in the public schools.[46] This resolution not only indicated the Crittenton position on the subject but also displayed a willingness on the part of Crittenton workers to involve themselves in public policy making in order to achieve the desired result. While Charles Crittenton had appealed primarily to ideas of Christian obligation, these later Crittenton workers demanded community action.

Vice reformers concerned about the spread of venereal disease joined those who worried about the White Slave Conspiracy in the belief that an end to the double standard of morals for men and women would contribute to the elimination of prostitution and reduce the number of cases of venereal disease. Clifford Roe proclaimed, "These standards always looked upon as rigid and firm must soon rot at the base and topple to the ground."[47] Roe, Addams, and their compatriots contended that the old view that sexual activity for men was necessary for good health resulted in sexual license and the spread of disease.[48] The white-slave revelations only served to confirm the Crittenton mission's outspoken opposition to the double standard, as expressed in "What of the Prodigal Girl?":

> We all have a heart for the Prodigal Boy,
> Who was caught in sin's mad whirl,
> And welcome him back with songs of joy
> But what of the Prodigal Girl?
>
> For the Prodigal Boy there's an open door
> And a father's bounteous fare;
> And though he is wretched, sick, and poor,
> He is sure of welcome there.
>
> But what of the girl who has gone astray
> Who has lost in the battle of sin?
> Say, do we forgive in the same sweet way,
> We've always forgiven him?
> Does the door stand ajar, as if to say
> Come enter, you need not fear;
> I've been open thus since you went away,
> Now close to the second year?
>
> Or, do we with hand of hellish pride
> Close and bolt the door,
> And swear, "While heaven and earth abide
> She will enter here no more?
>
> Oh Christ! It seems we have never learned
> The lesson taught in the sand.
> For even yet the woman is spurned
> And stoned in a Christian land.

> Down into the slough we hand her back,
>   Then turn around with a smile,
> And welcome the boy from sinful track
>   Though he may have been more vile.
>
> We all have a heart for the Prodigal Boy,
>   Who was caught in sin's mad whirl
> And we welcome him back with songs of joy
>   But what of the prodigal Girl?[49]

The poem reiterated the Crittenton view that women suffered more of a penalty than men, even though the man "may have been more vile," and it clearly pointed to the inequity of this situation. "What of the Prodigal Girl?" voiced the Crittenton call for society to change its attitudes in regard to both the girl's condition and the man's lack of responsibility. Florence Crittenton workers demanded a change in the traditional view of women and their sexuality. In doing so, FC women challenged long-established gender relationships.

In the wake of the white-slavery publicity, the Florence Crittenton workers became more militant in their opposition to the double standard as volunteers believed that it was responsible for the unequal treatment of male and female moral offenders. The NFCM contended that the punishment for a pimp or procurer should not depend on the past history of the girl involved, an early recognition of a still controversial principle. Margaret Luther and other workers were among the first to complain that the prostitute faced arrest while her customer went free. Luther was highly critical of plain clothes police officers who "tempted" street girls into solicitation, often out of fear of "taking a beating from a cadet who is watching her."[50] Complaints of entrapment were common among prostitutes and those sympathetic to their plight during the progressive period. Florence Crittenton people pointed out that raids on vice districts, a keystone of the progressive anti-vice crusades, always resulted in greater punishment for the women arrested than for the men. While the men involved usually were released on bond, the women remained incarcerated so that they would be able to testify in any trial. Vocal FC complaints of harsh treatment often served to soften the impact of the more militant anti-vice crusades on the prostitutes themselves, and the Crittenton workers offered a needed woman's viewpoint to the legal efforts to limit prostitution.[51] At the same time, the inability of Crittenton workers or other women reformers to significantly alter either the practice of prostitution in this country or the legal response to it is indicative of the relative powerlessness of women.[52] While Crittenton people could sometimes ameliorate the most burdensome effects of the vice crusade upon prostitutes, they were unable to redirect the white-slavery outcry toward men, despite their considerable efforts in that direction.

Progressives realized that prostitution was not new, but they were convinced that the phenomenal industrial expansion following the Civil War and the accompanying growth of urban areas had exacerbated the problem. With a typical progressive emphasis on environment, the vice reformers thought that the slums contributed to prostitution; groups such as the New York State Tenement House Commission, with its motto "The dwellings of the poor," helped instill this belief. Sexual license seemed to be a characteristic of slum life, and FC workers and their counterparts in other organizations supported improved housing conditions as a means of curbing it, a position in marked contrast to the organization's earlier emphasis on religious conversion as the primary concern of moral reform.[53]

Although many progressives were city-dwellers themselves, they expressed some revulsion for the city and all it symbolized. Certain that the cities' quick growth denied their inhabitants the tightly woven social fabric of small towns, the progressives wanted to restore a sense of community to the urban masses. The close living conditions in cities ensured young people of some contact with prostitution, and the impersonal nature of urban life made it easy for procurers to ply their trade. Jane Addams wrote, "Certainly only the modern city has offered at one and the same time every possible stimulation for the lower nature and every opportunity for secret vice."[54] Cities were particularly dangerous for those unaccustomed to them. Addams explained, "Mr. Clifford Roe estimates that more than half of the girls who have been recruited into a disreputable life in Chicago have come from the farms and smaller towns in Illinois and from neighboring states."[55] The NFCM advised girls to stay in their home towns rather than "come to the city and face the snares and dangers that await them," in recognition of the Crittenton workers' inability to guarantee absolute protection.[56] At the same time, Crittenton workers stepped up their efforts to aid women living in metropolitan settings.

Related to this belief that city life was conducive to immorality was the progressive realization that industrialization had so altered the economy that sometimes women viewed prostitution as an economic necessity. Maud Miner, a New York probation officer, claimed, "Another way to lessen moral wreckage among girls is by reducing the tremendous economic pressure to which many of them are subjected."[57] Barrett joined Miner, Addams, and others in calling for improved working conditions, higher wages, and job security for women. In an address before the National Council of Women entitled "Equal Standards of Morals," Barrett stated that many women entered lives of sin "to find bread to eat and the necessary clothes to wear," while "we never knew of a man to make such an excuse."[58] Barrett attacked the double standard of morals but also the inequality of economic opportunity for women and men. But Crittenton workers were cautious about placing all the blame on economics. They still considered moral lapses, ignorance, and the trickery of unscrupulous men as significant causes of prostitution, and the organization struggled to continue to address these issues as well.

Fear that family ties were disintegrating and that prostitution threatened the family institution inspired much of the anti-vice agitation.[59] Researchers claimed that prostitutes were more likely to come from broken homes, homes in which one or both parents had drinking problems or homes with a history of immorality.[60] Reformers therefore advocated a strengthening of the family and an improvement in home conditions. The NFCM had long recognized the importance of a healthy home and environment, and FC workers continued their labors to improve the family setting.[61] For example, in Boston, "Homes too unpleasant for girls to live in happily have been investigated, and in some instances conditions have been bettered and advice given." The Crittenton organization's reliance on urban mothers to help their own daughters was yet another indication of the FC faith in motherhood's power.[62] While FC workers feared for the family as an institution, they remained secure in their belief that mothers, regardless of their socioeconomic status, were capable of making the necessary adjustments to ensure that homes and families survived. This set Crittenton women apart from many of their reform colleagues, who were turning more and more to policies that advocated the removal of children from suspect families. Barrett's convictions regarding the bonds of motherhood shaped the Crittenton policy and made the Crittenton organization more likely to act as advocate for urban mothers.

Like much of the progressive reform agenda, the anti-vice movement was directed toward protecting women and children. The New York City Vice Commission found that the average age of girls at the time of their first offense was seventeen, and Jane Addams pointed out that "the bulk of the entire traffic is conducted with the youth of the community."[63] As a result, progressives lobbied to encourage states to raise the age of consent, or the age when the court considered a girl capable of deciding to participate in the sexual act. In some states the age of consent was as low as seven, and since 1893 the NFCM had been working to change these laws. The Crittenton organization renewed this campaign and urged its supporters to employ every means at their disposal to convince legislatures to change the laws.[64] The campaign to raise the age of consent represented an overt attack upon the privileged position men had enjoyed in sexual matters—yet another challenge to the double standard. As such, it resonated deeply within the Crittenton experience and provided a concrete method of at least partially achieving a long-term Crittenton goal.[65] In working to raise the age of consent, Crittenton women recognized that appeals to Christian virtue would not always have impact, so they turned to legal means to change behaviors.

The tremendous influx of immigrants into the United States heightened the progressive distrust of the urban environment. Nativists feared that the immigrants' presence was a divisive influence on the community, since foreigners brought with them different languages, cultures, and backgrounds. Addams studied immigrant families in the Hull House neighborhood and made several significant observations. She explained that immigrant families—ripped from the social stability and sense of community of their native lands and not understanding American customs—often failed to provide their children with proper supervision and direction. According to Addams and other progressives, this large group of people, ignorant of American traditions, contributed to the already deteriorating social control in cities.[66]

Foreign-born girls were particularly susceptible to white-slave procurers due to the language barrier and the girls' almost overwhelming desire to belong. Nativists insisted that large European organizations were devoted to sending women to serve as prostitutes in American cities. Although many Americans thus believed that the majority of prostitutes were foreign born, vice commission investigators reached other conclusions.[67] Florence Crittenton records showed that native-born Americans made up the largest group of home inmates by far. This was true in both rural and urban areas and in all geographic sections of the country. The Fargo home's 1910 annual report illustrated the Crittenton realization that immigrants represented only a small percentage of the problem: twelve foreign born inmates, fifteen girls of Scandinavian descent born in this country, and "HOW APPALLING 45 American girls." Other homes, such as those in Chicago and Washington, D.C., reported similar percentages.[68] So while a significant contingent of antiprostitution crusaders viewed Europe as the source of a considerable part of the white-slavery problem, the NFCM experience proved otherwise.

Many Crittenton workers treated immigrant women with considerable compassion. Boston workers told the story of Dora, one of several women they rescued from "a bleak hall-bedroom in a dingy lodging house, where she prepared her scrimpy meals on the smoky little gas jet." Dora had come to the United States without money or friends. Being alone, she had fallen into "intimacy with a fellow workman." The Crittenton women were sympathetic and sought to aid Dora because they recognized that her economic condition certainly contributed to her problems.[69] This Crittenton recognition of economic pressures that confronted many immigrant women is noteworthy.

Despite the fact that immigrant girls were in a minority, the Crittenton organization joined other women progressives in devoting considerable attention to the plight of immigrant women. Led by Jane Addams, progressives came to see that the immigrant girl was more often a victim than a conspirator. Xenophobes advocated deporting immigrant women suspected of prostitution, but others thought the United States had some responsibility for these women's conditions.[70] Addams pleaded, "Certainly the immigration laws might do better then to send a girl back to her parents, diseased and disgraced because America has failed to safeguard her virtue from the machinations of well-born but unrestrained criminals."[71]

Barrett shared Addams's views and, in fact, became a recognized authority on the subject of immigrant women and prostitution.[72] Her sympathies aroused, Barrett became an outspoken advocate for immigrant women. She emphasized how unjust it was that the immigrant woman faced deportation while those guilty of orchestrating her fall went free. Barrett appealed to Americans' sense of fair play, as well as to their practical nature: "Nothing is more in keeping with the wishes of a man who has gotten a woman in trouble then to have her deported and thus put the ocean between them, thus ridding him of his encumbrance." Crittenton workers also sympathized with the immigrant girl whose mother was "across the Atlantic Ocean."[73] In the absence of these girls' mothers, Crittenton women believed they had a responsibility to protect them.

The commissioner for immigration appointed Barrett a special agent to investigate the condition of immigrant women in Europe and to represent the U.S. government at conferences dealing with the problems of these women. In his yearly report to the secretary of labor, the commissioner considered the country fortunate to have Barrett's assistance in this "most important" endeavor, as she "occupies a leading place among the world's greatest benefactors."[74] Few of Barrett's contemporaries could boast either this kind of reputation or official government recognition of it.

The commissioner wanted Barrett to investigate the conditions that immigrant women met on ships bound for the United States and to suggest ways the government might ensure these women greater protection. Therefore, before she left for Europe, Barrett spent some time at Ellis Island interviewing women held for deportation to determine what the shipboard conditions were from their point of view. Her ability to analyze the situation from the women's perspective was invaluable.

From April 15 to June 30, 1914, Barrett visited Italy, Switzerland, Austria-Hungary, Serbia, Bulgaria, Turkey, Rumania, Bavaria, Saxony, Bohemia, Prussia, France, Belgium, the Netherlands, and England. Her diplomatic position assured her of government cooperation in each country, and her contacts with women's organizations stemming from her presidency of the National Council of Women further facilitated her research. However, Barrett reported that she gathered more information through informal contacts and was proud that she "drank goats' milk with them in tiny Swiss chalets, ate polenta and raw green peas with them in the vineyards of Italy, and goulash on the plains of Hungary, and drank coffee with them in Turkish baths in Constantinople."[75] Barrett suggested that her gender, as well as the fact that she herself was a mother, convinced many women to speak candidly about the immigration situation. Barrett implied that no male representative of the United States government would have been able to obtain such reliable information. Barrett attacked the traditional male power structure in this instance, and she was outspoken in her convictions regarding women's abilities and the influence women ought to wield.

At a meeting of the International Council of Women in Rome, Barrett discussed the United States government's aims for deported women and sought assistance in establishing groups of people in each country to assist them until the women could care for themselves. Her presentation was successful in that the International Council of Women unanimously passed resolutions calling upon each of its member organizations to form a committee to correspond directly with the U.S. government on the subject of the care and protection of deported women. The group also urged each national council to request its respective government to support an international conference of immigration officials.[76]

During her travels, Barrett conferred with authorities responsible for immigration in the various countries she visited, and she encouraged closer cooperation with U.S. officials in arresting the people responsible for knowingly sending women to the United States for immoral purposes. Barrett contended that the Bureau of Immigration ought to pay more attention to the problem of single woman immigrants. Previously, most female immigrants had been older or accompanied by their families, but Barrett found that many unattended young girls were among the new immigrants and she believed these women deserved protection.

As a result of her findings, Barrett made several recommendations to the commissioner of immigration. She suggested that steamship companies grant free passage to one woman supervisor for every one hundred female immigrants or fraction thereof on board each vessel. Barrett maintained that these supervisors should not be steamship employees who might hesitate to report anything uncomplimentary to the company, but rather better qualified people such as Bureau of Immigration employees. Barrett also recommended that deportees or immigrants who were refused admission to the United States receive passage back to the initial point of their journey rather than to the port of embarkation. This would help save women, stranded at their point of departure with no friends or money, from falling prey to the white-slave procurers. Moreover, according to Barrett, the steamship companies should provide separate quarters for men and women and not allow crew members to visit the steerage quarters except as their duties required. First- and second-class passengers should be forbidden to visit steerage under any circumstances. These recommendations stemmed from an experience Barrett had while returning from Europe when she witnessed a first-class male passenger attempting to convince three young female steerage passengers to accompany him once the ship landed in the United States. Despite Barrett's vocal objections, she could not influence the steamship company to intervene.[77]

Barrett also suggested that the government place a woman awaiting possible deportation in the hands of a private philanthropic organization of her own nationality and religion. Local officials would immediately inform the commissioner general of immigration so that he could correspond with the women's committee in the deportee's native land to determine the kind of conditions that girl would encounter on her return home. This information could have an important impact on the woman's sentence. These recommendations show a keen sense on Barrett's part of what would assist women immigrants and illustrate her faith in the ability of women everywhere to assess home life and help one another. Barrett called upon women's organizations in this country to aid in the effort to protect immigrant women.[78]

One of Kate Barrett's major criticisms of the Bureau of Immigration was that it deported a woman before she could testify against those "contributing to her delinquency." She believed men escaped punishment because immigration officials were "indefatigable in arresting women, but strange to say are very unsuccessful in finding the guilty male partner." Better treatment for women subject to deportation would, as Barrett saw it, make citizens more willing to report alien women guilty of moral offenses. She claimed that informants would not hesitate to identify alien prostitutes if they could be assured that the women in question would receive protection, be placed in the care of women officers, and placed in touch with "those of her own nationality."[79]

Local Florence Crittenton homes provided shelter for immigrant women without jobs and for women awaiting deportation. Many homes began to advertise in foreign languages in order to serve immigrant women better. The NFCM urged local workers to scrutinize immigration officials to determine whether or not immigrant women received just treatment. While NFCM policies and Barrett's recommendations to the commissioner of immigration underlined a concern for immigrant women, the Crittenton organization always considered these women as a separate class from old stock Americans.[80] Undoubtedly due to Barrett's efforts, many immigrant women were spared the worst aspects of the deportation process. At the same time, Crittenton involvement in this area accentuated the undercurrents of feminism that characterized Crittenton work. Barrett's policies point to her conviction that women bore responsibility for the well-being of other women, regardless of their nationality. According to the Crittenton mission, men were often spared the consequences of their actions, and governmental policy must rectify this omission.

Barrett's attitude toward immigrant women had an impact on Crittenton work and on progressive reform as well. She addressed the National Conference on Charities and Corrections on the topic of "The Deportation of Immigrant Girls" in 1912. She continued to speak out on behalf of immigrants. In 1925 she told a Greensboro audience that "a quality sometimes insisted upon as 100 percent Americanism is descent from the first comers. The speaker sees no especial distinction in being among the first ticket-buyers"—a noteworthy statement coming from an active member of the Daughters of the American Revolution. Barrett went on to say that she preferred Theodore Roosevelt's definition of a 100 percent American, which "says nothing about foreign blood, but describes a person who 'can lift his own weight, and then some.'"[81] Barrett encouraged other FC women to adopt this attitude toward immigrants.

Not content with these efforts to end prostitution, progressive anti-vice crusaders sought government assistance in their fight against white slavery. In 1908 anti-vice advocates in Congress prevailed upon the government to adhere to a 1902 "International Agreement for the Repression of Trade in White Women." The governments of Spain, France, Great Britain, Italy, the Netherlands, Portugal, Russia, Sweden, Norway, Switzerland, Austria-Hungary, Brazil, and the United States agreed to cooperate in identifying and returning to their homelands women victims of the white-slave trade. FC organizations worked for this government action.[82]

Due to Clifford Roe's influence, Illinois passed an anti-pandering law in 1908, and the NFCM urged its members in other states to work for similar legislation. When few states followed Illinois' lead, the progressives opted for a national act. The Mann Act, named for an Illinois congressman but largely the work of Roe, made it illegal to transport or aid, abet or cause the transportation of a woman across state lines for immoral purposes.[83] Opponents of the law attacked it on the grounds that it violated states' rights, but Barrett and other reformers believed the Mann Act was well within the bounds of federal jurisdiction. Barrett argued, "When the authority of the United States Government is not questioned when it puts its stamp of approval upon a beef or hog carcass to say whether it is suitable for interstate commerce—when it has authority to inspect oil which flows through pipelines, certainly it would seem as if it had the right to ask any men or women who are using common carriers whether it is for the despoiling of the youth of our land or not."[84] Barrett was convinced that women were at least as valuable as animal carcasses and oil, and she demanded that women receive consideration. She stated, "The passage of the Mann Law . . . is to my mind the most effective measure that has ever been passed in checking the social evil."[85]

The NFCM supported the Mann Act wholeheartedly. Barrett informed the Department of Justice that the organization would take charge of any woman involved in a Mann Act case. To this end, Barrett furnished the government with a complete list of all Crittenton homes and the addresses of their officers. If a local home could not accommodate these Department of Justice referrals, Barrett directed home officials to take the women temporarily and notify the national. In an article entitled, "The Government Needs Our Help," *Girls* declared, "Let our organization arise to the dignity of the position that the Red Cross Society takes on the field of battle, in this great battle the authorities are waging against the White Slave Traffic."[86] At the 1914 national conference delegates passed a resolution commending all district attorneys and judges who were "fearlessly enforcing the Mann Act." The resolution went on to assert that we "protest against any action or interpretation of the laws by our judges *or any*

body of Man [emphasis added] that will lesson its power and efficiency."
FC workers applied whatever political pressure they could on officials
with poor enforcement records.[87]

Florence Crittenton homes provided an important service in offering
sanctuary for witnesses in Mann Act trials. Authorities believed that
procurers and their agents tampered with witnesses on many occasions.
While detention in a home ensured a witness of freedom from procurers' pressure, the evidence also suggested that FC workers tried to influence the witnesses. At a Crittenton home, according to one worker, "the
girl's sense of justice and honor can be appealed to, so that she is not only
willing to remain during the period, but also her sense of truthfulness if
cultivated so that when she is put on the witness stand she has the strength
to tell the truth."[88] In a similar vein, a prosecuting attorney praised the
"value of the Florence Crittenton Home as an adjunct to the court" and
a place where witnesses "may be cared for and protected and developed
so that they can be put on a witness chair and give such clear and unequivocal testimony."[89] Crittenton workers also acted as probation officers for women Mann Act witnesses, thus allowing the women to avoid
incarceration while awaiting the trials. In Michigan, for example, the
Detroit home provided the only place in the state that accommodated
white-slave witnesses, except jails. Some Crittenton homes actually worked
to bring white slavers to justice. Mrs. Barclay Hazard reported that after much effort the New York City home had succeeded in securing the
conviction of a Hungarian couple guilty of exploiting young girls.[90]

Several cities moved to close red-light districts within their boundaries
as a response to the white-slave scare. Barrett committed the NFCM to
providing a place to live for every woman displaced by these closures.[91]
Crittenton homes cooperated with these ventures by offering shelter for
the displaced inmates of bawdy houses. A headline in a Wilkes-Barre,
Pennsylvania, paper announced, "Florence Crittenton Shelter of Park
Avenue Offers the Hospitality of that Institution for Those who desire
to Make a New Start in Life—None need be in Despair. The Doors of
the Home are Open."[92] In February 1911, Congress passed the Kenyon
Red-Light Bill, abolishing the Washington, D.C., vice district. President
Woodrow Wilson, before signing the bill into law, insisted on some pro-
vision for the district's former residents. When Barrett offered to take
charge of the women, Wilson signed the bill.[93] Barrett and her Crittenton
associates were determined to guarantee that vice legislation would not
impact women residents in vice districts more negatively than was absolutely necessary.

The NFCM went so far as to employ women who were experts in dealing with red-light district closures. These consultants traveled to cities at the request of local government officials to oversee vice area closures. Mayor Frank McCalin of Lancaster, Virginia, wrote to Barrett expressing his appreciation for the services of FC workers Robertson and Gooch, praising their efficiency and noting that their assistance "could not have been supplied so effectively in any other manner." They were "knowledgeable and compassionate," he said. "If all the persons, who, today, are engaged in the suppression of harlotry and associated forms of vice, possessed the qualities of mind and heart that Mrs. Robertson and Mrs. Gooch possess," he concluded, "reforms could be more promptly arrived at and more permanently secured."[94] McCalin's evaluation indicated that Barrett's aspirations for the Crittenton response to white slavery had been met.

Sometimes FC plans to help women displaced as a result of vice-district closures went awry. The Kansas City home reported that, despite the personal visit of one of its "leaders" to each house of prostitution, no inmates accepted the Crittenton invitation of shelter. The FC offer of a place to live nonetheless served to assuage any guilt local officials felt at turning women out into the street.[95] Crittenton efforts clearly represented practical solutions to difficulties vice-district closures created. The question Charles Crittenton had asked himself about New York City prostitutes in 1883—Where can she go?—remained a relevant one more than thirty years later.

A part of the white-slavery scare reflected middle-class objections to the developing culture of working-class women. For that reason, much of Crittenton activity in this period was focused on dance halls, movie theaters, and other public amusement locations. In fact, some historians have questioned just what portion of the white-slave campaign was directed toward behavior other than actual sexual intercourse, as some definitions of prostitution included any sexual contact outside of marriage. But to the Crittenton workers' credit, they were sympathetic to working women's desire for leisure time recreation. According to the Boston Crittenton organization's 1913 annual report, "They [girls] are the victims, in the first place, of a social order which has not even begun to adjust itself to the new demands of girl life. The mad clamors of business are surpassed only by the madder whirl of pleasure and we helplessly wonder and ponder and experiment. Until we can really satisfy the young girl's craving for a good time in some chaste and yet delightsome way social perils and social catastrophes will continue to multiply."[96] Rather than attempting to close these entertainments, Crittenton workers sought to make them safer for women, and in fact viewed this as another aspect of their campaign to improve women's condition in society. Barrett told a group of women's club members in Newark the story of a girl who wore a disguise every time she went to the park to avoid "being passed at." Barrett was outspoken in her belief that this young women should be able to enjoy the recreation the park provided without having to worry about unwanted sexual advances. She urged her audience to use their influence to foster the attitude that working girls should be able to participate in public entertainments without fearing for either their reputations or their safety.[97] In this instance, Crittenton policy was more understanding of working women's wishes than some other reform groups, and in fact, its view was a precursor to our modern one. Under Barrett's leadership, the Florence Crittenton organization sought to bridge the gap between old-fashioned notions of propriety and new attitudes of especially working-class women toward leisure time.

White-slavery crusaders thought that women were especially vulnerable to abduction when they were away from home and in large crowds. Consequently, the NFCM increased its efforts to protect such women. As the magazine pointed out, "Wherever a large number of persons gather for pleasure or for temporary employment, the danger to unprotected womanhood is great."[98] During the summer months the NFCM operated shelters at large resorts such as Atlantic City and Ocean Grove, Maryland; Coney Island, New York; and Cedar Point, Ohio. These FC "rest rooms" provided temporary housing and assistance to women so that they would not be susceptible to procurers. The rest rooms served a clientele composed mostly of women who had lost or used all of their funds, accidentally drank too much, or became separated from friends.

Some Crittenton contributors fretted that such assistance might actually be counterproductive. They reasoned that because unsavory people frequented these resorts, the Crittenton presence might appear to condone unwholesome entertainment. Critics particularly objected to Crittenton activity at Cedar Point, because the resort company provided the FC facility and paid for the worker. *Girls* commented, "We are very sorry that some of our friends who did not have a very high opinion of Cedar Point from an ethical standpoint did not understand the conditions under which we went there and were exceedingly critical of our having accepted any courtesies from the resort company."[99] The magazine dismissed this opposition by pointing out that Christ had also been called the friend of publicans and sinners. Barrett's tendency to temper idealism with practicality entered into this decision. She was convinced that it was better to improve conditions at Cedar Point than to do nothing, particularly since there was no likelihood that any Crittenton action would result in the popular resort's closure. Barrett also recognized that young women sought the excitement and entertainment that Cedar Point offered. It only made sense to work to guarantee that women would have access to assistance if they needed it, rather than to simply denounce the new forms of entertainment.

Expositions seemed to present an excellent opportunity for white slavers, and so the Florence Crittenton mission became interested in them. Barrett, who attended every great exposition from 1876 until her death, was convinced that fair employees faced danger. She wrote, "The excitement and other influences which were brought to bear upon them frequently unfitted them for future usefulness."[100] Therefore, the NFCM experimented with a fair grounds agent at the 1900 Paris Exposition. This endeavor met with such success that the boards of directors of several expositions requested FC aid in the "rescue of young girls from the clutches of the vultures who select exposition grounds for their nefarious work."[101]

The 1904 St. Louis Exposition set the pattern for Florence Crittenton efforts at world fairs. The mission headquartered at the Woman's Anchorage, which it shared with the King's Daughters, the National Council of Women, the WCTU, the Baptist Missionary Society, and several women's college fraternities. These groups feared an increase in the number of prostitutes in the fair city and worried that women coming to seek employment would be easy picking for white slavers. The NFCM opened an office in the downtown St. Louis business district, and the railroad car *Good News* stayed in St. Louis during the fair. The national solicited funds from all over the country, with the rationale that since the girls were coming from everywhere, so should rescue workers and money.[102]

As a result of its investigation, the NFCM asked Secretary of Commerce and Labor George Courtelou to supervise closely girls from foreign countries with prepaid tickets listing St. Louis as their destination. The mission thought many of these girls were victims of a European white-slavery ring operating to supply prostitutes to St. Louis. Shortly after Crittenton people contacted him, Courtelou asked them to send someone to St. Louis to take charge of eight German girls traveling under "suspicious circumstances." The girls were consigned to a German saloon keeper's wife. When she became aware that authorities were watching her, she pretended to seek employment for the girls at several respectable places. This action made it impossible for FC workers to gain a conviction, even though, according to Barrett, "no one who came in contact with her had the least doubt as to her guilt."[103]

FC workers also cared for fifteen Japanese girls from the "Fair Japan" concession. A man had asked the girls to travel from city to city "under conditions that led both the United States and Japanese Governments to feel they were not safe."[104] The mission saw to it that the girls returned to Japan unharmed. *Girls* advised any young woman traveling to St. Louis to be careful and listed safe places to stay. The magazine cautioned, "All persons, especially young women, are warned against taking directions from strangers, no matter what badges or signs they may wear on their persons."[105] This was a sensible response to the situation, as the Crittenton magazine did not advise women to avoid the exposition but to exercise caution.

The following year the Portland, Oregon, home employed a field worker for the Portland exposition, "as there are many cases which could be reached in no other way." The board members solicited a pass to the fair for the field worker and also ordered twenty-five specially designed badges for workers to wear.[106] Throughout the exposition's run, the Portland women made certain that their services were available to any woman who sought them, even if this meant only providing directions or giving advice as to suitable hotel accommodations.

The white-slave scare aided the NFCM in gaining respectability, support, and influence. Other reformers adopted the basic tenets of Crittenton philosophy, such as support for an end to the double standard of morals and belief in the value of sex education, while anti-vice crusaders copied the methods of Margaret Luther and other Crittenton workers. Kate Waller Barrett's association with the Bureau of Immigration also lent credibility to Crittenton work. The NFCM established a pattern of concern for women involved in prostitution that mitigated the most hostile aspects of the anti-vice crusade. Thus the white-slave fear thrust the NFCM to the forefront of reform after twenty years of relative obscurity. The anti-vice crusade was remarkably successful in arousing national indignation regarding prostitution and venereal disease. The NFCM benefited from this national obsession in terms of both recognition and monetary donations. The movement reached new heights with the onset of World War I, when the National Florence Crittenton Mission joined in the war effort.

Chapter 6

The Great War and After

In the shadow of the grave, where each woman stands when she gives
birth to an immortal soul, some of the greatest mysteries of life have
been solved and foundations for the most progressive steps in civilization have been made. Thus it will be at the end of this great cataclysm
when there shall be a new birth, a new world.
—Kate Waller Barrett, 1917

The European conflict of 1914 fostered disagreements among American
progressive social reformers while creating challenges for their reform
agendas. Some thought the United States should use its power to aid the
democracies, others were convinced that U.S. involvement in the war would
threaten progressive achievements. For the National Florence Crittenton
Mission, as for other social welfare groups, World War I indeed resulted
in significant and contradictory changes: while shrinking funds forced the
closing of some Crittenton homes, the NFCM's war-related activities
brought a reputation and influence wider than ever before. During the
postwar period further alterations in traditional Florence Crittenton activities accompanied experiments and new programs. By the time of Kate
Waller Barrett's death in early 1925, the NFCM was clearly in transition.

Barrett's affiliation with European women through the International
Council of Women led her to support Woodrow Wilson's initial attempts
to keep the United States out of the European war. She spoke in favor of
mediation of international conflicts, even when vital interests were involved, and she protested the "odious wrongs which women are the vic-

tims of in time of war."[1] Barrett praised the Women's Peace Party as "one of the most magnificent mobilizations of women that the world has ever seen." She claimed that only alarmists and men wanting to profit from war contracts advocated American entrance into the war, and she warned that "the country living by the sword shall perish by the sword."[2] Barrett's viewpoints placed her squarely within the woman's peace movement, and her involvement in international women's activities was partly responsible for her position.

However, as was the case with most of the organized women's movement in the country, once the United States officially entered the conflict in 1917, Barrett abandoned her pacifist position and rallied the NFCM to support the war effort in any way possible. According to one home official, her charges constructed six thousand garments for the Red Cross, and the Boston home reported that inmates had made 20,745 surgical dressings.[3] Barrett was active in Liberty Bond sales, and local homes scrimped in order to purchase the bonds.[4] The Chicago home took five hundred dollars from its building fund for that purpose.[5]

Barrett's pro-war rhetoric matched her earlier antiwar sentiments in its clarity and stridency. In a series of speeches with titles such as "Mother's Service to the Enlisted Man," "Ideals of American Womanhood in War Service," and "The Permanent Value of Patriotic and Spiritual Influence of Women on World Thought," Barrett urged patriotism upon American women.[6] She reminded her audiences that American soldiers carried "the reputation and the heart of American Womanhood" into battle with them, and she believed American women were worth the effort.[7] She was fond of pointing out that it was impossible to name five German women who had ever done anything of great import for humanity but simple to name five English, French, and American women who had made significant contributions.[8] Barrett thus applied a pro-woman perspective to her pro-American position, playing on the veneration of motherhood that accompanied the war.[9]

Barrett often recounted the story of a prewar visit to Germany, when she found that the government required mothers to breast-feed their children because naturally fed children allegedly made more enduring and better soldiers. At the time Barrett had not suspected that American boys would be fighting those German soldiers, but she was now glad that Americans had finally recognized the benefits of breast feeding. This association of breast feeding with patriotism increased Barrett's pride in Crittenton mothers, some of whom nursed two, three, or four children in addition to their own. Barrett especially praised one Crittenton inmate who breast-fed eight children daily and thus certainly did her part for the war effort.[10] Barrett and the NFCM consciously strived to associate traditional motherhood and its tasks with patriotism and support for the United States.

White-slave reformers feared that the preoccupation of the NFCM and other charity groups with war work would mark the end of the anti-vice crusade. In fact, the war intensified the fight against prostitution in ways that even the most optimistic reformer could not have predicted. Social-hygiene proponents joined together to protect American servicemen from the ravages of venereal disease and from prostitutes seeking to take advantage of young men away from home for the first time.

Anti-vice crusaders found powerful allies in their war against venereal disease. Secretary of War Newton D. Baker was a vocal advocate of shielding American fighting men with an "invisible armor" against disease and moral decay; and President Wilson agreed that American soldiers should return home "with no scars except those won in honorable warfare."[11] Baker entrusted Raymond B. Fosdick, a prominent anti-vice crusader, with the primary responsibility for ensuring American soldiers' purity. As head of the Commission on Training Camp Activities, Fosdick used the techniques pioneered during the antiprostitution campaigns to achieve "the cleanest army since Cromwell's day."[12]

Fosdick enlisted the assistance of the YMCA, the Russell Sage Foundation, and other private social organizations—including the NFCM—to make the Commission on Training Camp Activities a success. The commission's program emphasized an educational campaign to inform soldiers regarding venereal diseases, a sophisticated system of disease diagnosis and treatment, strict regulations to exclude prostitutes from the training camps, and an extensive program of alternative recreational activities at the camps.[13]

Florence Crittenton workers and other veterans of the earlier purity crusades were undoubtedly delighted with the commission's policy of closing red-light districts. Secretary Baker, in letters to the mayors and sheriffs of all cities and counties adjacent to training camps, expressed the government's intention to keep prostitutes away from the camps and his own determination not to tolerate red-light districts. Through the War Department, Fosdick ultimately closed red-light districts in Deming, New Mexico; El Paso, Waco, San Antonio, Fort Worth, and Houston, Texas; Hattiesburg, Mississippi; Spartanburg, Charleston, Columbia, and Greenville, South Carolina; Norfolk and Petersburg, Virginia; Jacksonville, Florida; Savannah, Georgia; Douglas, Arizona; Louisville, Kentucky; and Montgomery, Alabama.[14]

The commission's program also encouraged men who did consort with prostitutes to seek prophylaxis from army physicians and not rely on quack remedies. Not surprisingly, some of the moral-reform groups viewed this as an invitation to incontinence, but the army continued the treatments despite criticism.[15] Fosdick's program achieved a level of success that astonished even its staunchest supporters. By the time the war had ended the rate of venereal disease cases per thousand men was only thirty-five—a rate that no European nation had even approached.[16]

The NFCM devoted much time and effort to commission activities. Barrett even ordered new stationery bearing the letterhead "War Work Commission, National Florence Crittenton Mission."[17] She was, moreover, the only woman appointed to serve on the Virginia State Commission on Training Camp Activities.[18] Shortly after America's entry into the war, Margaret Louise Stecker, director of the American Institute of Social Service, asked Barrett if the NFCM would help to protect girls in communities located near training camps.[19] The NFCM responded with alacrity, notifying Secretary of War Baker and the commandants of each mobilization camp that the mission would take responsibility for the care of any girl arrested for loitering in the vicinity of the camps. This offer produced dual benefits: it saved many women from incarceration in jails and, according to the mission, it encouraged local officials to make more arrests because they had Crittenton facilities at their disposal.[20] Several local homes expanded their physical plants in order to accommodate the additional inmates.[21] Barrett claimed that the NFCM was the only private agency in a position to make this offer.

In keeping with established Crittenton practice, NFCM war work emphasized a decidedly woman's point of view. The Commission on Training Camp Activities and those associated with it stressed the dangers that prostitutes—both as seducers and disease carriers—posed for American servicemen.[22] The crack-down on prostitutes often meant in practice that any woman found in the vicinity of a training camp could be detained and possibly subjected to a test for venereal disease. The NFCM was cognizant of the potential threat to the armed forces that prostitutes represented, but the organization made it very clear that soldiers should not be protected at the "expense of the thoughtless, untrained, immoral girl" who was not a hardened prostitute.[23] Crittenton officials noted that observers criticized the NFCM for "receiving girls so lost to modesty as to run after 'those defenders of our country.'" However, Crittenton workers pointed out that their charges were not the ones who "deliberately lure the uniformed lads into clandestine relations," but were girls who were "swept off their feet" by men in uniform. These girls deserved the traditional Crittenton sympathy and assistance, and FC people spoke out against the excesses of wartime policies and sought to mitigate their effects vis-à-vis women. As the Crittenton workers pointed out, despite the unpopularity of their position, sometimes men "away from the restraining influence of home" would "take advantage of unsuspecting girls."[24] The conviction that men involved shared responsibility was in keeping with the longstanding Crittenton position, and even the patriotic zeal of many Americans could not convince the Crittenton organization to turn its back on women.

The NFCM and its local affiliates also joined in the campaign to promote purity for servicemen. A part of the Crittenton response was decidedly traditional. Mrs. A. E. Houseman of the Ocean Grove, Maryland, home suggested that local authorities discourage ball playing on the beach and place a ban on improper wearing apparel worn by bathers. Houseman believed these steps would guard against possible problems stemming from the fraternization of local women and soldiers from the nearby camp.[25] But other Crittenton groups tried a more contemporary approach. The Chicago home formed the Florence Crittenton Anchorage Morals Committee in connection with the Women's National Coast Defense League.[26] The Boston Crittenton organization paid for four patrol workers for the Boston Commons area in conjunction with a federal program there.[27] The Chicago and Boston workers thus joined with other groups and the federal government to establish programs designed to prevent unsupervised contact between servicemen and local women, while at the same time recognizing that some fraternization was bound to take place.

Barrett also traveled to Europe during the war as a delegate to the International Women's Congress in Zurich, Switzerland. *Girls* boasted of her recognition, noting that "at the time she was chosen to go to Europe there were other organizations representing more than 7,000,000 women meeting in Washington, all of whom were desirous of sending representatives 'over there,' and they wondered how she came to be selected." Barrett's status as an established authority on immigration, European conditions, prostitution, and the entire "girl problem" positioned her to achieve even more influence.[28]

Barrett visited fifteen of the sixteen cantonments and was able to send a "message of cheer" to the mothers of servicemen regarding the conditions in the camps.[29] She delivered speeches tying patriotism and purity together and reported that when she asked a group of young men what ought to be done with a soldier who wronged an American girl, the men replied,

"Shoot him."[30] This sentiment convinced Barrett that "many a man has made a braver fight on the battle fields of France because he left no nameless child on the door step of society."[31]

Unfortunately, not every American soldier could claim to belong to this category. Due to both the training camp work and increased maternity cases, Crittenton homes housed 8,679 girls during 1918–19, twice as many as in any previous year.[32] Each local home reported to the national which cases were due to "war conditions," but there were some discrepancies in these reports. According to one, 86 percent of the "soldier cases" were "street girls who were following our boys to ensnare them," while 14 percent were maternity cases. On the other hand, the Boston home attributed the increase to girls who fell victim to the allure of a man in uniform and claimed that these girls were "of the very highest type we have had all year."[33] At any rate, there was general agreement that a number of cases involved servicemen and that the demands upon Crittenton resources had increased substantially. At the same time, Crittenton officials believed that both patriotism and their commitment to helping other women required their continued efforts.

When the man involved was a member of the armed forces, workers often could not rely on the usual Crittenton solutions of marriage or a paternity suit to gain support for the illegitimate child. There were a distressing number of cases of young women such as Sadie ———, who entered the Chicago home after the man who impregnated her had sailed for Europe.[34] The Chicago board also discussed the case of Ruth ——— and a student at Lake Forest College. The student indicated that he was a draftee assigned to the Rockford, Illinois, camp. However, the board had reason to doubt his story, and board members suspected that the man had used the war as an excuse for deserting Ruth.[35] Thus the dislocations brought about by the wartime conditions made Crittenton work even more difficult.

One aspect of the Crittenton association with the Commission on Training Camp Activities caused controversy among Crittenton workers: the commission's emphasis on treatment for those suffering from venereal disease. Most FC workers deemed venereal disease victims as undesirable inmates for homes, and many still found the prospect of associating with "diseased" women distasteful.[36] To cooperate with the commission, the NFCM again tried to change longstanding attitudes on this subject but was only partly successful. The Boston home, for instance, cared for 1,375 girls involved with servicemen. Of these, workers examined 400 for venereal disease and found that 50 percent were infected. The home, despite reservations about the wisdom of sheltering the infected women, provided care for them until they had finished the prescribed course of treatment.[37] The Chattanooga, Tennessee, Crittenton organization took more dramatic steps. With Barrett's approval, workers sold their home and all its equipment and used the proceeds to purchase eleven acres from the city. There the organization erected a building for the sole purpose of caring for venereal disease patients.[38] Chattanooga workers followed the Commission on Training Camp Activities example of providing the best available treatment to women infected with sexually transmitted disease. The Chattanooga FC women wanted to ensure that their female charges had access to treatment without suffering the indignities they might face in a treatment center run by males. Mrs. Joe Brown, president of the Chattanooga home, wrote in her annual report that the board had been "much criticized" by both the public and the press for their decision, but that it had been worth it in the long run.[39]

The Boston and Chattanooga examples were exceptions to the rule, as most homes steadfastly refused to accept women infected with venereal disease. Minnie Burton Taylor, one of Barrett's assistants, complained about this obdurateness: "WE lost the opportunity to enlarge our vision by doing a necessary yet more difficult work where we were needed, and the GIRLS lost the opportunity to be handled by trained Christian women who have been doing this work for years."[40] Dr. Barrett went even further when she stated that had Crittenton homes worked at their potential, there would have been no need for the Fosdick commission at all. These comments revealed both the limitations of Crittenton work and the continued Crittenton conviction that FC workers had special empathy for the girls involved. As Crittenton workers later admitted, the debate over admitting patients with venereal disease was probably academic as many inmates suffered from venereal disease unbeknownst to the workers, who often did not have access to reliable tests and therefore identified the diseases only in their acute stages.[41] As Taylor noted, "It was easier to go on in our old way, just take the type of case that appealed to us," rather than to expand Crittenton work to meet the needs of the Commission on Training Camp Activities. According to Taylor, the Crittenton organization's failure to respond meant that the commission's funds went to temporary war work rather than being put to use in well-established Crittenton work. Once the war was over, there was no permanent organization left.[42]

Despite that failure, the Crittenton association with the Commission on Training Camp Activities was beneficial for the NFCM, even though wartime demands on people's generosity resulted in sharply reduced donations for most private charity groups and forced the Crittenton organization to curtail some activities, including the publication of *Girls*. The publicity the NFCM received from its work with the commission nonetheless provided the Crittenton organization with the widespread exposure and the acceptance workers had long strived to attain.[43] During the war, the mission became so well known that people from all over the country wrote letters seeking assistance for women in trouble. For example, a Pennsylvania couple sought refuge for their pregnant foster daughter, a victim of "aggravated assault and a hard losing fight trying to protect her honor."[44] The couple offered to pay for the girl's room and board if an FC home would accept her.

There were in fact more of these requests than the NFCM could handle—a situation that demonstrated the organization's popularity but also suggested administrative difficulties. Ironically, Barrett, who for years had been the chief source of strength for the Crittenton movement, was herself part of the problem. Her attempts to give her personal attention to all facets of Crittenton work caused the NFCM to falter under the growing number of requests. When a Cynthiana, Kentucky, attorney wrote Barrett regarding a fifteen-year-old girl whom the court wished to place in a Crittenton home, the attorney waited for over a month for Barrett to reply. In the meantime, the girl remained in limbo and it took a second, more desperate letter to elicit a response from Barrett.[45]

Barrett realized that the increased public acceptance accorded Crittenton work had caused her to overextend. Certain, however, that the national was responsible for Crittenton achievements, she did not want to relinquish her control. She feared that after her death the national organization might collapse and Crittenton work come to an end. Consequently, she devoted much of her energy during the postwar era to strengthening the bonds between local homes and the national.[46]

Some local leaders criticized Barrett's attempts to keep control at the national level on grounds that her motives were selfish. She denied these accusations and was especially incensed at speculation among some workers that she planned to name one of her children as her successor. Barrett wrote, somewhat defensively, "None of them have the desire or the taste, and while they will always be ready to help in the future as they have in the past, they certainly will not look for an office of any kind. When I lay down my office there will be plenty of people eager to take it up. I am glad to say that they will not have to face the difficulties that I have encountered."[47]

Barrett aimed to increase the involvement of local homes in NFCM activities, so when delegates to the 1919 national conference expressed their desire to expand Crittenton work and to publicize FC accomplishments more broadly, she suggested that the local homes assume the responsibility. The delegates formed the National Florence Crittenton Association, an organization composed of representatives from the local homes and from the national. The new association elected the Central Extension Committee, which was charged with strengthening ties between the NFCM and the local homes and among the various homes themselves. The committee members were Barrett; Lillian G. Topping, Fargo; Mrs. M. E. Kline, Chicago; Mrs. Frank White, Washington, D.C.; Mrs. Joseph Brown, Chattanooga; Mrs. W. E. R. Taylor, Baltimore; D. D. Spellman, Detroit; H. O. Chrysler, Detroit; Clifford Willey, Seattle; Clarence R. Preston, Boston; B. G. Tenneson, Fargo; Mrs. A. M. Donaldson, Denver; H. M. Hurd, Los Angeles; and Mrs. Anthony Camminnetti, San Francisco.[48] The committee's composition reflected both mission history and new realities. There were seven women and six men on the committee. While the committee included representation from all geographic areas, large urban organizations dominated the membership. The only real exceptions to this were the two representatives from Fargo. Lillian Topping's status as one of the Crittenton workers with the most seniority and as a Kate Waller Barrett confidante won her a committee position. The National Florence Crittenton Association and the Central Extension Committee represent the first decentralization of Crittenton work in its history. Charles Crittenton and then Kate Waller Barrett had directed the NFCM since its inception. Now a committee took on considerable responsibility.

The committee made a number of proposals, and Barrett acted on most of them. In response to a committee suggestion, the national employed more officials to visit local homes on a regular basis, tender advice, and suggest ways to improve local services. When the national found that publication of *Girls* was too expensive in both time and money, the committee recommended a less-ambitious alternative, and the national began to print the *Bulletin* to fulfill the committee's desire for a publication to serve as "a medium of exchange of ideas and which would be instrumental in strengthening the bond of fellowship between the various Homes."[49] At the committee's urging, the national took it upon itself to provide training for a few women each year in order to supply the local homes with a pool of experienced workers.[50] In a further effort to strengthen the administration of the NFCM, the board of trustees expanded from three to six members in 1925, thus allowing people outside the original circle of Crittenton followers, and people who lived in cities other than New York and Washington, D.C., to assume leadership positions.[51]

While the war-inspired increase in demand for Florence Crittenton work created some stress in the NFCM organization, the publicity the mission received during the war dramatically changed its approach to fundraising. The Washington, D.C., home staged an annual financial appeal on Flag Day to capitalize on the public association of Crittenton homes with patriotism; the authorized collectors presented each donor with a tiny American flag.[52] However important such strategies were, the fact was that by the 1920s it had become more fashionable than ever before to support Crittenton endeavors. Mrs. Calvin Coolidge's decision to become an FC patroness was only one example of the organization's enhanced appeal.[53] A gala entertainment and tea held at San Francisco's St. Francis Hotel and attended by the upper crust of that city's society netted $1,750, and the governor of Maryland was a contributor and attended the Baltimore home's twentieth anniversary party.[54] The NFCM had indeed come a long way from the days when homes held measuring parties. The organization's public role in both the anti-white-slavery campaign and the Commission on Training Camp Activities program had earned the NFCM recognition that the organization parlayed into increased donations.

Another aspect of the growing institutional evolution of the Crittenton movement was its alliance with the emerging community chest system. Most homes began their association with these groups during the war and found their systems more satisfactory than the old one of hiring solicitors or planning a series of fund-raising events. The chests were more efficient, did not cost the homes anything, and reached a greater number of potential donors. Participation led to a situation in which most Crittenton operating funds in many localities came from contributors to the community chest who knew little and perhaps cared nothing about Florence Crittenton work.[55] Barrett believed that the benefits of community chest involvement outweighed this drawback. She thought that the inclusion of Crittenton homes indicated a decisive improvement in the public's attitude toward the NFCM.[56] Financially, the association with community chests was beneficial. In fiscal year 1922–23, homes received $750,000 from these chests.[57] By 1923, although the NFCM's financial problems had not disappeared, all of the homes were free from debt and receipts approached $1 million.[58] Many homes erected new buildings during the 1920s, and several, including those in Detroit, Sioux City, and Philadelphia, built large hospitals designed to serve the community as well as the home.[59]

Crittenton membership in community chests and the expansion of Crittenton activities necessitated some changes in the operation of member

The Detroit Florence Crittenton Hospital, 1929. Courtesy of the Detroit Public Library, Burton Historical Collection.

institutions. Participation in the chests subjected Crittenton homes to greater outside scrutiny (usually male-dominated) and thus forced the adoption of more formal methods. This in turn dramatically altered the nature of the Crittenton organization. Public opinion became more important than ever, and Crittenton officials tended to follow the examples set by the social welfare establishment rather than pioneering new techniques as they had in the past.[60] When the Detroit Community Services Organization audited that city's Florence Crittenton home in 1920, they uncovered a number of irregularities. The auditor complained that it was "impossible" to even list assets and liabilities, since the books were "neither complete nor current." The auditor was surprised to find that the receipts from children's mite boxes and from some circle donations were simply stuffed in manila envelopes. The Community Services Organization patiently explained to the Crittenton people that they could neither budget nor plan for the next year without a sense of current financial standing. Obviously, the Detroit Crittenton organization had to revamp and regularize its financial dealings in order to qualify for the community chest monies. A more systematic and formal approach was required, and oftentimes paid professionals were called upon to provide it.[61]

Many early FC workers were volunteers, and Barrett had long believed that service given out of love was a hallmark of Crittenton work. Following World War I, however, the trend in social work continued toward a reliance on professional social workers. Some historians have portrayed Crittenton workers as opponents of this change, but this was not always the case. According to a recent study, the Chicago Crittenton home during the 1930s was an example of the clash between evangelical women and social workers; however, as the study notes, the Crittenton organization itself was pressuring Chicago to move forward and, in fact, the Chicago home had a long history of refusing advice from anyone, even from Barrett.[62] The Chicago experience was not typical of the Crittenton chain, and many FC homes moved in the direction of professional casework, and some were even at the vanguard of professionalization efforts. Many homes hired caseworkers to keep in contact with girls after they left, and several Crittenton institutions employed three or four professionals. Eventually, the paid professional superseded the volunteer in Crittenton work. Central Extension Committee member Clarence R. Preston told the 1926 annual conference, "Volunteers are dangerous and unless they are especially selected and trained and supervised themselves they may prove to be a liability rather than an asset."[63] Preston was one of the outspoken new guard among the Crittenton hierarchy, and his

gender supports Regina Kunzel's viewpoint that the move to professionalism also tended to force Crittenton institutions to include more men
in leadership positions.

Women Crittenton workers moved to protect their hegemony when
they could. The women in charge of homes became known as superin-
tendents instead of matrons, an acknowledgment of their primarily managerial role and their increased professional status. Even the once-power-
ful Florence Crittenton board became more of an honorary position as
homes could afford to hire workers to assume the board's former duties.
The Boston home, for example, hired a staff psychologist, and all girls
were examined upon admission. The Boston organization was instrumental in the founding of the Boston Council of Social Agencies. Workers
reported that not only had their work increased, but the "technique has
improved." The Boston home was the first maternity home in the city to
hire a casework supervisor, an action the officials described as "such a
forward step." The Detroit Crittenton organization played an active role
in that city's Committee for Case Cooperation, composed of representatives from the major charities.[64] Philanthropic organizations cooperated
and shared case information in an effort to provide the best services for
clients and to keep better track of help tendered to families.

These paid professional social workers emphasized casework and thus
the individual's responsibility to come to terms with her own problems.
This attitude was in striking contrast to the prewar Crittenton conception that had held that at least a part of an individual's difficulties resulted
from society's treatment and, therefore, that social reform would aid both
society and the individual.[65] Consequently, the reforming zeal that characterized prewar progressivism and Crittenton work waned.

Due to these changing approaches to social work, Barrett became a victim of her own philosophy. Since she had long argued that the NFCM ought
to be scientific and should particularly seek approval and recognition from
the social work community, she could hardly speak out against the new
attitudes. Her own reputation as an expert and professional made it difficult for her to reject professional social workers in favor of women volunteers, a painful situation in instances in which social workers criticized FC
practices. Barrett's own established position in the social-work community
served to shelter the NFCM from the most strident criticism, but Barrett's
personal leadership could not reach to every Florence Crittenton home.

Crittenton workers were well aware of the tensions that the new professional social work created. The organization's 1919 annual report
noted that there was a movement to "do away with certain features of

Florence Crittenton work" and a "reaction against our maternity work." The report urged FC people to cooperate with any organization studying the problem of unmarried mothers, and "if they can do it better than we, lets move up and either do it as well as anyone else or go out of existence. Methods of years ago are out of date at this time."[66] This statement indicates a willingness to experiment with new methods, not a determination to keep Crittenton practices unchanged. Crittenton workers did not want to be labeled old-fashioned and their methods outmoded, rather they hoped to continue at the cutting edge of social reform.

A great deal of the Crittenton agenda became an established part of the social welfare scene. Crittenton work was a highly respected and integral part of the Children's Bureau and other high visibility activities. In fact, Crittenton workers were on the cutting edge of those considered to be the epitome of professionalization. At the 1919 annual meeting, Miss Katherine Lenroot of the Department of Labor presented an address titled "The Handicap of Illegitimate Birth." Her discussion was a synopsis of what Crittenton leaders and been saying for years. Lack of prenatal care, lack of intelligence, and social ostracism were among the handicaps she listed. She noted, "We have had splendid cooperation from the Boston Florence Crittenton home, and also from national."[67] At the same meeting, Julia Lathrop, head of the Children's Bureau, told delegates, "There can be nothing better than for a mother and child to stay together if it is at all possible." She added that "the fundamental need of childhood is maternal care, no less for children of illegitimate birth than for others."[68] Certainly, Barrett agreed with that sentiment and had been preaching a similar message for years.

In 1919, following a series of conferences held throughout the country, the Children's Bureau set minimum standards for the "protection of children born out of wedlock." According to the bureau, both parents should be held responsible for support and maintenance of these children; the father was liable for expenses the mother incurred during pregnancy and confinement, and the father's obligation ought to be enforceable against his estate. The bureau also endorsed the 1916 Maryland law making it illegal to separate a child younger than six months from her mother.[69] The bureau combined this information to create the Uniform Illegitimacy Act of 1921, which the bureau urged each state adopt. So the social-work establishment and long-established Crittenton policies were actually very much in accord in some cases. Often a battleground between evangelical women and social workers did not exist, although Crittenton homes certainly experienced the tensions that accompany change.

The shift from volunteer workers coincided with the conclusions of many former anti-vice crusaders that the Commission on Training Camp Activities represented the ultimate victory for their viewpoint. The conspiracy of silence had certainly ended, and the War Department's closure of red-light districts finished the job the vice commissions had begun. Reformers believed they had defeated the white slavers.

Both the development of casework and the conviction that the anti-vice crusade had succeeded, plus a general move away from reform and toward the more relaxed moral standards of the 1920s, resulted in a drastic reduction of what had been a widespread public clamor to end prostitution. The NFCM virtually abandoned efforts to rescue and reform prostitutes. Local homes devoted their energies to the care of unwed mothers and juvenile offenders, and the national basked in its newfound status as the largest chain of maternity homes in the country. Detroit statistics illustrated the Crittenton homes' preeminent position. Of the 947 registered illegitimate births in Detroit during 1926, 164 were Florence Crittenton cases.[70] In many localities the terms *maternity home* and *Florence Crittenton home* became synonymous.

Perhaps as a result of the dramatic increase in the number of professional social workers employed at Crittenton homes, as well as the unparalleled growth in FC work, the ideals most often associated with Kate Waller Barrett became more difficult to maintain as policy. This was particularly true of the goal of keeping mother and child together. Many homes not only turned to foster placement or adoption but also reported their new policies to the national. The Los Angeles home superintendent stated, "I do not encourage a girl 14, 15, or 16 years old to keep her baby." Little Rock and Phoenix officials echoed her view.[71] The Boston Crittenton workers reported an adoption in the case of a young girl, Margaret, who had been attacked on her way to church; the adoption allowed Margaret to return to her parents. Perhaps more important, the organization reported that they "felt it best" for Margaret's baby to be placed for adoption. Once the adoption was completed, Margaret had entered nurses' training and was doing well.[72]

The mutiny against Barrett's cardinal rule became so widespread that delegates to the 1926 convention believed it was necessary to pass a resolution reaffirming the earlier policy. The resolution urged homes to "make every effort in each individual case to work out a plan by which mother and baby may be kept together." Practice, however, certainly fell short of earlier Crittenton requirements.[73] The Boston home's experience with Margaret indicated that workers were beginning to view adoption as a strategy for freeing unmarried mothers to pursue their own lives. Even more significant, workers expressed the idea that Margaret's child would be better off living with adoptive parents. This was a major departure from previous Crittenton attitudes.

On the other hand, Florence Crittenton workers' long experience with unmarried mothers led them to discover what contemporary observers recognize as an inherent problem with adoption. Mrs. T. E. Robertson reported that a woman born in the Washington, D.C., home in the 1890s came "begging for help to find her mother." The government contacted the NFCM on behalf of a woman "asking for help to find out about her own people."[74] Workers knew from experience the heartache and questions that adoption sometimes brought to the children involved.

The influence that professionals wielded in Florence Crittenton organizations, coupled with the more enlightened views regarding venereal disease that characterized the postwar period, finally resulted in Crittenton boards reevaluating their positions on the acceptance of venereal disease cases. FC workers realized that while the former exclusion policy had banned women suffering from venereal disease in the acute stages, homes had probably unknowingly sheltered disease victims all along. Jean Cole of the Washington, D.C., home admitted, "We were ostrich like, hiding our heads in the sand and probably fifty percent of our family were at that very same time suffering from venereal disease."[75] Several empirical studies confirmed Cole's estimate.[76] Many Crittenton homes instituted a requirement that prospective residents submit to a Wasserman test for syphilis. Delegates to the 1923 convention passed a resolution calling upon each home to follow suit and urging that diseased girls "be not turned away, but be given proper treatment."[77] In response to this resolution, Crittenton homes began to provide care for venereal disease patients in surroundings that were certainly more pleasant than those of public institutions.

During the 1920s sufferers of sexually transmitted diseases accounted for a large segment of the population in some homes. Crittenton institutions established sophisticated procedures directed toward curing pregnant victims before their unborn children contracted the disease. The Denver home and hospital cared for four hundred such patients in one year and were the subject of a study of venereal disease and pregnancy published in the *American Medical Association Journal*.[78] Surgeon General Hugh Cummins praised Crittenton efforts to identify, treat, and report to health officials all cases of venereal disease in each home. In his pamphlet *The Florence Crittenton Missions and their Relation to Public Health*, published in 1924, Cummins suggested that if all public and private institutions did likewise, the number of venereal disease cases in the United States would decrease dramatically.[79] Once again, the Florence Crittenton organization provided leadership for other social welfare agencies.

Crittenton workers also found themselves at odds over whether to provide contraception information to inmates. Measured against the contemporary debate on this topic, Crittenton workers were surprisingly silent on the issue of birth control. The years the current study encompasses coincided with the criminalization of contraception or reproduction-control information. This crack-down made it extremely difficult to even obtain information, much less distribute it.[80] However, a 1917 issue of *Girls* included a lengthy discussion of Alfred Knopf's pro-birth-control article that appeared in *Survey,* as well as a critical response letter written by a Mrs. Hopkins. The *Girls* editors came down firmly on the side of Dr. Knopf.[81] On the other hand, prominent Boston Crittenton worker Clarence Preston remarked at an annual meeting that Crittenton girls were "more innocent than thousands of others who are wise enough, or rather foolish enough to use contraceptive measures or have an abortion and then hold their heads up and look down on the girl with a nameless child." It may be a coincidence that Preston was a man and *Girls* was under the direction of women, but clearly there was a wide gap between the two viewpoints. It is probable that some Crittenton homes provided birth control information while others did not.[82] The NFCM may have adopted a policy of silence on the topic in an effort to avoid controversy.

The growing independence of local homes, and especially the failure of some homes to adopt a more tolerant policy toward venereal disease patients, influenced Barrett's sponsorship of a Florence Crittenton experiment that led to a promising NFCM venture. In 1914, Mrs. Ella Shaw, later Mrs. LaMont A. Williams, read a series of articles that Barrett wrote for the *Washington Times*. The articles impressed Shaw so much that she donated her 264-acre farm, residence, and eight hundred fruit jars to the mission. The property was located in Clifton, Virginia, about thirty miles from Washington, D.C., and Shaw named the farm Ivakota, after the three states where she had lived: Iowa, Virginia, and South Dakota. Later, the NFCM received a neighboring farm as a further bequest from Shaw, and when added to some land the mission had purchased, the Ivakota Farms comprised over four hundred acres.[83]

Initially, the NFCM used Ivakota primarily as a summer retreat for FC inmates from the Washington, D.C., home, but World War I conditions altered Ivakota operations. Crittenton workers believed that rural living and "contact with the soil" had a curative effect on both the souls and bodies of their charges.[84] As *Girls* explained, at the farm "mothers and children have the benefit of the right sort of living." This attitude reflected a progressive period conviction that life in rural America provided a tonic for counteracting the ill effects of the urban environment.[85] Each girl who visited Ivakota received her own garden plot and learned how to can the produce for winter consumption at the home; the Federal Farm Management Bureau provided direction for this activity.[86]

During World War I, Crittenton girls grew and preserved food as a demonstration of patriotism in furthering the war effort.[87] When the NFCM was unable to persuade all local homes to accept venereal disease sufferers referred to it by the Commission on Training Camp Activities, the mission made Ivakota a haven for these women. The Crittenton organization was proud that these patients received the most up-to-date medical treatment, coupled with "the training of heart and hand" so that they could be "socially and economically" fit.[88]

Ivakota Farms became Barrett's pet project, and she tried to get the entire Florence Crittenton "family" involved. Barrett appealed to Crittenton inmates to give a little something so that the Ivakota girls could have a Christmas tree in 1919. According to Barrett, this would show "the world" that Florence Crittenton girls were interested in helping the Ivakota inmates. Barrett noted that the thirty Ivakota girls had not been accepted at Crittenton homes due to their diseases and "there was no other place except a clinic or a jail" for them. Barrett appealed to FC residents to help in the effort to nurse the Ivakota girls back to "health and usefulness."[89] Due to Barrett's interest and effort, Ivakota Farms grew and flourished.

Following World War I, the farms began year-around operations, which included additional services for women. A worker summed up Ivakota's goal:

> If I can dry one tear today
> Hold back one girl that wants to stray
> Or show to one the higher way
> My life will fuller be.[90]

As such, Ivakota was a combination of traditional FC work with more modern objectives. The farms included a hospital building to treat not only Ivakota residents but also all women referred by the Virginia Public Health Service. The hospital featured a maternity ward along with its venereal disease treatment facilities. Ivakota Farms accepted maternity cases only when the mother had venereal disease and, therefore, when the infants required special facilities.

190

Barrett believed the farms land provided the perfect location for the extension of Crittenton work among African Americans. While homes located in northern cities were integrated, in many southern states' laws forbade mixing races in one institution. Since 1914 the "colored home" in Topeka, Kansas, had served African American women, and homes that did not admit African Americans sometimes sent black women there. This arrangement was far from satisfactory; as Barrett noted, "The call has come to us almost daily to rescue some self-respecting girl who could be readily placed on a self-supporting basis if she had the proper surroundings."[91] Barrett's language is indicative of her attitudes toward African American Crittenton charges: the terms *self-respecting* and *self-supporting* were the same ones Barrett used in reference to white Crittenton girls.

Barrett proposed to build a cottage at Ivakota capable of accommodating forty black women. In 1919 the NFCM set aside one thousand dollars for that purpose and sought to raise an additional nine thousand dollars to build and equip the facility. To that end Barrett appointed Sarah Malone, former matron of the Topeka home, "Field Secretary of Colored Work for the National Florence Crittenton Mission."[92] Barrett provided Malone with a letter of introduction to aid her fund-raising efforts, and she assured potential donors that "the excellent results which have followed the small efforts which we have been able to put forth on behalf of our colored sisters, assures us of a remarkable return for money invested."[93] Barrett appealed to the practical inclinations of contributors, and the tone of her letter clearly indicates that FC programs for African American women in no way threatened the status quo. As in the case of venereal disease patients, Barrett's concern for African American women was ahead of her time, although she did not contemplate challenging Virginia's tradition of racial segregation. Barrett did not live to see this part of her Ivakota dream fulfilled.

A children's home for boys and girls under the age of twelve did become a reality, as did a model school. The children occupied two cottages—one for children with venereal disease and one for the others. Recreational as well as educational activities marked the regimen of the farm, which also boasted its own Scout troop.[94]

Ivakota staff members worked to improve rural life and to study Virginia women's country life. The farms cooperated with the Agricultural College of Blackburg, and the County Extension Agent maintained offices at the farms.[95] This interest in scientific farming methods reflected a nationwide movement aimed at preparing young Americans to go "back to the land." Before World War I, the Department of Agriculture and the YMCA had experimented with methods of imparting agricultural skills to city youths as had various private philanthropies.[96] The Ivakota experiment continued along these lines and in some ways was a precursor to New Deal programs such as the Civilian Conservation Corp. The care of female juvenile delinquents became Ivakota's major function since the farms provided delinquent girls with a rural environment, in keeping with the popular view that preparation for farm life was a satisfactory antidote for delinquency. Since the juvenile delinquent had already succumbed to the temptations of city life, it seemed best to remove her from the city to the wholesome atmosphere of a farm.[97]

Incorrigible juveniles that other institutions had failed to reach became Ivakota inmates. Virginia courts committed many of the farms' inmates, but FC workers from across the country sent girls as well. The Lexington, Kentucky, home superintendent wrote to Barrett regarding a "bright and promising girl," explaining that some of the females in the Lexington home had "gone the limit" and that exposing the girl to them was bad. "Socially it would not do," she noted, for the girl in question to attend public school, so she requested that her charge receive acceptance to Ivakota, and the staff welcomed her.[98] Ivakota thus provided an opportunity for Crittenton workers to expand their established interest in delinquent girls from its earlier ad hoc basis to a more structured format.

Margaret Luther, the longtime Florence Crittenton New York and Boston night court worker, assumed the position of Ivakota supervisor. The farms had no fences, reflecting Luther's conviction that some self-expression was fundamental to development and that it was necessary to "direct but not to repress young people."[99] Luther believed that "independence" was a vital component in dealing with her charges. She wanted them to develop their own ideas and not "just become machinery carrying the plans of others."[100] Luther's philosophy reflected Crittenton ideas that Barrett had pioneered at the training school for workers. Fostering independent thought among women, even women who were in trouble with the law, was a key tenet of Crittenton ideology.

Margaret Luther succeeded in establishing a nurturing environment at Ivakota Farms. A Red Cross worker from Pennsylvania wrote, "When I visited Ivakota it seemed more like a vacation camp than a reformatory."[101] Ivakota boasted its own store where the girls could purchase toiletries, candy, and special clothing. Instead of money, the inmates traded in merits earned for good behavior, extra work, or through special projects. Ivakota recaptured some of the old Florence Crittenton keenness for aiding unfortunate girls; perhaps that is why Barrett and Luther devoted so much time to it.[102]

In typical FC fashion, life at the farms was structured. Ivakota adopted the cottage system increasingly prevalent at many reformatories and other children's institutions. "Difficult" girls lived in the Shaw-Colo Cottage, while the "least troublesome" girls occupied the House-that-Jack-Built.[103] The inmates participated in a more sophisticated educational program that stressed home economics and nursing. The Progressive Club for home economics held open forums each Monday night. A typical program included talks on making paper, baking bread and rolls, making butter, caring for milk, and taking measurements for sewing a dress. Forums dealt with subjects such as What are cutworms and how do you get rid of them? What can you put in water to brighten silver? How do you take paint specks off window glass? What will prevent the smell of cabbage in the house when cooking?[104]

Every Tuesday night Ivakota residents combined entertainment with instruction on first aid and home nursing, as the following agenda indicates:

I. Piano solo
II. Tell how to fumigate a room . . . . One of the Class
III. Demonstrate the wrong and right way to change a patient
in bed . . . . The Red Cross Nurse
IV. Duet . . . . Two girls from class
V. Tell what is meant by isolation and how it is done . . . . Girls from class
VI. Demonstrate the wrong and right way to serve a tray
to an invalid The Red Cross Nurse
VII. Recitation "Aunt Doleful's Visit"
VIII. Tell the benefit of massage in constipation
IX. Solo
X. How should a nurse prepare for the night?
XI. Reading . . . . Principles of Bandaging
XII. Bandaging . . . . Head, shoulder, arm
XIII. Tableau . . . . The Road to Health
XIV. Song . . . . "Carry Me Back to Old Virginny."[105]

On Wednesdays the girls conducted Christian Endeavor Night. Thursdays the domestic science teacher led calisthenics, marches, and games, and on Fridays the inmates presented playlets. Saturday was devoted to miscellaneous songs, recitations, and readings, while Sunday was taken up with church services.[106] The program indicates the wide variety of

Flag raising at Ivakota Farms, c. 1920. Courtesy of the National Florence Crittenton Mission.

concerns that had come to characterize Crittenton work. Demonstrations and oral presentations provided an opportunity for Ivakota residents to hone the skills that Barrett and Luther believed were vital for all women. In keeping with traditional Crittenton interests, nursing skills and domestic science enjoyed a prominent place in the Ivakota curriculum.

Ivakota inmates worked hard. The laundry processed over 52,000 pieces of clothing each year, and the inmates put up 15,000 cans of vegetables, 3,000 cans of pickles, and gathered and canned 580 quarts of berries. These activities paid for about one-third of Ivakota's operating costs.[107] The farming was under the direction of Miss Leaf, whom the NFCM's annual report described as a "fine farmerette."[108] Besides cooking, sewing, and nursing, Ivakota inmates took classes in shoe repair, picture framing, carpentry, carpet weaving, cement work, and animal husbandry.[109] The NFCM built a gymnasium equipped with dumbbells, Indian clubs, horizontal bars, and rings for use in the physical education classes.[110] The "New Woman" had replaced the lady of traditional Crittenton work; skills Ivakota residents learned equipped them for more than domestic service.

The girls' slogan was "I am an American girl and I am going to make the world know that I am worth something."[111] This implied a more self-centered attitude than previous Crittenton mottoes, as well as a feminist undertone. One of the inmates wrote the Ivakota song:

> We are the girls of Ivakota, and here we love to stay.
> We cook and sew, and wash and scrub, and then again we play.
> We fell the trees and grub the stumps and haul the wood each day.
> And then we saw it into sticks
> To shoo Jack Frost away!
>
> Oh, Jolly Ivakota, Ivakota, Ivakota tra, la, la!
> Oh, Jolly Ivakota, Ivakota tra, la, la!
> We are the girls of Ivakota and here we love to stay.
> We will always think of you as home
> When we are far away.[112]

Ivakota combined many of the curriculum areas that had been features of the training school—physical education, domestic science, and nursing—with an active outdoor life. It is difficult to imagine workers in the early period of Crittenton activities allowing inmates to fell trees and make firewood, and yet the idea of the Crittenton institution as home is still evident. Workers hoped to instill those qualities of home life that had always been at the center of Crittenton work while also embracing a more modern approach that included a healthy dose of fun. The local normal school provided classes in domestic science, and also in agriculture.[113] The adjective *jolly* is consistent with Barrett's aspirations for the Ivakota atmosphere.

Although Barrett's influence on local homes was diminishing in the wake of the postwar takeover by professional social workers, she maintained control of Ivakota Farms. Most of the workers were longtime Crittenton associates, and they found that FC methods were more successful with juveniles than they had been with hardened prostitutes. This was a source of satisfaction for Barrett and her followers. Reba Barrett Smith, Barrett's daughter, wrote of the farms, "Discarding their makeup boxes, their sheer hose, and high heel slippers, of necessity renouncing cigarettes, they subconsciously respond to the regular hours and routine, the simple wholesome food, the vitalizing country air, and they grow to like the place, like the pursuits, like those in authority, like being decent."[114] In 1926 the mission published a pamphlet entitled *What Happens to the Girls Who Leave Ivakota?* The leaflet included the case histories of fifty girls who went on to successful lives following their stay at the farms.[115] The practical nursing program graduated fifteen women a year.[116] As a further indication of Ivakota's achievements, an FC official claimed that 53 percent of the former inmates married within six months of their departure.[117] Ideas of motherhood and home as central aspects of women's lives remained prominent in Crittenton thinking, but in combination with vocational and practical considerations.

Barrett's highly praised war work, the new widespread acceptance of Crittenton work, and Ivakota Farms' success finally brought Barrett the national recognition she had long coveted. Crittenton accomplishments thrust Barrett into a position of leadership among American social reformers, and she reveled in her enhanced status. In recognition of her contributions to the war effort she was a delegate to the 1919 Zurich Peace Conference and was elected the second national president of the American Legion Auxiliary. More than ever, she became a sought-after public speaker and a respected authority on a wide variety of social welfare issues. In this context she served as vice-president of the Virginia Conference on Social Work and was the Virginia delegate to the 1921 Congress of the American Prison Association.[118] During 1920 alone Barrett visited sixty-four U.S. cities and delivered sixty major addresses, including speeches before the National Prison Association, the National Congress of Mothers, the Public Health Service, and the American Suffrage Association. She also spoke to more than ten thousand school children.[119] Her public appearances were well attended, and major newspapers carried full accounts of her speeches. In his introduction of Barrett, a Greensboro man remarked, "Certainly she is one of three or four of America's foremost women, and she is as much admired and beloved in many of the countries of the world. She combines the qualities which distinguish modern women, a virile, intellectual and aggressive womanhood, with the best qualities of the women of old, high ideals, love of home, culture, innate charm and womanliness." This introduction is to the point, Barrett was both a traditional "true woman" and a "New Woman."[120]

The ideas she sought to convey were the same ones she had always advocated, and in so doing she came to speak for a broad coalition of Americans who viewed the rapid changes apparent in American society with alarm. Barrett feared that the revolution in American manners and mores following the war threatened woman's role as wife, homemaker, and mother. She theorized that civilization was becoming too complex for sentiment and that many artificial interests kept people from pursuing the old goals of love and marriage. From her perspective, the "terrible extravagance of dress" that women "plunged" into during the 1920s was a desperate last gasp attempt to attract men and thus restore marriage to its former position.[121]

For Barrett, marriage remained the central event in each woman's life; she considered matrimony so sacred that a second marriage was unthinkable, even for widows.[122] Convinced good marriages boasted companionship and a community of interests, if not always great passion, she wrote, "A girl who does not marry misses one of the greatest things in life."[123] In response to an interviewer's question, Barrett contended that if a man and a woman were not in love but both wanted a home, they should marry to gain their common goal.[124] At one point she even suggested a return to the practice of arranged marriages as a solution to the rising divorce rate.[125]

While few people took Barrett's advice seriously enough to act on it, her outspoken affirmation of marriage and the family struck a popular chord at a time when many Americans fretted over the apparent breakdown of traditional values; consequently, her popularity and status increased. Fellow Democrats elected her a delegate to the 1924 national convention. In urging Senator Claude Swanson to support Barrett's inclusion in the delegation, the head of the Virginia American Legion gushed, "Her personality is magnetic and her oratory is brilliant and persuasive."[126]

Barrett seconded the presidential nomination of Virginia's favorite son, Carter Glass, and in so doing became the first woman to speak before a Democratic national convention; her effort earned rave reviews in newspapers across the country. She quipped, "There is nothing in the world I am so fond of as men. And I want to tell you that if I had enough votes I would vote for every candidate that has been presented here, because they are all worthy."[127] Certainly her comment ingratiated Barrett to other party members, did not threaten anyone, and at the same time illustrated her political savvy. She realized that she had nothing to lose and everything to gain by covering all of the political bases, and at this stage in her career, Barrett was adept at doing just that.

In recognition of Barrett's diplomacy as well as her achievements, some prominent Virginians urged her to run for governor in 1925. Henry F. Byrd wrote to her: "Very frankly I do not know of anyone better prepared for this office both by reason of your own great ability and the commanding position you occupy as well as the splendid public service that you have rendered in many ways."[128] She declined to enter the gubernatorial race, but the support she received pleased her immensely. While most party officials no doubt knew that Barrett would not run since her health was poor and she was sixty-eight years old, the fact that she received mention as a possible candidate illustrated the esteem Virginians had for her.

On February 23, 1925, only a few days after she announced her decision not to run for public office, Kate Waller Barrett died following a short illness. Obituaries appeared in newspapers and magazines throughout the United States, including a cover story in the *Trained Nurse and Hospital Review*.[129] These tributes and the hundreds of sympathy letters the Barrett family received praised her social work and her ability to combine her philanthropic endeavors with successfully raising a family. One said, "Here was a woman of the broadest national and international activities without infringement of the tenderest family ties." The author claimed that while few could match Barrett's "public service for good in this generation" on both the national and international scene, Barrett had accomplished this without jeopardizing her "beautiful home life, her motherhood, or her womanhood."[130] Even in death, Barrett's motherhood was paramount. The governor of Virginia ordered the state flag over the capital building to be lowered to half mast, making her the first woman ever to receive that honor. He wrote to Barrett's son, "I felt her distinguished career merited this token of appreciation on the part of the people of Virginia."[131]

Kate Waller Barrett's career had been distinguished indeed. She had moved from a sheltered plantation upbringing to the pinnacle of social welfare work. Her philosophy of motherhood not only shaped Florence Crittenton efforts, but influenced social workers' attitudes toward unmarried mothers and their children. Barrett presided over a nationwide network of homes that offered a variety of services for women, including medical care, shelter from abuse, day-care facilities, and vocational training. Her organizational skills were largely responsible for keeping the far-flung Crittenton organization operating at a high level of efficiency. Under her direction, the NFCM came to play a crucial public policy role during the white-slavery scare. Barrett had established an international reputation as an advocate for women, regardless of their ethnic background. For many, Barrett epitomized what was best of American motherhood, and she used her status on behalf of women of all classes.

News of Barrett's death shocked and saddened Crittenton workers everywhere. Barrett had been associated with the National Florence Crittenton Mission for more than thirty years, and for many people her name was almost always identified with FC activities. As one Crittenton worker lamented, "In Crittenton can any fill her place? / In Christendom who will relay her race?"[132] For the Florence Crittenton movement, a long and seminal era had ended.

Conclusion

In the forty years that separated the National Florence Crittenton Mission's founding and Kate Waller Barrett's death, the organization moved from an evangelical enterprise on the fringe of reform to a mainstream social welfare organization. Crittenton assets topped $4.5 million, and throughout 1924, homes cared for 5,359 girls and 3,005 babies. Charles Nelson Crittenton's dream of a string of homes covering each geographic area of the country was a reality; a third of all maternity homes in the United States were affiliated with the NFCM, making it the largest chain of homes in the country.[1] These accomplishments alone warrant the historical study of the organization, but the NFCM's development also illustrates several significant elements of reform and women's history.

Charles Crittenton's evangelistic fervor motivated him to devote his life to helping women and girls. His well-attended sermons and revival meetings helped to publicize the moral reform movement all across the United States. For many Americans, the image they held of prostitutes and unmarried mothers came from Crittenton's sermons and writings. His emotional public appeals recruited many, especially women, to join his efforts to rescue prostitutes, end the double standard of morals for men and women, and champion sex education programs. His financial support enabled the NFCM to spread quickly from New York to California. Crittenton's status as the only male officer of the Women's Christian Temperance Union symbolized his prominence among moral reformers as well as his cutting-edge position on gender issues. He appreciated the title "Brother of Girls" in its several dimensions—protector, close associate, and sympathetic advocate. Crittenton worked to redefine manliness and masculinity vis-à-vis women, arguing that true men treated women of all classes and walks of life with respect.

His career as a preaching evangelist consumed Crittenton and enabled him to introduce the missions to the public. Realizing that his busy schedule kept him from overseeing the administration of the NFCM, he chose Dr. Kate Waller Barrett as his colleague, recognizing in her a talent for organization and a personal charisma that would inspire and motivate Crittenton workers. It turned out to be a fortuitous choice.

One of the most prominent women of her time, Kate Waller Barrett is today a virtually unknown historical character. This reveals much regarding the nature of women's history, as historians have recently stressed the importance of women to progressive reform. Historical attention has centered on settlement house residents and on women social scientists who tended to be single, career women. Certainly, as a physician and trained nurse, Barrett's professional status was on a par with any progressive reformer, male or female. However, unlike many of her contemporaries, Barrett relied on her role as wife and mother to establish her credentials. She and other so-called maternalists recognized the special nature of motherhood, its essential contribution to society, and used it to gain access to power and influence, even as the forces of industrialization and urbanization conspired to curtail women's sphere in the home. Barrett's veneration of home and motherhood, recorded in her theoretical work *Motherhood as a Means of Regeneration,* struck a chord with middle-class women who identified with Barrett. As president of the National Council of Women and the American Legion Auxiliary, and as a leader in the National Congress of Mothers, Barrett represented mainstream American womanhood. She was a vocal advocate of cooperation among women's groups. Recent studies of maternalism have made it clear that middle-class women often used the rhetoric of motherhood to make inroads toward achieving changes favorable to women. Barrett and the NFCM illustrate this phenomenon in several ways.

Moral reform and the campaign to fight prostitution are symbolic of late-nineteenth- to early-twentieth-century efforts to reshape American society. Keeping in mind the prescribed notions of women's place, reformers' involvement with prostitutes appears to be an anomaly. In fact, women reformers took considerable risks to both their reputations and their personal safety when they engaged in work with prostitutes. Even discussing the topic challenged accepted notions of appropriate female behavior.

Nevertheless, Crittenton women braved society's censure, and in so doing they took a step toward their own personal liberation. Through their association with women from other classes, Crittenton volunteers often adopted a more sympathetic and understanding viewpoint. In one poignant case, a prostitute told workers she plied her trade only when she was "very hungry."[2] Her statement put women's inferior economic status and limited employment opportunities in bold relief. Crittenton workers did not see this woman as a whore or harlot, but rather as deserving of their sympathy and, more importantly, their assistance. Sometimes these middle-class women underestimated the fissure that separated them from working-class women. Nonetheless, bridging that gap was a central element of the progressive mindset.

The continuing strength of the double standard of morals accentuated former prostitutes' trouble regaining a respectable position in society. Crittenton workers were determined to combat that attitude. As one wrote, "We receive them as members of the family and not as criminals and from the very first day they are given to understand that their past will not stand in the way of their advancement."[3] As Crittenton women assessed the plight of prostitutes and battled for their rights, they were led to examine their own relationships with men—especially their lack of power to alter those relationships. In 1906 Barrett participated in a symposium on white slavery that included such well-known male reformers as Anthony Comstock, the Reverend Charles Sheldon, and Dr. G. Stanley Hall. When asked whether or not there was ever "any justice or expediency" in the double moral standard, Barrett's quick and definite response was "none," whereas some symposium members equivocated. Her conviction that the double standard was unfair was one of Barrett's earliest motivations and continued to be so throughout her career.[4]

Aware that rescuing prostitutes required tremendous effort and results were not easily measured, Florence Crittenton endeavors came more and more to center on the unmarried mother. Pregnancy outside of marriage was a catastrophe for women; it often alienated them from family and friends, made it difficult if not impossible for them to earn a living, and banished them from society. Many of these women lacked even the necessary vocabulary to describe their trouble or request assistance. In desperation, a woman might resort to infanticide or child abandonment. Poverty and even homelessness could await the woman who kept her child. At a time when no government safety net was ready to catch these women or their children, Florence Crittenton homes provided an alternative. Social worker Francis Emerson compared maternity homes to the medieval church, as an easily found asylum or "refuge" for pregnant girls, and this is an apt analogy.[5] Certainly, middle-class Crittenton workers sometimes forced their own values and life-style upon women of another class, and perhaps race. These actions sometimes resulted in negative effects on the women involved. Nevertheless, Crittenton homes served a purpose and filled a void that provided a real service to women enduring considerable personal turmoil.

Responding to the crisis of unmarried motherhood became a primary Crittenton objective. Barrett's philosophy of motherhood demanded no less. She and many of her colleagues reveled in their roles as wives and mothers, and the Florence Crittenton homes provided an opportunity to expand their influence. While historians have labeled Crittenton efforts as conservative, punitive, and motivated by evangelical conviction rather than professional efficiency, the Crittenton program was in fact more far-ranging, innovative, and even feminist than historians have recognized.

The Crittenton philosophy demanded that unmarried mothers receive all of the considerable respect that motherhood deserved. Barrett was adamant in her claim that Crittenton charges were not just adequate mothers but mothers in every sense of the word. She labored to guarantee that every Crittenton mother possessed the wherewithal to support herself and her child, and she was tireless in her efforts to ensure that former Crittenton girls encountered no barriers to full acceptance as mothers. This mindset defines the Florence Crittenton agenda. Barrett and her cohorts argued that motherhood and independent wage earning were not mutually exclusive, and in doing so made important inroads on behalf of women. While traditionalists found the notion of single parent families "reprehensible," the NFCM described them as families in the truest and finest sense of the word.[6] Barrett's ideas regarding motherhood were thus almost revolutionary, but her faith in maternalism resonated deeply with other middle-class women and allowed Crittenton workers to contemplate what would otherwise have been the unthinkable. Even today, the organization's efforts to bring inmates to self-support and independence would find critics, but the Crittenton position was sensitive to women's needs and the reality of the situation.

Crittenton workers were up against formidable odds as they tried to prepare their charges. Critics have noted that sometimes Crittenton efforts resulted in little more than training inmates in basic domestic skills. However, even this was no small feat. Workers warned outsiders that teaching the rudiments of domestic work and child care required considerable commitment. Joe Klein wrote recently in *Newsweek* that his investigation of contemporary programs for unmarried mothers demonstrated to him just how much effort was needed to help them even to be good mothers.[7] Certainly, it was no easier for Crittenton workers and their successes are noteworthy.

By calling their institutions *homes,* a term designed to produce favorable and nonthreatening images, Florence Crittenton women appealed to a broad cross-section of their peers. Crittenton homes were physical spaces that women controlled and directed for the benefit of other women. Barrett and her associates administered a substantial organization that included considerable real estate and other assets. Women presided over the day-to-day operation of the homes, they set policy, they raised funds. The care and thought the workers gave to decoration, furnishings, holiday celebrations, and other home activities provides a clue as to how Crittenton women viewed the institutions they built. While historians and sometimes inmates compared the Crittenton establishments to prisons, Crittenton workers patterned them on their own homes, and photographs of Crittenton institutions reveal this. Homes were what most Crittenton workers knew best, and it stands to reason that they would try to duplicate them for their charges.

Florence Crittenton regimes emphasized a thoughtful and organized approach to domestic tasks, punctuated with a large dose of scientific knowledge. FC volunteers were quick to praise their charges when they acquired these requisite skills, and in so doing helped to increase inmate self-esteem and self-satisfaction. In the process, Crittenton workers undoubtedly favored their own values over those of their charges. While it is incumbent for the historian to recognize this, it is equally necessary to point out that any other response would be unexpected.

Child bearing and rearing were the pursuits that separated women from men. So, not surprisingly, in the female enclave of the maternity home, workers were often able to transcend class and moral divisions and reach out to women engaged in these distinctly womanly activities. The relationship between workers and inmates was complex, but examination of case records and Crittenton board minutes indicates that Crittenton inmates often had their own ideas and could ameliorate even the harshest of regimes. In most cases, inmates had a choice, and they chose the Crittenton home over other alternatives. Florence Crittenton workers could not force their charges to follow rules, or even to continue their residence. I think the evidence is clear that Crittenton women engaged in maternity work out of a legitimate desire to help others; there were dozens of more attractive and popular avenues for social service available. While life in a Florence Crittenton home was less than idyllic, the alternatives for unmarried mothers and former prostitutes were often grim. Crittenton homes served a useful purpose for inmates, and also an important role in providing opportunities for women workers.

Partly through Florence Crittenton efforts, the condition of illegitimate children in society had grown as a public issue during the progressive era. By stressing the regenerative properties of motherhood as a fundamental principle, Barrett's speeches and writings influenced others, especially such important child-saving groups as the Russell Sage Foundation and the Children's Bureau. Although many experts then and later turned to adoption as the best solution available to the unmarried mother, by the late twentieth century Barrett's views were again in vogue. Crittenton efforts contributed to improved conditions for illegitimate children.

Much has been written regarding the development of professional social work and the associated decline of evangelical benevolence. Molly Ladd-Taylor and Regina Kunzel have argued persuasively that evangelical women and female professional social workers operated from different blueprints during the period under consideration. However, Barrett and her associates were often an exception to this dichotomy. Evangelicalism, professionalism, and maternalism "coexisted naturally" in Barrett's career and in the operation of most FC homes. It was not a question of whether what Peggy Pascoe has called "female moral authority" or Kunzel's "professional expertise" would win out, but rather how the two forces could combine in Crittenton work.[8]

Barrett was conscious of the importance of a scientific approach to rescue work from the very beginning of her career. She attended medical school for three years and completed a graduate course in nurses' training with the sole purpose of bringing expertise to her reform efforts. While she never practiced either profession, and had no intention of doing so, she recognized that the initials "M.D." behind her name gave weight to her viewpoints. She purposefully set about to provide direction to rescue work and her *Some Practical Suggestions for the Conduct of a Rescue Home* served as a primer for workers across the country. When she formalized her approach and committed it to writing, Barrett expanded her influence beyond the usual personal contacts of traditional benevolence.

Professional social work in the early twentieth century is usually identified with casework. While not abandoning their faith in religious conversion, Crittenton homes gradually evolved casework strategies. Barrett was a pioneer in formal training for Crittenton workers through the training school, and she fostered professional growth within the organization.

First as a participant in the White House Conference on Children and then as a frequent speaker at the National Conference on Charities and Corrections, Barrett's professional credentials were clearly established. I suspect that Barrett might have been exactly right when she attributed the greater esteem that the new social workers garnered with the considerable effort they put into publicizing their own accomplishments. A good public relations policy, rather than superior methods for dealing with unmarried mothers, accounted for the difference.

In fact, I would argue that it was this melding of evangelicalism and professionalism that allowed Dr. Barrett and the NFCM to develop as they did. Jane Addams and other progressive professional women relied on alliances with middle-class club-women types to further their reform agenda. People such as Barrett helped provide the bridge that connected these two groups of women. The fact that the Children's Bureau adopted most of the Crittenton pattern for dealing with unmarried mothers and their children is a telling one. Even the official NFCM historian wrote that Barrett "took hold of a movement whose single driving force was an evangelical enthusiasm, all too frequently fitful and uncertain in action, and without abating in the least the Christian character of the project, she steadied it into sound and sane courses, which more than any other influence, perhaps, established it with the public and ensured its survival and enormous growth."[9] Most Florence Crittenton workers did not dream of separating the religious impulse that led them to work with unfortunate women, from the practical side of Crittenton institutions, and historians must guard against this.

As Barrett and her colleagues worked to gain recognition for Crittenton charges as mothers and to improve their situations, they sometimes encountered roadblocks thrown up in the name of women's established place in society. Barrett was determined to break down these barriers, not only to continue her work for women but also for herself and her peers. She firmly believed that women could make a difference in society and in their own lives. Motherhood imbued women with the power to make changes and the right and responsibility to advocate reform. During her numerous speaking engagements and public appearances, Barrett implored women to embrace work for their sisters. She argued that women's role as mother and nurturer entitled them to put their knowledge into practice for all women. When tradition stymied her efforts, Barrett was willing to combat it in the name of women. Florence Crittenton workers emphasized gender identity, even as they recognized that class and race created boundaries between women. Whatever their differences with their charges, FC volunteers were keenly aware that their gender provided a community of interest as a subjugated segment of society. As a result, the NFCM was often at the forefront of what would in contemporary language be a called feminist campaign.

Barrett's vision for the NFCM was a broad one, and historians have not given attention to many aspects of Crittenton endeavor. Crittenton women attempted to make the claim that they engaged in "women's work for women," a reality. Barrett fostered efforts at middle-class/working-class solidarity that were contemporary to better-known activities such as the Consumer League. Florence Crittenton homes sheltered victims of abuse, domestic violence, and incest; and Florence Crittenton workers often acted as advocates for women victims in courtrooms and elsewhere. Crittenton dealings with young women described as "problem girls" featured some decided differences from standard progressive reformers. Barrett was more forward looking in her assessment of entertainments and leisure activities and advocated a more sympathetic attitude towards the girls themselves—refusing to brand them as the culprits responsible for a societal decline. This was also true when Crittenton women worked with Mann Act witnesses and residents of red-light districts. Crittenton women campaigned to make sure that these women did not bear the brunt of attacks. Especially during World War I, when wartime patriotism and zeal led many reformers to villainize prostitutes, Barrett and Crittenton workers lobbied for a more moderate viewpoint. They resented what they viewed as an effort on the part of some segments of society to blame the victims of vice.

Crittenton homes were havens for women in other ways as well. They were pioneers in day care for working women, recognizing that it benefited not just the children but also the mothers. Realizing that worrying about children was debilitating and counterproductive, Crittenton women were vocal in their claims that safe day care was a necessary component for the mother's successful independent wage earning and sought to provide that care at a time when few other groups did. While the necessity of day care for women working outside the home now seems obvious, Florence Crittenton workers challenged accepted ideas of proper motherhood when they advocated and supplied this service.

As a physician, Barrett was in a position to lobby for women's health care. Florence Crittenton homes and hospitals pioneered in the women's health care field. Crittenton nurses training programs not only provided inmates with the means of earning a living but ensured that women's health received the attention it deserved, made use of current medical knowledge (especially in the field of obstetrics), and was responsive to women's needs and preferences. Even today, women's health does not receive the same attention as men's, and Barrett fought to close that gap.

Barrett fostered important relationships with African American women. For the southern born and bred Barrett, this represents a considerable accomplishment. At a time when few white organizations interacted with black women, Barrett facilitated the efforts of middle-class African American women to engage in rescue and maternity home work. When cross-race cooperation was "virtually unknown," the NFCM welcomed the Topeka home and its matron Sarah Malone and included them in the organization.[10] Photographs provide irrefutable evidence that African Americans were included in Crittenton programs. The FC approach was neither revolutionary nor radical, and both white and black Crittenton workers failed to confront or challenge predominant views of race. At the same time, the Crittenton organization made inroads against racism that deserve to be recognized.

When many in the United States were caught up in the white-slavery hysteria, Barrett and the NFCM pushed to help the victims of prostitution rather than to punish them as offenders. Crittenton women lobbied for sex education, continued to fight against the double standard, and campaigned for changes in the age of consent. NFCM public proclamations denounced attempts to place the blame for prostitution solely on women, and the organization was tireless in its efforts to bring the full force of Mann Act penalties to bear on the men involved.

Barrett established herself as an authority on issues of immigration and deportation of women. As a special agent of the Immigration Service, Barrett received official recognition of her expertise and established a relationship with an official government bureaucracy that few women could boast in 1914. Despite the xenophobia that was popular, Barrett remained stalwart in her advocacy on behalf of immigrant women. Crittenton publications presented straightforward statistics to demonstrate that immigrant women were in the minority among prostitutes and unmarried mothers. The organization denied that members of ethnic groups were somehow more likely to engage in illicit sexual activity.

During World War I, while the NFCM enjoyed recognition as one of the social service agencies best equipped to help keep American servicemen "fit to fight," the organization never abandoned its conviction that women deserved respect. Several Crittenton homes were at the forefront of efforts to provide treatment for venereal disease victims.

Ivakota Farms represents the pinnacle of Barrett's career. She built the farms from scratch as a place to deal with venereal disease and delinquent girls. The farms were certainly more responsive to inmate needs than many public institutions, and were a model of progressive institutional development that looked forward to later developments in social work for girls.

As an individual, Barrett played a dynamic role. Linda Gordon has described late-nineteenth-century moral reform as "punitive and moralistic," but Barrett pursued a course that was both more humanitarian and more practical.[11] Under her leadership, the NFCM became an established social service organization that provided a wide spectrum of services to women. The mission initiated activities that many now consider essential services for women and children. Florence Crittenton homes pioneered women-oriented policies in the areas of health care, employment for women, and children's rights. The organization campaigned for equality for women and for a recognition of women's needs.

Florence Crittenton workers were justifiably pleased with the job they did, and their self-esteem and self-confidence are a key element of a feminist viewpoint. Despite differences in class and race with most of their clients, FC volunteers tried to emphasize gender identity. Crittenton women saw needs within American society, and they tried to fill them, often with long-term repercussions. Crittenton workers harnessed the power of motherhood and used that power for both themselves and other women. It would be a long time before a group of women had the resources to duplicate Crittenton efforts.

Epilogue

Kate Waller Barrett's earlier promises to the contrary, the National Florence Crittenton Mission remained a Barrett family operation. The leadership responsibilities were again split as they had been while Charles Crittenton lived. Barrett's son, Robert, became NFCM president, taking charge of fund raising and extension work and serving as spokesperson for the mission. His sister, Reba Barrett Smith, assumed her mother's role as general supervisor, assuring proper treatment and care for the residents of every home and overseeing dealings between the local homes and the national. It became Smith's task to referee the petty disagreements and grumblings that had occupied so much of her mother's time.

Moving into the 1930s, Florence Crittenton efforts turned almost exclusively to maternity cases, as the homes offered assistance and shelter to women of high school age who had "made their first mistake." During the twenties almost every home had constructed its own maternity ward, so that inmates could receive prenatal, obstetrical, and postnatal care without leaving the premises. Reflecting the Crittenton determination to guarantee the best possible care for both mother and child, the maternity wards featured the most up-do-date equipment available, and homes featured the latest methods of maternity care.

In 1929 Robert Barrett published *The Care of the Unmarried Mother*, designed to supersede his mother's *Some Practical Suggestions for the Conduct of a Rescue Home* as the guidelines for Crittenton operations. Robert Barrett included many quotations from Kate Waller Barrett's earlier work, but the differences between the two books illustrated changes within the Crittenton system. There was a pronounced change in the attitude toward the unmarried mother. Early Crittenton workers believed that considerable effort was needed for Crittenton girls to completely overcome their past. Robert Barrett was matter-of-fact when he advised workers to assure their charges that the situation was not bleak and to remind the girls that they had not made "an irrevocable mistake." He urged workers to point out that "thousands of girls have gone through a similar experience" and many were living "normal lives" with children who "turned out to be fine men and women."[1]

When Robert Barrett found it impossible to stem the tide toward adoption that his mother had hoped to control, he established criteria for workers to determine when adoption was an acceptable alternative for a Crittenton resident. He stressed that in most cases workers should encourage a girl to keep her child but admitted that adoption was often the choice of both workers and their clients.

Moreover, rather than trying to train inmates for their future role in society, Crittenton workers sought to enable their charges to resume their lives once their pregnancy was complete. Inmates attended high school classes so that they could return to school following the births of their babies, although the homes continued to provide instruction in child care for those who kept their infants.[2]

Although Crittenton homes maintained their interest in the plight of illegitimate children, the FC staff was concerned with making certain that both the illegitimate child and the mother did not become burdens upon the rest of society. Efficiency and economics sometimes superseded other considerations. While the Crittenton preoccupation with the inmates' souls ended, workers tried to offer a healthy environment for their charges' bodies. Robert Barrett encouraged home officials to provide nutritious meals, plenty of exercise, and happy surroundings for Crittenton girls.

Throughout most of the 1940s, the NFCM was isolated from social workers and other welfare agencies. However, as Robert Barrett and Reba Barrett Smith came to the end of their careers, there was yet another reorganizational effort. In 1950, the Florence Crittenton Homes Association (FCHA) was founded in Atlantic City, New Jersey; the National Florence Crittenton Mission remained a separate organization. FCHA headquarters were in Chicago, while the mission continued in Alexandria, Virginia. The NFCM continued to give grants to a number of agencies, including the FCHA, which in 1960 changed its name to the Florence Crittenton Association of America (FCAA).

During the 1960s, the Florence Crittenton Association of America pursued a broad agenda of social-service work, including efforts to obtain legislation more favorable to unmarried mothers. In association with the National Conference of Catholic Charities and the Salvation Army, the FCAA received a major grant from the Children's Bureau to develop a project on data collection in agencies serving unwed mothers. In 1966, the Comprehensive Care Center in Chicago sponsored by the Chicago Board of Health and administered by the Florence Crittenton Association of America, became the first project in which a national private charity worked with local, state, and federal agencies to serve unmarried mothers. During the 1970s, FCAA work turned more to family services, and in 1976 the organization merged with the Child Welfare League of America to become the Florence Crittenton Division of that organization.[3]

Notes

Introduction

1. Francis V. Emerson, "The Place of the Maternity Home," *Survey* 42 (30 Aug. 1919): 772.

2. Barbara Dafoe Whitehead, "Dan Quayle Was Right," *Atlantic Monthly,* Apr. 1993, 47–84. Even President Bill Clinton's secretary of health and human services, Donna Shalala, declared that Murphy Brown "set a bad example by having a fictional baby out of wedlock." Carol Jouzaitis, "Demos Now Claim Single Moms Are Legitimate Concern: Welfare Reform or Murphy's Law?" quoted in *Spokesman Review* (Spokane, Wash.), 19 July 1994, p. 1.

3. See Linda Gordon, *Pitied but Not Entitled: Single Mothers and the History of Welfare, 1890–1935* (New York, 1994), 55–56. Gordon argues persuasively that feminists used the maternal perspective militantly. See also Sonya Michel and Seth Koven, "Womanly Duties: Maternalist Politics and the Origins of the Welfare State in France, Great Britain and the United States, 1880–1920," *American Historical Review* 95 (Oct. 1990): 1076–1108; Eileen Boris, "Regulating Industrial Homework: The Triumph of 'Sacred Motherhood,'" *Journal of American History* 71 (Mar. 1985): 745–63; Guida West and Rhoda Lois Blumberg, eds., *Women and Social Protest* (New York, 1990), 209–24; Karen Offen, "Defining Feminism: A Comparative Historical Approach," *Signs* 14 (Autumn 1988): 119–57.

4. Regina Kunzel, "The Professionalization of Benevolence: Evangelicals and Social Workers in the Florence Crittenton Homes, 1915–1945," *Journal of Social History* (1986): 21–43; Regina Kunzel, *Fallen Women, Problem Girls: Unmarried Mothers and the Professionalization of Social Work, 1890–1945* (New Haven, 1993), 1–64. See also Marian J. Morton, *And Sin No More: Social Policy and Unwed Mothers in Cleveland, 1855–1990* (Columbus, Ohio, 1993), 56–65.

5. Robyn Muncy, *Creating a Female Dominion in American Reform, 1890–1935* (New York, 1991).

6. Using Jill Conway's paradigm of women leaders concentrating on their professionalism and expertise or their image as sage or prophet, Barrett belongs in the former camp. See Jill Conway, "Women Reformers and American Culture, 1870–1930," *Journal of Social History* 5 (1971–72): 167–69.

7. See Ellen Fitzpatrick, *Endless Crusade: Women Social Scientists and Progressive Reform* (New York, 1990). Fitzpatrick discusses Sophonisba Breckinridge, Edith Abbott, Katharine Bement Davis, and Frances Kellor. Clarke A. Chambers has pointed out that most prominent female social workers "remained unmarried." Clarke A. Chambers, "Women in the Creation of the Profession of Social Work," *Social Service Review* (Mar. 1986): 17.

8. Linda Gordon, "Family Violence, Feminism, and Social Control," *Feminist Studies* 12 (Fall 1986): 466. For an excellent discussion of the difficulties associated with case files as source material, see Regina Kunzel, "Pulp Fictions and Problem Girls: Reading and Rewriting Single Pregnancy in the Postwar United States," *American Historical Review* 100 (Dec. 1995): 1468.

9. Gordon, *Pitied but Not Entitled*, 33–35.

10. See Joan Jacobs Brumberg, "'Ruined Girls': Changing Community Responses to Illegitimacy in Upstate New York, 1890–1920," *Journal of Social History* 18 (Winter 1984): 247–72; Maris Vinovskis, "An Epidemic of Adolescent Pregnancy? Some Historical Considerations," *Journal of Family History* 6, no. 2 (1981): 204–30; Daniel Scott Smith and Michael S. Hindus, "Premarital Pregnancy in America, 1640–1971: An Overview and Interpretation," *Journal of Interdisciplinary History* 5, no. 4 (1975): 537–70; Barbara Meil Hobson, *Uneasy Virtue: The Politics of Prostitution and the American Reform Tradition* (New York, 1987), 59.

11. Rickie Solinger, *Wake Up Little Susie: Single Pregnancy and Race Before Roe v. Wade* (New York, 1992), 87.

12. Nancy F. Cott, *The Grounding of Modern Feminism* (New Haven, 1987), 4–5.

13. See Barbara J. Berg, *The Remembered Gate: Origins of American Feminism, The Woman and the City, 1800–1860* (New York, 1978).

14. See Estelle Freedman, "Separatism as Strategy: Female Institution Building and American Feminism, 1870–1930," *Feminist Studies* 5 (Fall 1979): 512–29.

15. Karen Blair, *The Clubwoman as Feminist: True Woman Redefined, 1868–1914* (New York, 1980).

16. See Berg, *Remembered Gate*, 149; Lori D. Ginzberg, *Women and the Work of Benevolence: Morality, Politics, and Class in the Nineteenth-Century United States* (New Haven, 1990).

17. See, for example, Department of Labor, Children's Bureau, *Illegitimacy as a Child-Welfare Problem*, part 2, *A Study of Original Records in the City of Boston and in the State of Massachusetts*, pub. no. 75, by Emma O. Lundberg and Katherine F. Lenroot, Pub. No. 75 (Washington, D.C., 1921); Children's Bureau, *Illegitimacy as a Child-Welfare Problem*, part 3, *Methods of Care in Selected Urban and Rural Communities*, pub. no. 128 (Washington, D.C., 1924).

18. Department of Labor, Children's Bureau, *Children of Illegitimate Birth Whose Mothers Have Kept Their Custody*, pub. no. 190, by Madorah Donahue (Washington, D.C., 1928), 8.

Chapter 1. The Merchant Evangelist

1. Charles N. Crittenton, "Autobiography," *Florence Crittenton Magazine* 7 (1905): 36 (hereafter cited as *FCM*).

2. Otto Wilson, *Fifty Years' Work with Girls 1883–1933: A Story of the Florence Crittenton Homes* (Alexandria, Va., 1933), 92. See also Charlton Edholm, *Traffic in Girls and the Florence Crittenton Missions* (Chicago, 1893), 108. The story of Crittenton's business origins appeared in many sources, and there were some discrepancies. According to an article in *World Today* 18 (1910): 20, he began his business with $863.

3. Edholm, *Traffic in Girls,* 109.

4. Crittenton, "Autobiography," 351.

5. Ibid., 351–52. See also Wilson, *Fifty Years' Work,* 39; Edholm, *Traffic in Girls,* 110.

6. Crittenton, "Autobiography," 354. See also Edholm, *Traffic in Girls,* 112–15.

7. "Crittenton is Here," *Knoxville Journal,* 29 Jan. 1898, McClung Collection, Lawson McGhee Library, Knoxville, Tennessee (hereafter cited as McClung Collection). Because he believed they should not have the exalted title *women,* Crittenton, as well as his followers, used the term *girl* to describe a fallen woman. I have followed this precedent in order to differentiate between Crittenton clients and the female Florence Crittenton volunteers.

8. Carol Smith-Rosenberg, "The Hysterical Woman: Sex Role Conflict in Nineteenth Century America," *Social Research* 39 (1972): 655; Barbara Welter, "The Cult of True Womanhood: 1820–1960," *American Quarterly* 18 (1966): 154–64; Ginzberg, *Women and the Work of Benevolence,* 11. According to Kirk Jeffrey, "The Family as Utopian Retreat from the City, The Nineteenth Century Contribution," *Soundings* 55 (1972): 22, "Certainly three utopian themes—retreat, conscious design, and perfectionism—pervade nineteenth century writings about the family."

9. Carol Smith-Rosenberg, "Beauty, The Beast and the Militant Woman: A Case Study in Sex Roles and Social Stress in Jacksonian America," in *The Private Side of American History: Readings in Everyday Life,* ed. Gary Nash (New York, 1975), 223.

10. Charles E. Rosenberg, "Sexuality, Class and Role in Nineteenth Century America," *American Quarterly* 25 (1973): 140–45 and Smith-Rosenberg, "Beauty," 223.

11. David Kennedy quoted in Carl Degler, "What Ought to Be and What Was: Women's Sexuality in the Nineteenth Century," *American Historical Review* 79 (1974): 1468. Karen Lystra, *Searching the Heart: Women, Men and Romantic Love in Nineteenth-Century America* (New York, 1989) argues persuasively that passion was in fact a key element in many Victorian marriages. However, the stereotype remains evident in much literature of the time.

12. Robert E. Riegel, "Changing American Attitudes Toward Prostitution (1800–1920)," *Journal of the History of Ideas* 29 (1968): 440–41; Ruth Rosen, *The Lost Sisterhood: Prostitution in America, 1900–1918* (Baltimore, 1982); John D'Emilio and Estelle B. Freedman, *Intimate Matters: A History of Sexuality in America* (New York, 1988), 130–46; Hobson, *Uneasy Virtue,* 21–111.

13. Rosenberg, "Sexuality, Class and Role," 145; Smith-Rosenberg, "Beauty," 217.

14. Ginzberg, *Women and the Work of Benevolence,* 18.

15. Riegel, "Changing American Attitudes Toward Prostitution," 441; Hobson, *Uneasy Virtue,* 49.

16. Smith-Rosenberg, "Beauty," 215–21; Ginzberg, *Women and the Work of Benevolence,* 21.

17. *New York Times,* 10 May 1859, p. 5. See also Riegel, "Changing American Attitudes Toward Prostitution," 443; Smith-Rosenberg, "Beauty," 217.

18. Smith-Rosenberg, "Beauty," 226; David J. Pivar, *Purity Crusade: Sexual Morality and Social Control, 1868–1900* (Westport, Conn., 1973), 64; Rosenberg, "Sexuality, Class and Role," 145, Allan M. Brandt, *No Magic Bullet: A Social History of Venereal Disease in the United States Since 1880* (New York, 1985); Kathy Peiss and Christina Simmons, ed., *Passion and Power: Sexuality in History* (Philadelphia, 1989).

19. Pivar, *Purity Crusade,* 78, 255–56. This book contains information on the purity movement throughout the nineteenth century.

20. Wilson, *Fifty Years' Work,* 1; Charles N. Crittenton, "A Plea for the Erring," *FCM* 3 (1901): 5.

21. L. Howard, "A Famous Night Mission in New York," *Westminster Review* 140 (1893): 274.

22. Ibid., 276–78.

23. Wilson, *Fifty Years' Work,* 365 and 119.

24. Edholm, *Traffic in Girls,* 119–24.

25. Ibid., 136–41.

26. For a first-rate discussion of the "seduced and abandoned" scenario, see Regina G. Kunzel, *Fallen Women, Problem Girls,* 19–25.

27. Wilson, *Fifty Years Work,* 36–38; Edholm, *Traffic in Girls,* 219–24.

28. Edholm, *Traffic in Girls,* 213.

29. Ibid., 218.

30. "Mr. Crittenton Arrives," *Knoxville Tribune,* 29 Jan. 1898; "Crittenton Is Here," *Knoxville Journal,* 29 Jan. 1898; "Mr. Crittenton Arrives Tonight," *Knoxville Sentinel,* 21 Jan. 1898, McClung Collection: Crittenton, "Autobiography," 283; Crittenton, "President's Letter," *FCM* 5 (1903): 84. Another example of Crittenton's influence in the business community is that fifty-six businesses closed between 4:00 and 5:00 P.M. to hear him when he made a 1901 appearance in Atlanta. "Mr. Crittenton's Revival Meeting in Georgia," *FCM* 3 (1901): 37.

31. *Spokesman Review* (Spokane, Wash.), 14 Oct. 1909, p. 11.

32. "Self Denial," *FCM* 3 (1901): 69.

33. Crittenton, "President's Letter," 572.

34. *FCM* 2 (1900): 65.

35. Charles N. Crittenton, "A Plea for Friendless Girls," *FCM* 1 (1899): 30.

36. Howard Morton, "Magdalen," *FCM* 3 (1901): 149.

37. See John Higham, "The Reorientation of American Culture in the 1890s," in *The Origins of Modern Consciousness*, ed. John Weiss (Detroit, 1965), 25–48.

38. C. S. Carr, M.D., "Our Fallen Girls." *FCM* 4 (1902): 7.

39. "Pathetic Scene," *Knoxville Tribune*, 30 Jan. 1898, McClung Collection.

40. See the inside cover of any issue of *FCM* or *Girls*.

41. Crittenton, "Plea for the Erring," 7.

42. R. T. Sunderland, "Keep Yourself Pure," *FCM* 2 (1900): 226.

43. Charles N. Crittenton, "From Lips Usually Sealed to the World," *Ladies Home Journal* 26 (1909): 23.

44. Ibid. See Brandt, *No Magic Bullet*, 29.

45. Edholm, *Traffic in Girls*, 89–90.

46. Ibid., 90–92.

47. *FCM* 1 (1899): 4.

48. "The Twenty-First Annual Conference," *FCM* 6 (1904): 133.

49. F. May Gordon, "The Necessity of Consecration in Rescue Workers," *FCM* 7 (1905): 163.

50. Crittenton, "President's Letter," 351.

51. "Are You Discouraged?" *FCM* 2 (1900): 188.

52. Crittenton, "President's Letter," 88.

53. Clara Howard, "Instances of the Power of God's Love, as Seen Among the Lowly," *FCM* 4 (1902): 246. See John T. Cumbler, "The Politics of Charity: Gender and Class in Late Nineteenth Century Charity Policy," *Journal of Social History* 14 (Fall 1980), 106.

54. *FCM* 3 (1902): 196.

55. *FCM* 1 (1899): 76; *Spokesman Review* (Spokane, Wash.), 13 Apr. 1899, p. 5.

56. Edholm, *Traffic in Girls*, 129. Crittenton workers often claimed that they could identify a fallen woman by looking at her.

57. Hobson, *Uneasy Virtue*, 18.

58. Edholm, *Traffic in Girls*, 136–37.

59. "A Form Constitution Desirable for Florence Crittenton Homes and Circles," *FCM* 1 (1899): 108.

60. "Suggested Programme for F.C. Circles," *FCM* 3 (1901): 129; "Reports from Circles—Santa Barbara," *FCM* 1 (1899): 17.

61. See "Reports from Circles—Newburyport, Mass. and Zanesville, Ohio," *FCM* 7 (1905): 309; "Circle Notes," *FCM* 7 (1905): 92.

62. Prof. H. P. Van Lieu, "The Slums by Flashlight," *FCM* 1 (1899): 31.

63. Laura Morgan, M.D., "The Necessity of Preventive Work," *FCM* 5 (1903): 243.

64. "Reports from Circles—Milton, Mass.," *FCM* 7 (1905): 246. Mark Connelly refers to this as "vicariously titillating." *Responses to Prostitution in the Progressive Era* (Chapel Hill, 1980).

65. "Should Young People Do Rescue Work?" *FCM* 2 (1900): 3.

66. Ann Booth, "Reports from Circles," *FCM* 7 (1905): 28, cites the Akron group's publication, *Rescue Work*.

67. *FCM* 7 (1905): 277.

68. "Let Your Light Shine," *FCM* 2 (1900): 236. See also *What the Florence Crittenton Home Does for Girls,* a pamphlet prepared by the Board of Managers of the Florence Crittenton Home, Florence Crittenton Anchorage Collection, box 3, folder 4, University of Illinois Library at Chicago Circle Campus (hereafter cited as Anchorage Collection). The Florence Crittenton homes located in the North were open to women of all races; southern homes were segregated.

69. "Circle Notes," *FCM* 7 (1905): 61. See Solinger, *Wake Up Little Susie,* 106.

70. Crittenton, "President's Letter," 572.

71. "Lynchburg, Virginia," *FCM* 1 (1899): 220–21.

72. "Work on the Street and in Houses of Ill-Fame," by Sister Charlotte, in *Fourteen Years' Work Among Erring Girls,* a pamphlet printed by the National Florence Crittenton Mission about 1901, p. 32, box 4, folder 2, Florence Crittenton Collection, Social Welfare History Archives, University of Minnesota, Minneapolis (hereafter cited as SWHA). See Hobson, *Uneasy Virtue,* 66–70.

73. "A Touching Incident," *FCM* 1 (1899): 18.

74. Case #161, *Annual Report of the Florence Crittenton League of Compassion, Inc., 1896,* 7, Boston Public Library (hereafter cited as *Annual Report, 1896*).

75. "The Florence Crittenton Rescue League," *FCM* 6 (1904): 118–19.

76. Orrin Booth, "The Florence Crittenton Rescue League," *FCM* 5 (1904): 343–48.

77. Ibid.

78. Orrin Booth, "Visitation on the Streets and in Houses of Sin," *FCM* 5 (1903): 138.

79. Mother Prindle, "How Shall We Reach the Street Girls?" in *Fourteen Years' Work Among Erring Girls,* 37.

80. *Annual Report, 1896,* 7.

81. *Our Girls,* 1907, box 3, folder 3, Anchorage Collection.

82. "Reports from Homes," *FCM* 3 (1901): 20.

83. *FCM* 3 (1901): 63.

84. *FCM* 7 (1905): 269.

85. "What Some Circles Are Doing," *FCM* 7 (1905): 177.

86. Jane Addams, *A New Conscience and an Ancient Evil* (New York, 1912), 141.

87. Wilson, *Fifty Years' Work,* 38.

88. *FCM* 1 (1899): 71.

89. "Form Constitution Desirable," *FCM* 1 (1899): 106.

90. Ibid.

91. "Annual Report of the F.C. Home, Lynchburg, Va.," *FCM* 1 (1899): 199; "Reports from Homes—Scranton, Pa.," *FCM* 7 (1905): 58; "Reports from Homes—F.C. Anchorage, Chicago, Ill.," *FCM* 3 (1901): 19.

92. *FCM* 2 (1900): 1.

93. "Self-Denial Week, Phila., Pa.," *FCM* 3 (1901): 67.

94. "Home versus Mission," *FCM* 1 (1899): 24.

95. "Letters from Girls," *FCM* 3 (1901): 73.

96. "Reports from Homes, Savannah, Ga.," *FCM* 7 (1905): 59.

97. Mary Odem, *Delinquent Daughters: Protecting and Policing Adolescent Female Sexuality in the United States, 1885–1920* (Chapel Hill, 1995), 51–52.

98. "Crittenton Bequests to Aid His Mission," *New York Times,* 14 Dec. 1909, p. 5.

Chapter 2. Kate Waller Barrett

1. The idea of maternalism and its relationship to feminism and women's history in general, has recently begun to receive historians attention. See Michel and Koven, "Womanly Duties," 1076–1108; Mary G. Dietz, "Citizenship with a Feminist Face: The Problem with Maternal Thinking," *Political Theory* 13 (Feb. 1985): 19–37; Theda Skocpal, *Protecting Soldiers and Mothers: The Political Origins of Social Policy in the U.S.* (Cambridge, 1992). *Journal of Women's History* 5 (Fall 1993) is devoted to "Maternalism as a Paradigm." Works that link maternalism and reform include Molly Ladd-Taylor, *Mother-Work: Women, Child Welfare, and the State, 1890–1930* (Urbana, 1994); Estelle B. Freeman, *Maternal Juscie: Miriam Van Waters and the Female Reform Tradition* (Chicago, 1996); Katherine Kish Sklar, *Florence Kelley and the Nation's Work: The Rise of Women's Political Culture, 1830–1900* (New Haven, 1995).

2. Kate Waller Barrett, "Maternity Work—Motherhood A Means of Regeneration," in *Fourteen Years' Work Among Erring Girls,* by Kate Waller Barrett (Washington, D.C., 1897), 52–62.

3. Alice Lee Moque, "On the Other Side," *FCM* 1 (1899): 33. Barbara Leslie Epstein discusses antimale aspects of the Women's Christian Temperance Union in *Women, Evangelicalism and Temperance in Nineteenth Century America* (Middleton, Conn., 1981), 443.

4. Wilson, *Fifty Years' Work,* 39, 139–41; Edward T. James, ed., *Notable American Women 1607–1950: A Biographical Dictionary* (Cambridge, Mass., 1971), 1:97–99; Martha M. Dore, "Organizational Response to Environmental Change: A Case Study of the National Florence Crittenton Mission" (Ph.D. diss., University of Chicago, 1986).

5. Edholm, *Traffic in Girls,* 249–58.

6. Wilson, *Fifty Years' Work,* 139–41; James, *Notable American Women* 1:97–98.

7. James, *Notable American Women* 1:98. Joan Jacobs Brumberg, "Zenanas and Girlless Villages: The Ethnology of American Evangelical Women, 1870–1910," *Journal of American History* 69 (Sept. 1982): 347–71 discusses the foreign missionary work of evangelical women which was closely related to rescue work in many ways. The Episcopal Church was at the forefront of the social gospel movement and her husband's position in the church no doubt facilitated Kate Waller Barrett's exposure to it. See Estelle B. Freedman, *Maternal Justice: Miriam Van Waters and the Female Reform Tradition* (Chicago, 1996), 13–14; Sklar, *Florence Kelley,* 200.

8. "Happenings," *FCM* 3 (1901): 193.

9. Women's role in progressive reform has only recently received much attention. See especially Fitzpatrick, *Endless Crusade*, xii–xiii, and Muncy, *Creating a Female Dominion*.

10. *FCM* 8 (1906): 76.

11. "What Has the National Done for the Homes?" *FCM* 1 (1899): 5; "From Our Field Workers," *FCM* 8 (1906): 886.

12. National Florence Crittenton Mission Folder, Kate Waller Barrett Papers, Library of Congress, Washington, D.C. (hereafter cited as KWB Papers, LC).

13. Ginzberg, *Women and the Work of Benevolence*, 48–49, discusses the importance of charters for nineteenth-century woman reformers.

14. Orrin B. Booth, "The Relation of the Local Homes to the Training School," *FCM* 6 (1904): 94; Kate Waller Barrett, "A Forward Step," *FCM* 7 (1905): 292. Cott, *Grounding of Modern Feminism*, 119, notes that feminists connected wage earning to independence.

15. Muncy, *Creating a Female Dominion*, 20.

16. "Editorial," *FCM* 4 (1902): 220.

17. *The National Florence Crittenton Training School for Christian Workers*, a pamphlet published by the National Florence Crittenton Mission, 14, box 4, folder 1, Florence Crittenton Collection, SWHA.

18. "Our Training School," *FCM* 1 (1899): 27.

19. *The National Florence Crittenton Training School for Christian Workers*, 16.

20. See Roy Lubove, *The Professional Altruist: The Emergence of Social Work as a Career, 1880–1930* (Cambridge, 1965), 6.

21. "National Florence Crittenton Training School for Christian Workers," *FCM* 6 (1904): 60–62.

22. "Editorial," *FCM* 8 (1906): 580.

23. Kate Waller Barrett to Chicago Florence Crittenton Anchorage, 24 Apr. 1907, reprinted in *Our Girls*, box 3, folder 3, Anchorage Collection.

24. "Our Training School," *FCM* 1 (1899): 25–27; *National Florence Crittenton Training School for Christian Workers*; "The National Florence Crittenton Training School for Christian Workers," *FCM* 3 (1901): 270–71; "The National Florence Crittenton Training School for Christian Workers," *FCM* 6 (1904): 60–62; "Trained Workers—The Need of the Hour," *FCM* 7 (1905): 215–17. For physical education, see Roberta Frankfort, *Collegiate Women: Domesticity and Career in Turn of the Century America* (New York, 1978); Gai Ingham Berlage, *Women in Baseball: The Forgotten History* (Westport, Conn., 1994), 1–22.

25. Letter from Training School graduate Callie Tarkington, Superintendent, Florence Crittenton Home, Roanoke, Virginia, "The Florence Training School," *FCM* 8 (1906): 289.

26. "Seventh Annual Commencement," *FCM* 7 (1905): 65; Kate Waller Barrett, "Closing Exercises of the Training School," *FCM* 4 (1902): 68; "Training School Commencement," *FCM* 8 (1906): 532; "Training School Items," *FCM* 7 (1905): 78.

27. Booth, "Relation of the Local Home," 93.

28. "Opening of Training School," *FCM* 8 (1906): 948.

29. "Editorial," *FCM* 5 (1903): 281.

30. Kunzel, *Fallen Women, Problem Girls,* 123, indicates that the Training School began to teach the "rudiments" of social work in the 1930s.

31. "The Conference," *FCM* 7 (1905): 77.

32. See *FCM* 5 (1903): 121–47.

33. "Why People Should Take the Florence Crittenton Magazine," *FCM* 4 (1902): 51; *FCM* 6 (1904): 5, 62.

34. Mrs. M. H. Gephart, "Reports from Homes," *FCM* 7 (1905): 372.

35. Ella Higginson, "M'Liss' Child," *FCM* 8 (1906): 502–7, 545–59, 575–79.

36. See Hobson, *Uneasy Virtue,* 56–58. Kunzel's *Fallen Women, Problem Girls* includes an excellent analysis of what she describes as the "seduced and abandoned" scenario (19–25).

37. May Gordon, "Discussion: Snares and Pitfalls for Girls," *FCM* 5 (1903): 122.

38. See, for example, the annual reports of the Florence Crittenton Anchorage, box 3, folder 3, Anchorage Collection.

39. See "Reports from Homes," *FCM* 5 (1903): 27; "Reports from Homes—Baltimore, Maryland," *FCM* 4 (1902): 90; "Reports from Homes—New Haven, Conn.," *FCM* 4 (1903): 372.

40. "Our Blessing Boxes," *FCM* 4 (1902): 76; *FCM* 7 (1905): 269.

41. "National Headquarters," *FCM* 5 (1903): 97.

42. "What Some Circles Are Doing," *FCM* 7 (1905): 177.

43. *FCM* 6 (1906): 880.

44. Ibid., 905.

45. Kate Waller Barrett, "Letter from Our General Superintendent," *FCM* 3 (1901): 272.

46. Michel and Koven, "Womanly Duties," 1078. See Skocpal, *Protecting Soldiers and Mothers,* 365; Deitz, "Citizenship with a Feminist Face," 19.

47. "Of Interest to Mothers," *FCM* 3 (1901): 290. See Maxine Van de Wetering, "The Popular Concept of 'Home' in Nineteenth Century America," *Journal of American Studies* 18 (1984): 5–28 for a discussion of the "home" phenomenon. Glenna Mattews has recently shown that while women such as those involved in Florence Crittenton work were advocating an expansion of women's influence due to their roles as mothers, the actual women's domestic sphere was declining. See Glenna Matthews, *"Just a Housewife": The Rise and Fall of Domesticity in America* (New York, 1987).

48. *FCM* 3 (1901), 220.

49. *FCM* 6 (1905): 259; Richard Jensen, "Family, Careers, and Reform: Women Leaders of the Progressive Era," in *The American Family in Social-Historical Perspective,* ed. Michael Gordon (New York, 1973), 267–80, indicates that mothers were more likely reformers than other women. For a discussion of this maternalism notion see Gordon, *Pitied but Not Entitled,* 325 n. 2; Skocpal, *Protecting Soldiers and Mothers,* 317–18; Gordon, "Family Violence," 466; Barbara Ehrenreich and Deirdre English, *For Her Own Good: 150 Years of the Experts' Advice to Women* (New York, 1978), 174. The official history of the National Congress of Mothers (later the National Congress of Parents and Teachers)

explained, "From the start the Congress was community minded. It was not enough that individual mothers should be taught how to care for individual children; there were other deep concerns to hold the attention of all mothers," National Congress of Parents and Teachers, *The Parent-Teacher Organization: Its Origins and Development* (Chicago, 1944), 140.

50. "The Home Department," *FCM* 3 (1901): 43.

51. "How to Make a Home," *FCM* 6 (1905): 437.

52. Mrs. David O. Means, Vice-President, National Congress of Mothers, "The First International Congress in America for the Welfare of the Child," held under the auspices of the National Congress of Mothers, Washington D.C., 10–17 Mar. 1908, National Congress of Mothers 1908, 147. For the National Congress of Mothers see, David J. Rothman and Sheila M. Rothman, ed., *National Congress of Mothers: The First Conventions* (New York, 1982).

53. "The Home Department," *FCM* 4 (1902): 11; "The Home Department," *FCM* 3 (1901): 87.

54. *FCM* 3 (1901): 6.

55. Kate Waller Barrett, *Some Practical Suggestions for the Conduct of a Rescue Home* (reprint; New York, 1974), 36.

56. *What the Florence Crittenton Home Does for Girls,* a pamphlet prepared by the Board of Managers of the Florence Crittenton Home, Chicago, 2, box 3, folder 3, Anchorage Collection; *Condensed Statement from the Annual Report, August 1917, Florence Crittenton Home,* Burton Historical Collection, Detroit Public Library (hereafter cited as BHC).

57. "Reports from Homes—Hot Springs, Arkansas," *FCM* 8 (1906): 822.

58. Linda K. Kerber, "Separate Spheres, Female Worlds, Women's Place: The Rhetoric of Women's History," *Journal of American History* 75 (June 1988): 34. Sklar, *Florence Kelley,* 200, discusses the evolution of some settlement houses from earlier missions. Christine Stansell has argued that domesticity was an "element of bourgeois consciousness," see Christine Stansell, *City of Women: Sex and Class in New York, 1789–1860* (Urbana, 1987), xii.

59. "Happenings," *FCM* 3 (1901): 218. The article concluded, "We pray that the lesson from the jar of peaches may go forth and return a harvest of many fold and that all who read may awaken and listen to the Master's words, 'Inasmuch as ye have done it unto the least of these my brethren, ye have done it unto me.'"

60. Kate Waller Barrett, "The Country Girl in the City," *Girls* 15 (Aug. 1912): 124.

61. "Form Constitution Desirable," *FCM* 1 (1899): 109. For example, the Enoch Pratt Library sent a box of books to the Baltimore Home once a week, Mrs. W. S. Gephert, Corresponding Secretary, "Report of the Baltimore F.C. Home," *FCM* 5 (1903): 162.

62. See, for example, "Wilmington, Delaware, Report 1898," *FCM* 1 (1899): 13; "Reports from Homes—Florence Mission, N.Y.2," *FCM* 3 (1901): 51.

63. "Work in the District of Columbia," *FCM* 8 (1906): 931.

64. Board Minutes of the Portland Oregon Florence Crittenton Home (hereafter cited as Portland Board Meeting Minutes), 9 Feb. 1904, Oregon Collection, University of Oregon Library, Eugene (hereafter cited as Oregon Collection).

65. "Form Constitution Desirable," *FCM* 1 (1899): 109.

66. "Queries," *Girls* 20 (1917): 12.

67. Mrs. A. D. Parry, Matron of F.C. Home, Baltimore, Maryland, "A Matron and Her Duties," *Fourteen Years' Work Among Erring Girls*, 8.

68. See, for example, "Reports from Homes—Parkersburg, West Virginia," *FCM* 7 (1906): 1025.

69. "Reports from Homes—Wilmington, Delaware," *FCM* 8 (1906): 818.

70. Barrett, *Some Practical Suggestions*, 26.

71. "Discussion—Industrial Training for Girls," *FCM* 5 (1903): 114–15; "Reports from Homes," *FCM* 7 (1905): 23.

72. "Reports from Homes—Hot Springs, Arkansas," *FCM* 7 (1905): 336.

73. "Discussion—Industrial Training for Girls," *FCM* 5 (1903): 112–13. Estelle Freedman has pointed out that training in domestic work was common in women's prisons. Other reformers also turned to domestic training, see Wendy Mitchinson, "The YWCA and Reform in the Nineteenth Century," *Social History* (Canada) 12 (1979): 278.

74. *Boston Florence Crittenton League of Compassion Annual Report for 1919*, Boston Public Library, 12.

75. *FCM* 6 (1904): 121.

76. Sklar, *Florence Kelley*, 177.

77. Hobson, *Uneasy Virtue*, 65; Stansell, *City of Women*, 159–67.

78. "Encouragement in Our Work," *FCM* 3 (1902): 348.

79. "Scranton, Pa. Home," *FCM* 2 (1900): 74; "Reports from Homes—Lynchburg, Virginia," *FCM* 2 (1900): 117.

80. Barrett, *Some Practical Suggestions*, 50.

81. "Reports from Homes—Savannah, Georgia," *FCM* 7 (1905): 335.

82. *FCM* 4 (1902): 233.

83. Hobson, *Uneasy Virtue*, 97; Susan Porter Benson, "Business Heads and Sympathizing Hearts: The Women of the Providence Employment Society," *Journal of Social History* 12 (Winter 1978): 304 points out that while servants provided middle-class women with the leisure time needed for reform activities, they also provided an opportunity to hone management skills that were vital to reform efforts. For statistics on women in domestic work see Department of Commerce, *Women in Gainful Occupations, 1870–1920*, ed. Joseph A. Hill (Washington, D.C., 1929), 36–39.

84. "Our Babies," *FCM* 5 (1903): 466.

85. Kate Waller Barrett, *Motherhood: A Means of Regeneration*, a pamphlet published by the National Florence Crittenton Mission, 4, box 4, folder 1, SWHA.

86. Kate Waller Barrett, "The Unmarried Mother and Her Child," *Proceedings of the National Conference of Charities and Corrections, 1910*, 96. As Marian J. Morton has noted, Barrett's "principle of redemptive maternity became an article of faith for both rescue workers and child-care professionals for the next three decades." Morton, *And Sin No More*, 59.

87. Michael W. Sedlak, "Young Women and the City: Adolescent Deviance and the Transformation of Educational Policy, 1870–1960," *History of Education Quarterly* 23 (Spring 1983): 18.

88. Harriet Philips, "Our Little Mothers," *FCM* 1 (1900): 233.

89. Moque, "On the Other Side," 38.

90. Matilda Robbins, "An Incident in Social Work (The Adoption)," box 1, folder 26, Matilda Robbins Papers, Archives of Labor and Urban Affairs, Wayne State University, Detroit (hereafter cited as Archives of Labor and Urban Affairs).

91. "Reports from Homes—Peoria, Illinois," *FCM* 7 (1906): 1024.

92. "Reports from Homes," *FCM* 7 (1906): 513.

93. "Report of Charities and Reformatory Institutions of the District of Columbia: Florence Hope and Help Mission, 15 Feb. 1898, #2-7, University of Virginia, Charlottesville (hereafter cited as KWB Papers, U.Va.).

94. *Annual Report of the Florence Crittenton League of Compassion, Inc., 1919*, 12, Boston Public Library.

95. Portland Board Meeting Minutes, 29 Jan., 9 Feb. 1904, Oregon Collection.

96. M. E. Luther, "Bettie and the Baby," *FCM* 7 (1906): 851.

97. "Reasons We Have for Rejoicing," *FCM* 3 (1902): 322.

98. *Our Girls*, 2, box 3, folder 3, Anchorage Collection.

99. Barrett, "Letter from Our General Superintendent," 277.

100. "Boise, Idaho," *FCM* 4 (1902): 335.

101. Rev. W. P. Huntington, Grace Church, New York City to Kate Waller Barrett, 29 Nov. 1896, KWB Papers, LC.

Chapter 3. A Well-Run Home

1. The homes were located in Atlantic City, New Jersey; Akron, Ohio; Alexandria, Virginia (two); Atlanta, Georgia (two); Augusta, Georgia; Baltimore, Maryland; Boston Massachusetts (two); Boise, Idaho; Charleston, South Carolina; Charlotte, North Carolina; Chattanooga, Tennessee; Chicago, Illinois; Columbus, Georgia; Denver, Colorado; Detroit, Michigan; Erie Pennsylvania; Fargo, North Dakota; Harrisburg, Pennsylvania; Helena, Montana; Hot Springs, Arkansas; Houston, Texas; Huntsville, Alabama; Kansas City, Missouri; Knoxville, Tennessee; Little Rock, Arkansas; Los Angeles, California; Lynchburg, Virginia; Meridian, Mississippi; Minneapolis, Minnesota; Mt. Vernon, New York; Nashville, Tennessee; Newark, New Jersey; New Haven, Connecticut; New York, New York (two); Norfolk, Virginia; Ogden, Utah; Old Orchard, Maine; Ossining, New York; Parkersburg, West Virginia; Paterson, New Jersey; Peoria, Illinois; Philadelphia, Pennsylvania; Phoenix, Arizona; Pittsburgh, Pennsylvania; Portland, Oregon; Reno, Nevada; Roanoke, Virginia; San Francisco, California; San Jose, California (two): Savannah, Georgia; Scranton, Pennsylvania; Seattle, Washington; Sioux City Iowa, Swampscott, Massachusetts; Spokane, Washington; Trenton, New Jersey; Topeka, Kansas (for white women); Topeka, Kansas (for black women); Terre Haute, Indiana; Washington, D.C.; Watertown, Massachusetts; Wheeling, West Virginia; Wilkes-Barre, Pennsylvania; Williamsport, Pennsylvania; Wilmington, Delaware; and Youngstown, Ohio.

2. See Peter G. Filene, "An Obituary for 'The Progressive Movement,'" *American Quarterly* 22 (1970): 20–34; David P. Thelen, *The New Citizenship: Origins*

of Progressivism in Wisconsin, 1885–1900 (Columbia, Missouri, 1972); Clyde Griffen, "The Progressive Ethos," in *The Development of an American Culture*, ed. by Stanley Coben and Lorman Ratner (Englewood Cliffs, N.J., 1970), 138, John C. Burnham, "Essay," in John D. Buenker, John C. Burnham, Robert M. Crunden, *Progressivism* (Cambridge, Mass., 1977); Daniel T. Rodgers, "In Search of Progressivism," *Reviews in American History* 10 (Dec. 1982): 111–32; Blair, *Clubwoman as Feminist*, 105; Hobson, *Uneasy Virtue*, 39.

3. Muncy, *Creating a Female Dominion*, 27; Fitzpatrick, *Endless Crusade*, xi; Skocpal, *Protecting Soldiers and Mothers;* Ladd-Taylor, *Mother-Work;* Freedman, *Maternal Justice;* Sklar, *Florence Kelley.*

4. Kate Waller Barrett remarks in "National Conference in Detroit," *Girls* 17 (1914): 2. See Robert H. Wiebe, *The Search for Order 1877–1920* (New York, 1967); Kunzel, *Fallen Women, Problem Girls,* 42.

5. See Wilson, *Fifty Years' Work,* 136; Crittenton's obituary, *New York Times,* 17 Nov. 1909, 9; "An Important Letter from Our President," *Girls* 13 (1910): 23; *New York Times,* 14 Dec. 1909, 5.

6. See Kate Waller Barrett to Judge Benjamin Lindsey, 26 Mar. 1906, box 7, Lindsey Papers, Library of Congress (hereafter cited as Lindsey Papers); Hastings H. Hart to Kate Waller Barrett, 13 Apr. 1912, National Florence Crittenton Mission Folder, KWB Papers, LC.

7. Hastings H. Hart to Kate Waller Barrett, 13 Apr. 1912, KWB Papers, LC.

8. Katharine Bement Davis served on the board of the Boston home, and Jane Addams delivered the keynote address at the 1910 national Crittenton convention in St. Louis. Barrett attended countless meetings of social workers, including the White House Conference on the Care of Dependent Children and the National Conferences of Charities and Corrections. See Barrett, "Unmarried Mother and Her Child," 100.

9. Flora Freeman, "Practical Methods of Uplifting Humanity," *FCM* 8 (1906): 631. On efficiency and progressivism see Burnham, "Essay," 13, 19; Lubove, *Professional Altruist,* (Cambridge, 1965), 6; Samuel Haber, *Efficiency and Uplift: Scientific Management in the Progressive Era, 1890–1920* (Chicago, 1964), 52.

10. Wilson, *Fifty Years' Work,* 7. Other institutions followed a similar pattern, see Steven Ruggles, "Fallen Women: The Inmates of the Magdalen Society Asylum of Philadelphia, 1836–1908," *Journal of Social History* 16 (Summer 1983): 65–82; Richard D. Sexton, "The San Diego Woman's Home Association: A Volunteer Charity Organization," *Journal of San Diego History* 29 (Winter 1983): 41–53; Peggy Pascoe, *Relations of Rescue: The Search for Female Moral Authority in the American West, 1874–1939* (New York, 1990); Kunzel, *Fallen Women, Problem Girls;* Morton, *And Sin No More.*

11. "Discussion—Shall Girls Who Are Able to Pay Be Received into Florence Crittenton Homes? If so, How Can We Prevent the Homes from Becoming Lying-in Hospitals?" *FCM* 5 (1903): 142.

12. Odem, *Delinquent Daughters,* 24. See D'Emilio and Freedman, *Intimate Matters,* 199–200.

13. Kunzel, "Pulp Fictions and Problem Girls," 1468.

14. Kathy Peiss, *Cheap Amusements: Working Women and Leisure in Turn of the Century New York* (Philadelphia, 1986); Joanne Meyerowitz, *Women Adrift: Independent Wage Earners in Chicago, 1880–1930* (Chicago, 1988); Ruth M. Alexander, *The "Girl Problem": Female Sexual Delinquency in New York, 1900–1930* (Ithaca, 1995); Stansell, *City of Women*, 125, 155; Brumberg, "Ruined Girls," 248; Janet Farrell Brodie, *Contraception and Abortion in Nineteenth-Century America* (Ithaca, 1994), 288; Odem, *Delinquent Daughters*, 57.

15. *Thirty-seventh Annual Report of the Florence Crittenton Anchorage, 1923*, 6, box 3, folder 3, Anchorage Collection.

16. Portland Board Meeting Minutes, "Reports, January 1, 1905–January 1, 1907," 191, Oregon Collection.

17. "Reasons We Have for Rejoicing," *FCM* 4 (Jan. 1902): 321.

18. "Annual Report of the Pittsburgh Home," *FCM* 4 (1902): 227–28.

19. *Annual Report of the Florence Crittenton League of Compassion, Inc., 1915*, 13, Boston Public Library (hereafter cited as *Annual Report, 1915*); *Annual Report of the Florence Crittenton League of Compassion, Inc., 1911*, 5.

20. "Reports from Circles," *FCM* 4 (Oct. 1903): 270

21. *Thirty-seventh Annual Report of the Florence Crittenton Anchorage, 1923*, 7.

22. "Reports from Homes, Savannah, Ga.," *FCM* 7 (Apr. 1905): 59.

23. Percy Gamble Kammerer, *The Unmarried Mother: A Study of Five Hundred Cases* (Boston, 1918; reprint, Monclair, N.J., 1969); LeRoy Ashby, *Saving the Waifs: Reformers and Dependent Children, 1890–1917* (Philadelphia, 1984); Susan Tiffin, *In Whose Best Interest: Child Welfare Reform in the Progressive Era* (Westport, Conn., 1982); Joseph M. Hawes, *The Children's Rights Movement: A History of Advocacy and Protection* (Boston, 1991), xi–26; Sheila M. Rothman, *Woman's Proper Place: A History of Changing Ideals and Practices, 1870 to the Present* (New York, 1978), 98. See also, Steven J. Schlossman, *Love and the American Delinquent: The Theory and Practice of "Progressive" Juvenile Justice, 1825–1920* (Chicago, 1977); Gordon, *Pitied but Not Entitled*, 29–32.

24. "Registration of Births," *Girls* 20 (1917): 7. Dr. Kate Waller Barrett was a long-time member and chair of the National Council of Women's Committee on the Care of Dependent and Delinquent Children, see *Program of the 5th Triennial Meeting of the National Council of Women of the United States, 1905* and May Wright Sewall, ed., *National Council of Women of the United States, Report of Its Tenth Annual Executive and Its Third Triennial Sessions*, Library of Congress.

25. "Our Nursery," *FCM* 5 (1903): 383.

26. Muncy, *Creating a Female Dominion*, 113.

27. Molly Ladd-Taylor, *Raising a Baby the Government Way: Mothers' Letters to the Children's Bureau, 1915–1932* (New Brunswick, N.J., 1986), 37.

28. "Our Nursery," *FCM* 5 (2903): 383. See Tiffin, *In Whose Best Interest*, 281.

29. "Our Babies," *FCM* 5 (1903): 88.

30. Kate Waller Barrett to Women's Society of the Vermont Avenue Christian Church, 15 Apr. 1914, box 17, folder 7, Florence Crittenton Collection, SWHA.

31. Barrett, *Some Practical Suggestions*, 45.

32. Sheila Rothman discussed this progressive redefinition of motherhood at length in *Woman's Proper Place,* 97–109; Muncy, *Creating a Female Dominion,* 56. The concept of "maternalism" has received considerable attention. See Gordon, *Pitied but Not Entitled,* 55–56; Michel and Koven, "Womanly Duties," 1076–1108; Boris, "Regulating Industrial Homework," 745–63. For an analytical discussion see Offen, "Defining Feminism," 119–57.

33. "A Mother's Work and Hope," *Girls* 13 (1911): 214.

34. *FCM* 6 (1904): 194.

35. Hastings H. Hart, "Duty of the Community to Illegitimate Children," *FCM* 6 (1904): 195.

36. Kate Waller Barrett, "Conservation of Childhood," undated newspaper clipping, #2-63, KWB Papers, U.Va.

37. Kate Waller Barrett, "Protection for the Innocents," undated newspaper clipping, #2-2, KWB Papers, U.Va.

38. "Our Nursery," *FCM* 1 (1899): 191; "Our Babies," *FCM* 5 (1903): 47. See Solinger, *Wake Up Little Susie,* 149.

39. *Girls* 20 (1917): 1–3.

40. Ibid., 5.

41. "Mother and Child," *Girls* 20 (1917): 7.

42. "Shall Girls Who are Able to Pay Be Received into Florence Crittenton Homes? If so, How Can We Prevent the Homes from Becoming Public Lying-In Hospitals?" *FCM* 5 (1903): 144. See Ladd-Taylor, *Raising a Baby the Government Way,* 37–39.

43. "Mother and Child," *Girls* 20 (1917): 6.

44. The Chicago Florence Crittenton Anchorage Board decided that wet-nursing was not a suitable occupation for its girls since some of them were of questionable character and therefore should not have contact with respectable children. See Board Meeting Minutes, 3 July 1913, box 2, folder 8, Anchorage Collection. According to Harvey Levenstein, "'Best for Babies' or 'Preventable Infanticide'? The Controversy over Artificial Feeding of Infants in America, 1880–1920," *Journal of American History* 70 (June 1983): 75–94, it was actually more common for working class mothers to breast feed their babies than it was for their middle-class counterparts. See also, Rima D. Apple, *Mothers and Medicine: A Social History of Infant Feeding, 1890–1950* (Madison, Wisconsin, 1987).

45. Muncy, *Creating a Female Dominion,* 111–22.

46. *FCM* 8 (1906): 469.

47. Ibid., 7 (1905): 142.

48. Kate Waller Barrett, "Conservation of Childhood," *Girls* 17 (1914): 119; Oral History interview with Douglas Smith (son of Kate Waller Barrett's daughter, Reba Barret Smith), quoted in Nancy Fifield McConnel and Martha Morrison Dore, *1883–1983: Crittenton Services, The First Century* (Washington, D.C., 1983), 27.

49. Barrett, "Unmarried Mother and Her Child," 100.

50. Barrett, "Conservation of Childhood," 119.

51. Children's Bureau, *Illegitimacy as a Child-Welfare Problem,* pt. 2, 188. See also Children's Bureau, *Children of Illegitimate Birth,* 3–12.

r, *Wake Up Little Susie,* 106; Sedlak, "Young Women and the City," *Woman's Proper Place,* 80–81.

ne and Baby," *Girls* 13 (1910): 18.

r Exhibit," *Girls* 17 (1914): 69–71.

e Waller Barrett to Women's Society of the Vermont Avenue Christian 5 Apr. 1914, box 17, folder 7, Florence Crittenton Collection, SWHA.

56. Muncy, *Creating the Female Dominion,* 42.

57. Children's Bureau, *Illegitimacy as a Child-Welfare Problem,* pt. 3, 154.

58. Muncy, *Creating the Female Dominion,* 37–48.

59. Kate Waller Barrett, "The Need of State Supervision for Both Public and Private Charities," *Proceedings of the National Conference of Charities and Corrections, 1908,* 32.

60. *Annual Report of the Florence Crittenton League of Compassion, Inc., 1914,* 2, Boston Public Library (hereafter cited as *Annual Report, 1914*).

61. Lubove, *Professional Altruist,* vii; Regina Kunzel discusses the professionalization of social work in *Fallen Women, Problem Girls,* 36–64.

62. *Proceedings of the Conference on the Care of Dependent Children Held at Washington, D.C., June 24–26, 1909* (Washington, D.C., 1909).

63. *Forty-Fifth Annual Report of the National Florence Crittenton Mission and Its Affiliated Branches for the Year 1927,* box 2, folder 7, Florence Crittenton Collection, SWHA.

64. Barrett, "Need of State Supervision," 30.

65. *Girls* 20 (1917): 13.

66. "Report of Superintendent of Charities Hon. Herbert W. Lewis, 1899," #2-10, KWB Papers, U.Va.

67. See *Girls* 15 (1912): 128.

68. *Report of the National Florence Crittenton Mission and Its Affiliated Branches for the Year 1914,* 38, box 2, folder 4, Florence Crittenton Collection, SWHA (hereafter cited as *Affiliated Branches, 1914*).

69. Wilson, *Fifty Years' Work,* 68.

70. *Girls* 15 (1912): 109. See Sol Cohen, *Progressives and Urban School Reform: The Public Education of New York City, 1895–1954* (New York, 1964), 72.

71. *Girls* 20 (1917): 5.

72. Chicago Board Meeting Minutes, 5 Feb. 1914, box 2, folder 8, Anchorage Collection.

73. National Conference Report (Apr. 1906), 497.

74. Hobson, *Uneasy Virtue,* 97.

75. Chicago Board Meeting Minutes, 5 Sept. 1912, box 2, folder 8, Anchorage Collection. According to Sheila Rothman, *Woman's Proper Place,* 16, whereas in 1870 one out of every eight families had a servant, by 1900 the number had fallen to one in fifteen.

76. Mrs. W. Starr Gephert, "The Value of Technical Training and Industrial Training in Moral Reform," *FCM* 8 (1905): 143.

77. Ibid., 185.

78. "Practical Cookery Course of the F.C.H.," legal box 1, folder 5, Florence Crittenton Collection, SWHA; *Annual Report, 1915,* 24. Progressive-era voca-

tional training was sometimes nothing more than thinly disguised institutional maintenance. See David J. Rothman, *Conscience and Convenience: The Asylum and Its Alternatives in Progressive America* (Boston, 1980), 269.

79. "Laundry," legal box 1, folder 5, Florence Crittenton Collection, SWHA.

80. "First and Second Dining Rooms," 1, legal box 1, folder 5, Florence Crittenton Collection, SWHA.

81. *Annual Report of the Florence Crittenton League of Compassion, Inc., 1913,* 12, Boston Public Library (hereafter cited as *Annual Report, 1913*); "Erie Home," *Girls* 20 (1917): 10.

82. Blair, *Clubwoman as Feminist,* 84; Ehrenreich and English, *For Her Own Good,* 136.

83. "Reports from Homes—Nashville, Tenn.," *FCM* 7 (1905): 243.

84. *FCM* 7 (1905): 274.

85. "Training," *Girls* 17 (1914): 15.

86. "Hospital Department," legal box 1, folder 5, Florence Crittenton Collection, SWHA.

87. *Spokesman Review* (Spokane, Wash.), 3 Feb. 1905, p. 7.

88. "Special Features of Florence Crittenton Work," *Girls* 15 (1912): 174; "Training," *Florence Crittenton League of Compassion Annual Report, 1909,* 15. On the history of the nursing profession, see Barbara Melosh, *The Physician's Hand: Work, Culture, and Conflict in American Nursing* (Philadelphia, 1982).

89. "Annual Report of the Florence Crittenton Home of Lynchburg, April 1916 to April 1917," *Girls* (Apr. 1917): 13.

90. *Girls* 16 (1913): 56.

91. United Community Services of Metropolitan Detroit Files, "A Christmas Appeal for the Florence Crittenton Home, 1913"; Linda Gordon, *Pitied but Not Entitled,* 22–23.

92. Mrs. W. S. Gephart, "Report of the Baltimore Home," *FCM* 5 (1903): 163; Chicago Board Meeting Minutes, 1 Nov. 1917, box 3, folder 1, Anchorage Collection; "New York," *Girls* 15 (1912): 55; Chicago Board Meeting Minutes, 24 Jan. 1903, box 2, folder 8, Anchorage Collection.

93. Kate Waller Barrett, "Professions Open to Women Retrieved from the Underworld," *Girls* 16 (1913): 33. See Ruth Rosen, ed., *The Maimie Papers* (Old Westbury, N.Y., 1977). In this remarkable group of letters written by prostitute Maimie Pinzer between 1910 and 1922, Maimie frequently pointed out that she would rather continue in her profession than become a domestic servant. However, Maimie did want to learn secretarial and business skills.

94. "Reports from Homes, Little Rock," *Girls* 13 (1910): 108, 62.

95. Gordon, "Family Violence," 475. For a discussion of mothers' pensions, see James T. Patterson, *America's Struggle Against Poverty, 1900–1994* (Cambridge, 1994), 27–32.

96. Barrett, *Some Practical Suggestions,* 46.

97. R. R. Reeder, "Institutionalism," *Charities* 11 (1903): 7–8. Reeder wrote a series of articles on the same topic for *Charities* between 1903 and 1908. I am grateful to LeRoy Ashby for pointing out these articles.

98. Barrett, *Some Practical Suggestions,* 107.

99. Ibid., 19.

100. Chicago Board Meeting Minutes, 2 Jan. 1913, box 2, folder 8, Anchorage Collection.

101. "Washington, D.C., Application for Admission," box 12, folder 6, Florence Crittenton Collection, SWHA.

102. "Extracts from the 1912 Report of the Mother Mission, N.Y.C.," *Girls* 15 (1913): 54.

103. "Application Form," box 12, folder 6, Florence Crittenton Collection, SWHA.

104. See for example, "President's Annual Report of the Florence Crittenton Home in Lynchburg, Virginia," *Girls* 13 (1910): 140; "Portland, Oregon," *FCM* 6 (1905): 23.

105. "Contract," box 12, folder 6, Florence Crittenton Collection, SWHA.

106. Portland Board Meeting Minutes, 12 July 1904, Oregon Collection.

107. Chicago Board Meeting Minutes, 8 Jan. 1906, box 2, folder 8, Anchorage Collection.

108. Barrett, *Some Practical Suggestions,* 13, 106; "Dormitory Rules and Recreation," legal box 1, folder 5, Florence Crittenton Collection, SWHA.

109. "Erie Home," *Girls* 20 (1917): 10.

110. Barrett, *Some Practical Suggestions,* 31.

111. "Florence Crittenton Home Grades," legal box 1, folder 5, Florence Crittenton Collection, SWHA.

112. Kate Waller Barrett, "Professions Open to Women Retrieved from the Underworld," 37.

113. Portland Board Meeting Minutes, 8 Aug. 1905, Oregon Collection. Kunzel's *Fallen Women, Problem Girls,* 92–102, is a first-rate discussion of the relationship between inmates and workers. One of the first works to examine this significant question was Barbara Benzel, *Daughters of the State: A Social Portrait of the First Reform School for Girls in North America, 1856–1905* (Cambridge, 1983).

114. Portland Board Minutes, 5 Aug. 1905, Oregon Collection.

115. "Reports from Homes—Chattanooga, Tenn.," *FCM* 8 (1906): 889.

116. "Reports from Homes—Bismarck, North Dakota," *FCM* 8 (1906): 858.

117. *Annual Report of the Florence Crittenton League of Compassion, Inc., 1918,* 13, Boston Public Library (hereafter cited as *Annual Report, 1918*).

118. Portland Board Minutes, 5 Aug. 1905, Oregon Collection.

119. Chicago Board Meeting Minutes, Aug. 1908, box 2, folder 8, Anchorage Collection. See also *Girls* 17 (1914): 75.

120. "Reports from Homes—Denver, Colorado," *FCM* 8 (1906): 670.

121. *Annual Report of the Florence Crittenton League of Compassion, Inc., 1900–1901,* 21, Boston Public Library.

122. Chicago Board Meeting Minutes, 7 Nov. 1912, box 2, folder 8, Anchorage Collection. Regina Kunzel speculated that concerns over lesbian behavior may have prompted the Chicago board decision. The wording "connecting link with the underworld" suggests to me what was a widespread middle-class concern over dancing and its effects. See Kunzel, *Fallen Women, Problem Girls,* 83; Peiss, *Cheap Amusements,* 181.

123. Chicago Board Meeting Minutes, 6 Nov. 1913, box 2, folder 8, Anchorage Collection.

124. Ibid., 5 Sept. 1912.

125. Portland Board Meeting Minutes, 14 Mar. 1905, Oregon Collection.

126. Ibid., 5 Aug. 1905; 15 Nov. 1905.

127. "Reports from Homes, Detroit," *FCM* 8 (1906): 408.

128. Chicago Board Meeting Minutes, 31 July, 4 Sept., 2, 23 Oct. 1913, box 2, folder 8, Anchorage Collection.

129. Portland Board Meeting Minutes, Dec. 1904, Oregon Collection.

130. Barrett, *Some Practical Suggestions,* 100.

131. Rothman, *Woman's Proper Place,* 80; Kunzel, *Fallen Women, Problem Girls,* 92–101, 112–14.

132. Barrett, *Some Practical Suggestions,* 100.

133. *Annual Report, 1918,* 12.

134. Ibid., 26.

135. Ibid., 20. See Peiss, *Cheap Amusements.*

136. Fannie Blakely, "Why Should Young Women Engage in Rescue Work?" *FCM* 6 (1906): 8.

137. *Girls* 12 (1910): 30.

138. "Superintendent's Annual Report," *Annual Report, 1915,* 8.

139. Sedlak, "Young Women and the City," 8.

140. Portland Board Minutes, June 1907, Oregon Collection.

Chapter 4. Helping Hands

1. "Report of the First General Convention of the National Florence Crittenton Mission and School of Methods, July 13 to 19, 1897," 119.

2. The whole concept of "women's sphere" is controversial. See Kerber, "Separate Spheres," 9–39. See also Ginzberg, *Women and the Work of Benevolence,* 1–18; Sklar, *Florence Kelley,* xiv–xv; Freedman, *Maternal Justice,* 22.

3. Wilson, *Fifty Years' Work,* 13.

4. "Reports from Homes—Augusta, Georgia," *Girls* 8 (1906): 663.

5. "Corner Stone of Los Angeles California Home is Laid," *Girls* 17 (Aug. 1914): 121.

6. "Individual Responsibility in Moral Issues," *FCM* 3 (1901): 8.

7. Edna Fry, Matron, "Reports from Homes—Newark, New Jersey," *Girls* 8 (1905): 238. See Estelle Freedman, *Their Sisters' Keepers: Women's Prison Reform in America, 1830–1930* (Ann Arbor, 1981), 20. In *Women and the Work of Benevolence,* 61, Lori Ginzberg discusses how difficult and unsentimental women's reform work could be.

8. Kate Waller Barrett, *Fourteen Years' Work Among Erring Girls* (Washington, D.C., 1897), 141.

9. "National Field Secretaries," *Affiliated Branches 1914,* 36, Florence Crittenton Collection, SWHA. Margaret Luther served as the New York Night Court worker, Boston Home matron, and Superintendent of Ivakota Farms. Grace

Nieman served as matron for the Roanoke, Virginia and Washington, D.C., homes, and Grace Topping was matron in Spokane, Washington, and Fargo, North Dakota.

10. Mary Heartwell's obituary, *Detroit Free Press,* 30 Aug. 1929, Burton Collection.

11. "Minutes of the Annual Conference," *Report of the National Florence Crittenton Mission and Its Affiliated Branches for the Year 1926,* 39, box 2, folder 7, Florence Crittenton Collection, SWHA (hereafter cited as *Affiliated Branches, 1926.*)

12. May Arkwright Hutton to Mrs. Jean Reeves, Bonners Ferry, Idaho, 24 Apr. 1911, May Arkwright Hutton Papers, Eastern Washington Historical Society, Spokane, Washington, MS SC 55 11.

13. *FCM* 7 (1906): 13.

14. Tiffin, *In Whose Best Interest,* 255. See, for example, the yearly reports of the Chicago home, box 1, folder 2, Florence Crittenton Anchorage Papers, Anchorage Collection; "Denver Treasurer's Report," *Girls* 15 (1912): 172.

15. *FCM* 1 (1899): 26.

16. See *Annual Report of the Florence Crittenton League of Compassion, Inc., 1904,* 5, and *Annual Report, 1896,* 5; "Items of Interest to Workers," *FCM* 7 (1906): 810; Chicago Board Minutes, box 2, folder 8, Anchorage Collection.

17. Catherine Wheat, "Reports from Homes—Los Angeles," *Girls* 13 (1910): 137.

18. "The Summer's Campaign," *FCM* 8 (1906): 872–73.

19. "Reports from Homes—Phoenix, Arizona," FCM 8 (1906): 475.

20. "Reports from Homes—New Haven, Conn.," *FCM* 8 (1906): 963.

21. *Spokesman Review* (Spokane, Wash.), 13 Apr. 1899, p. 5. For information on Cornelia Rockwell, see Franz Stenzel, M.D., *Cleveland Rockwell, Scientist and Artist, 1837–1907* (Oregon Historical Society, 1972); Cornelia Rockwell's obituary, *Portland Oregonian,* 23 Mar. 1922.

22. This was often a self-conscious decision. See *Reports of the Citizens' Rescue Board for 1895–6, Florence Crittenton Home for 1896,* 12, Boston Public Library: "The gentlemen who have aided by their counsel and money have decided to relinquish active participation in the work just as soon as the Ladies' Auxiliary is prepared to assume the responsibility."

23. Portland Board Meeting Minutes, Sept. 1905, Oregon Collection; Chicago Board Meeting Minutes, 26 June 1902, box 2, folder 8, Anchorage Collection.

24. Portland Board Meeting Minutes, July 1906, Oregon Collection; Chicago Board Meeting Minutes, 30 May 1912, box 2, folder 8, Anchorage Collection.

25. Portland Board Meeting Minutes, Aug. 1906, Oregon Collection.

26. Ibid.

27. Berg, *Remembered Gate,* 201.

28. Chicago Board Meeting Minutes, 16 Nov. 1906, box 2, folder 8, Anchorage Collection.

29. Kate Waller Barrett to Mrs. N. H. Bardwell, 28 May 1906, National Florence Crittenton Mission Folder, KWB Papers, LC.

30. *Constitution and By-Laws of the Detroit Circle of the Florence Crittenton Home,* pamphlet, E&M File, BHC.

31. Alice Manning, "A King's Daughters Circle," *Girls* 13 (1910): 205.

32. "Reports of Circles—Parkersburg, West Virginia," *Girls* 7 (1906): 485. See Cumbler, "Politics of Charity," 104; Nancy Cott, *The Bonds of Womanhood: "Woman's Sphere" in New England, 1780–1835* (New Haven, Conn., 1977); Benson, "Business Heads and Sympathizing Hearts," 301–12.

33. Portland Board Meeting Minutes, Apr. 1906, Oregon Collection. Barbara Berg has noted that a shared sense of mission "energized" women and drew them together, Berg, *Remembered Gate*, 161.

34. Rothman, *Woman's Proper Place*, 60.

35. Berg, *Remembered Gate*, 155.

36. Kate Waller Barrett, "A Three Months' Tour," *Girls* 12 (1910): 197.

37. *Annual Report, 1914*, 2. Single motherhood was an "extremely difficult situation" according to Linda Gordon and Ellen Dubois, "Seeking Ecstasy on the Battlefield: Danger and Pleasure in Nineteenth Century Feminist Sexual Thought," *Feminist Studies* 9 (Spring 1983): 4.

38. *Annual Report, 1913*, 13.

39. Charles Nelson Crittenton to Columbus Ohio Home, 16 Oct. 1906, box 21, folder 13, Florence Crittenton Collection, SWHA.

40. "Report from Homes—Denver," *FCM* 7 (1905): 237.

41. "Reports from Homes—Phoenix, Arizona," *FCM* 8 (1906): 475. See Berg, *Remembered Gate*, 169.

42. "In the Night Court," *Girls* 12 (1910): 56.

43. "The Tragedies of Human Lives," *Girls* 12 (1910): 165.

44. Cumbler, "Politics of Charity," 106.

45. *FCM* 1 (1899): 117.

46. "Some Preventive Measures," *Girls* 17 (1914): 97.

47. *FCM* 1 (1899): 41.

48. "Some Preventive Measures," 99.

49. Kate Waller Barrett, "The Woman of Today," *Girls* 17 (1914): 146.

50. "Some Typical Cases," *Girls* 15 (1912): 10.

51. Ibid., 12.

52. "Some Preventive Measures," 99. Berg, *Remembered Gate*, 224, indicates that women sought to translate this recognition into action.

53. "That Class of Girls," *Girls* 20 (1917): 11.

54. C. S. Carr, M.D., "Our Fallen Girls," *FCM* 4 (1902): 7. The Sanger survey of two thousand New York women imprisoned on charges of prostitution found that the majority cited "inclination" as their primary motivation. See Laura Hopke, "The Late Nineteenth Century American Street Walker, Images and Realities," *Mid-America* 65 (1983): 156.

55. Barrett, *Some Practical Suggestions*, 75; Mrs. Moore, Minneapolis Matron, "Rescue Work in the Northwest," *FCM* 5 (1903): 146. Richard Wade, introduction to Berg, *Remembered Gate*, vii.

56. For "social feminism," see William O'Neill, *Feminism in America: A History,* 2d rev. ed. (New Brunswick, N.J., 1989). Some historians have questioned the this term, see Nancy Cott, "What's In a Name? The Limits of 'Social Feminism':

On Expanding the Vocabulary of Women's History," *Journal of American History* 76 (Dec. 1989): 809–29. However, I believe the term is still useful. For a further discussion of the suffrage campaign, see Ellen Carol DuBois, *Feminism and Suffrage: The Emergence of an Independent Women's Movement in America, 1848–1869* (Ithaca, 1978). While some conservative women advocated woman suffrage in an attempt to limit the influence of African American men and working class men, Kate Waller Barrett and most Florence Crittenton women were part of an older, less conservative branch of the suffrage campaign.

57. "A Woman's Cry," *FCM* 3 (1901): 287; *Twenty-ninth Annual Convention Report,* 5 June 1912, Anchorage Collection; *Girls* 20 (Mar. 1917): 10.

58. Lida Keck Wiggins, "Woman's Rights," *Girls* 20 (1917): 2.

59. "Why I Am a Suffragist," *Girls* 20 (1917): 3.

60. See Cott, *Grounding of Modern Feminism,* 46.

61. *Girls* 14 (1911): 191.

62. "Love in Daily Life," *FCM* 3 (1901): 31; Sklar, *Florence Kelley.*

63. *Affiliated Branches, 1914,* 134–36; "Employment Agencies," *FCM* 8 (1906): 606.

64. "National Florence Crittenton Mission," *FCM* 7 (1906): 492.

65. *Girls* 15 (1912): 10–12; "Reports from Homes," *Girls* 13 (1910): 128.

66. C. S. Carr, "The Servant Girl Question," *FCM* 4 (1902): 180. See Benson, "Business Heads and Sympathizing Hearts," 304.

67. Barrett, *Some Practical Suggestions,* 43.

68. "Words of Commendation for our Girls," *FCM* 3 (1901): 14. Carol Lasser discussed the antecedents of this "chasm" between domestic servants and employers in "The Domestic Balance of Power: Relations Between Mistress and Maid in Nineteenth Century New England," *Labor History* 28 (Winter 1987): 5–22. See also Kenneth Kusmer, "The Functions of Organized Charity in the Progressive Era: Chicago as a Case Study," *The Journal of American History* 60 (1973): 663.

69. "Twenty-third Annual Conference in Boston: Discussion—What Can Be Done to Make Domestic Service Safer and More Desirable," *FCM* 8 (1906): 614. For a discussion of this topic that includes more of the domestic workers' perspective see David Katzman, *Seven Days a Week: Women and Domestic Service in Industrializing America* (New York, 1978), and Alice Kessler-Harris, *Out to Work: A History of Wage-Earning Women in America* (New York, 1982).

70. "Twenty-third Annual Conference in Boston: Discussion—What Can Be Done to Make Domestic Service Safer and More Desirable," *FCM* 8 (1906): 613–14.

71. *Report of the National Florence Crittenton Mission and Its Affiliated Branches for the Year 1918–1919,* 31, box 2, folder 6, Florence Crittenton Collection, SWHA (hereafter cited as *Affiliated Branches, 1918–1919*).

72. *FCM* 2 (1900): 93; Kate Waller Barrett to Mrs. Bliss, Chicago, 24 Apr. 1907, reprinted in *Our Girls,* box 43, folder 3, Anchorage Collection.

73. "Two Sinners," *Affiliated Branches, 1918–1919,* 9.

74. Barrett, "Country Girl in the City," 117.

75. Adelaide Abbott, M.D., "Whose Daughter?" *FCM* 8 (1906): 625.

76. "Equal Standard of Morals," *FCM* 8 (1906): 831–37.

77. *Girls* 20 (1917): 7.

78. "Annual Report of the Superintendent, Florence Crittenton Home, Fargo, North Dakota," *Girls* 15 (1912): 150.

79. "Reports of Homes—New Haven, Conn.," *FCM* 7 (1905): 306. Regina Kunzel correctly has described support of a female-headed family during this period as "a bold gesture." *Fallen Women, Problem Girls, 33.*

80. *FCM* 8 (1906): 497.

81. *Girls* 15 (1912): 101.

82. Ibid., 39. Even some reformers supported the idea that a woman's sexual history could preclude her from protection, see Odem, *Delinquent Daughters,* 71.

83. Chicago Board Meeting Minutes, 6 Sept. 1917, box 3, folder 1, Anchorage Collection.

84. Chicago Board Meeting Minutes, 5 Sept. 1912, box 2, folder 8, Anchorage Collection.

85. *Boston Annual Report, 1920,* 15.

86. Hart, "Duty of the Community," 196.

87. "Annual Report of the Superintendent, Florence Crittenton Home, Fargo, North Dakota," *Girls* 15 (1912): 150.

88. *Annual Report, 1915,* 23.

89. *Girls* 20 (1917): 10. See Odem, *Delinquent Daughters,* 72.

90. Michel and Koven, "Womanly Duties," 1079.

91. "Reports from Homes—Spokane, Washington," *FCM* 7 (1905): 305.

92. See Blair, *Clubwoman as Feminist,* 117;; Dr. M. E. Blackburn, "The Physician in the Crittenton Home," *Girls* 8 (1907): 1010. For a discussion of other women's hospitals see David Rosner, *A Once Charitable Enterprise: Hospitals and Health Care in Brooklyn and New York, 1855–1918* (Cambridge, 1982).

93. Freedman, *Their Sisters' Keepers,* 38; Berg, *Remembered Gate,* 207. While I was unable to determine the percentage of women doctors in any empirical way, the evidence indicates that a significant number of women physicians engaged in Crittenton work. I identified these women through either a direct discussion of their gender or the use of the female pronoun: Drs. Gray, Ester Dobe, Mari Cardwell and Emma J. Lelty in Portland, Dr. Ida V. Beers and Dr. Mary Hawes, Denver; Mrs. Dr. Clark, Massachusetts, Dr. Sleight, Mount Vernon; Dr. Anna Clark, Scranton; Dr. Jennie Young, Meadville, Pennsylvania, Dr. Genevieve Stout, Parkersburg, Virginia, Dr. Rachel Staunton, Charleston, West Virginia, Drs. Elizabeth Irwin and C. N. Ritter, Williamsport, Pennsylvania; Claire S. Shellhamer and Mildred Williams, Detroit; Dr. Agnes Eichelberger, Sioux City, Iowa; Drs. Nelson and Willitts, San Francisco; Drs. Phoebe Norris, Ada Thomas, Sophia Norduff-Jung, Louise Taylor-Jung and Anna Wilson, Washington, D.C.; Dr. Alice Purvis, Boston, Dr. Kate Bushnell, Chicago, Dr. Myra Everly and Dr. Harriet J. Clark, Seattle, and Dr. Ellen Smith, San Diego. Women's quest for health care that is responsive to female needs continues in the present, and the Florence Crittenton advocacy of female controlled hospitals and woman physicians would find numerous supporters today.

94. Berg, *Remembered Gate*, 240; Ladd-Taylor, *Raising a Baby the Government Way*, 15, states that fewer than 5 percent of women delivered their children in hospitals in 1900 and about half of births took place in hospitals by 1940 (almost three-quarters of those in cities).

95. Portland Board Meeting Minutes, Apr. 1904, Oregon Collection; *Girls* 13 (1910): 31. See Regina Morantz-Sanchez, *Sympathy and Science: Women Physicians in American Medicine* (New York, 1988), 308 and Mary Roth Walsh, *Doctors Wanted: No Women Need Apply* (New Haven, 1977), 88–94. Crittenton people make mention of abortion only infrequently, and usually unfavorably. See Charles N. Crittenton, "Snares and Pitfalls for Girls," *FCM* 5 (1903): 127.

96. Ada R. Thomas, "The Opportunity for the Christian Physician to Aid Unfortunate Girls," *FCM* 5 (1904): 179. See Freedman, "Separatism as Strategy," 518; Walsh, *Doctors Wanted*, 260.

97. *Boston League of Compassion Annual Report for 1922*, 73.

98. Gerda Lerner, *The Female Experience: An American Documentary* (Indianapolis, 1977), 424, indicates that only two Homes were integrated. According to Kunzel (*Fallen Women, Problem Girls*), "The early homes also strived to be racially homogeneous," 29.

99. *Our Girls*, 1907, box 3, folder 3, Anchorage Collection.

100. *FCM* 2 (1901): 255; Mrs. W. Starr Gephart, Baltimore, "The Value of Technical and Industrial Training in Moral Reform," *FCM* 6 (1905): 146.

101. "Twenty-third Annual Conference in Boston, *FCM* 7 (1906): 162.

102. Wilson, *Fifty Years' Work*, 146. The classic study of paternalism and slavery is Eugene D. Genovese, *Roll, Jordan, Roll: The World the Slaves* Made (New York, 1974).

103. "Letter from the Secretary," *Girls* 17 (1914): 107. Many progressive reformers exhibited no interest in African Americans, see Fitzpatrick, *Endless Crusade*, 139.

104. *FCM* 3 (1901): 228–29.

105. W. E. B. Du Bois, *The Negro American Family* (New York, 1968), 41. See Gordon, *Pitied but Not Entitled*, 130.

106. See Paula Giddings, *When and Where I Enter: The Impact of Black Women on Race and Sex in America* (New York, 1984), 178–79. For African American maternity homes see Darlene Clark Hine, ed., *Black Women in United States History* (Brooklyn, 1990), 501; W. E. B. Du Bois, ed., *Efforts for Social Betterment Among Negro Americans*, Atlanta University Publication No. 14, (Atlanta: 1909), 96–102. Maternity Homes for African American women were located in New York City, Topeka, St. Louis, Los Angeles, Kansas City, and Indianapolis.

107. Darlene Clark Hine, ed., *Black Women in America: An Historical Encyclopedia* (Brooklyn, 1993), 1:671. Historians have only just begun the process of examining African American women's organizations and philanthropy. See Anne Frior Scott, "Most Invisible of All: Black Women's Voluntary Associations," *Journal of Southern History* 56 (Feb. 1990): 3–22; Darlene Clark Hine, "'We Specialize in the Wholly Impossible': The Philanthropic Work of Black Women,"

in *Lady Bountiful Revisited: Women, Philanthropy and Power,* ed. Kathleen D. McCarthy (New Brunswick, N.J., 1990); Eileen Boris, "The Power of Motherhood: Black and White Active Women Redefine the 'Political,'" in Seth Koven and Sonya Michel, eds., *Mothers of the New World: Maternalist Politics and the Origins of the Welfare States* (New York, 1993); Cynthia Neverdon-Morton, *Afro-American Women of the South and the Advancement of the Race, 1895–1925* (Knoxville, 1989).

108. "Reports from Homes, Mrs. Malone, Topeka, Kansas (Colored) *Girls* 13 (Nov. 1910): 190.

109. Ibid.

110. "Minutes of 43rd Annual Conference of Florence Crittenton Homes, Columbus, Ohio, May 23–25, 1926," 39, box 2, folder 7, Florence Crittenton Collection, SWHA.

111. Jacquelyn Dowd Hall, *Revolt Against Chivalry: Jessie Daniel Ames and the Women's Campaign Against Lynching* (New York, 1979), 1; Kate Waller Barrett to Whom It May Concern, 20 June 1919, box 19, folder 12, Florence Crittenton Collection, SWHA.

112. "Minutes of Conference of the National Florence Crittenton Mission, Held at Atlantic City, New Jersey, May 30, 31, 1919," *Affiliated Branches, 1918–1919,* 106.

113. Ibid.

114. "Topeka Kansas," *Girls* 16 (1913): 113.

115. Solinger, *Wake Up Little Susie,* 66.

116. Chicago Board Meeting Minutes, 6 June 1905, box 2, folder 8, Anchorage Collection; "Report of the Citizens Rescue Band for 1895–6 and Florence Crittenton Home for 1896" (Boston), 9; "New York Court Work," *Girls* 113 (1913): 60, "A number of colored girls under sixteen have been sent to us directly from the children's court as means of caring for this class is so limited." Photographic evidence of black inmates: Trenton, *FCM* 7 (1905): inside front cover; *Annual Report of the Florence Crittenton League of Compassion, Inc., for December 31, 1904–February 28, 1906,* 5, Boston Public Library.

117. According to the 1912 Los Angeles annual report, the home housed twenty-seven Americans, seven Spanish, three "colored," two German, two French, two Canadian, and one Jewish inmate. For population figures, see Department of Commerce, Bureau of Census, *Thirteenth Census of the United States Taken in the Year 1910,* vol. 2, *Population* (Washington, D.C.: GPO, 1913), 163.

118. "Detroit's Report, Miss Mary E. Heartwell," *Affiliated Branches, 1918–1919,* 118.

119. *Girls* 15 (1912): 72.

120. Portland Board Minutes, Sept. 1905, Oregon Collection.

121. Chicago Board Minutes, 1 Sept. 1904, box 2, folder 8, Anchorage Collection.

122. Chicago Board Minutes, 1 Oct. 1904 and 4 Mar. 1906, box 2, folder 8, Anchorage Collection.

123. Chicago Board Minutes, May 1914, Feb. 2, 1905; 2 Mar. 1905; 6 Apr. 1905, box 2, folder 8, Anchorage Collection.

124. Trouble Case no. 409, box 13, folder 7, United Community Services Collection, Archives of Labor and Urban Affairs (hereafter cited as UCSC). I have used numbers rather than names in citing cases in order to protect the privacy of families.

125. Box 7, folder 5, UCSC.

126. Case #490, box 13, folder 3, UCSC.

127. Case #28, Trouble Cases, box 9, folder 4, UCSC.

128. See *Girls* 15 (1912): 10–12.

129. "Florence Crittenton Circle and Shelter of Wilkes-Barre, Penn.," *Girls* 14 (1911): 235.

130. *FCM* 6 (1904): 29.

131. *FCM* 1 (Aug. 1899), 143.

132. "Volunteers Wanted," *Girls* 20 (1917), 1.

133. Linda Gordon, "Single Mothers and Child Neglect, 1880–1920," *American Quarterly* 37 (Summer 1985): 185; in "Black and White Visions of Welfare: Women's Welfare Activism, 1890–1945," *Journal of American History* 78 (Sept. 1991), Gordon noted, "Virtually no northern white welfare reformers endorsed such programs [day nurseries] as long-term or permanent services until the 1930s and 1940s," indicating the importance of this aspect of Crittenton work. Some other groups experimented with day care, see Ruth Bordin, *Women and Temperance: The Quest for Power and Liberty, 1873–1900* (Philadelphia, 1981), 103.

134. *Annual Report of the Florence Crittenton Mission of Detroit, 1918,* 3, BHC; Gordon, *Pitied but Not Entitled,* 23.

135. Ibid.; Matilda Robbins, "From the Life of a Wage Earning Woman," and "My Story," Archives of Labor and Urban Affairs, box 1, folder 6 are helpful here. Robbins was an unmarried mother herself and demonstrated the difficulty working women had in locating child care and the real mental torment this created.

136. *Constitution and By-Laws of the Detroit Circle.*

137. Trouble Case #10595, box 9, folder 10; Trouble Case #394, box 12, folder 1, UCSC.

138. Wilson, *Fifty Years' Work,* 261.

139. *Spokane (Wash.) Spokesman Review,* 3 Feb. 1905, p. 7. Linda Gordon has pointed out that many women labeled "deserted" during this period would today be called "separated." Nevertheless, they were women who needed help. See Gordon, *Pitied but Not Entitled,* 20. The Crittenton concern for abuse victims was part of a feminist concern that was often subsumed by the antiprostitution campaign, Elizabeth Pleck, "Feminist Responses to 'Crimes Against Women,' 1868–1896," *Signs* 8 (1983): 451–70.

140. Trouble Case #218, box 10, folder 2; Trouble Case #392, box 11, folder 2, UCSC.

141. "Reports from Homes," *Girls* 13 (1910): 172.

142. Case #336, Trouble Cases, box 11, folder 9, UCSC.

143. Trouble Case #207, box 9, folder 16, UCSC.

144. Lola Zell, "Reports from Homes—Peoria," *FCM* 7 (1905): 302; *Annual Report, 1913,* 17.

145. *Affiliated Branches, 1914,* 136.

146. "Report of Shelter," *Annual Report, 1913,* 17.

147. *Affiliated Branches, 1918–1919,* 55.

148. "Trouble Cases no. 286," CS0, box 10, folder 16, UCSC.

149. Michigan State Welfare Commission, 26th Biennial Report, 1921–22, 38.

150. *FCM* 7 (1905): 273, 306.

151. "Reports from Homes," *Girls* 13 (1910): 11. See Hobson, *Uneasy Virtue,* 135. Several historians have examined the issue of so-called delinquent girls and the court system. See Odem, *Delinquent Daughters;* Alexander, *"Girl Problem,"* and Freedman, *Maternal Justice.*

152. Lillian Grace Topping, "Annual Report of the Fargo, North Dakota Florence Crittenton Home," *Girls* 13 (1910): 124.

153. Judge Ben Lindsey to Miss Blanche Stalling, 24 Aug. 1906, box 8, Lindsey Papers.

154. *Affiliated Branches, 1918–1919,* 47.

155. Trouble Cases, box 9, folder 4, and box 10, folder 16, no case numbers, UCSC.

156. *Girls* 13 (1910): 172.

Chapter 5. The National Florence Crittenton Mission and "White Slavery"

1. According to Egal Feldman, "Prostitution, the Alien Woman and the Progressive Imagination, 1910–1915," *American Quarterly* 19 (1967): 192. *The Readers' Guide to Periodical Literature* had 36 listings under the subject heading "Prostitution" between 1890 and 1909, 156 from 1910 to 1914, and 41 for the years 1915–24. See also Roy Lubove, "The Progressives and the Prostitute," *Historian* 24 (1962): 309; Laura Hapke, "The Late Nineteenth Century Streetwalker: Images and Realities," *Mid-America* 65 (1983): 155–62; Timothy J. Gilfoyle, *City of Eros: New York City, Prostitution, and the Commercialization of Sex, 1790–1920* (New York, 1992); Hobson, *Uneasy Virtue.*

2. See Pivar, *Purity Crusade,* 62; Brandt, *No Magic Bullet.*

3. "Moral Reform," *Girls* 15 (1912): 24.

4. "The White Slave Traffic," *Girls* 15 (1912): 58.

5. John C. Burnham, "The Social Evil Ordinance—A Social Experiment in Nineteenth century St. Louis," *Bulletin of the Missouri Historical Society* 24 (1971): 203–17; John C. Burnham, "Medical Inspection of Prostitutes in America: The St. Louis Experiment and Its Sequel," *Bulletin of the History of Medicine* 24 (1971): 203–18; Vern L. Bullough, *The History of Prostitution* (New Hyde Park, New York, 1964), 173 discuss the St. Louis law in detail.

6. Charles Walter Clarke, *Taboo: The Story of the Pioneers of Social Hygiene* (Washington, D.C, 1961), 14. See also Bullough, *History of Prostitution,* 171.

7. Bullough, *The History of Prostitution,* 130; Clarke, *Taboo,* 25–27. Stead's enemies convinced the "virgin's" father to charge Stead with abduction, and as a result Stead served a six month jail sentence.

8. B. S. Steadwell, "Introduction," in *The Great War on White Slavery or Fighting for the Protection of Our Girls,* by Clifford G. Roe (copyright 1912 by Clifford Roe and B. S. Steadwell), 13. Steadwell was president of the American Purity Federation. William Stead's Chicago appearances served as a catalyst for many American reform movements, see Sklar, *Florence Kelley,* 201.

9. Edholm, *Traffic in Girls,* 13–65. Stead later helped to arouse interest in this topic in America when he visited Chicago. His account of vice in that city was similar in nature to his work dealing with London. See William T. Stead, *If Christ Came to Chicago! A Plea for the Union of all Who Love in the Service of All Who Suffer* (Chicago, 1894).

10. George J. Kneeland, *Commercialized Prostitution in New York City* (New York, 1913), 4–142. The investigator could not determine the price at two of the houses of prostitution visited. This report was published under the auspices of the Rockefeller led New York City Vice Commission. Between 1902 and 1916, 102 cities appointed vice commissions.

11. Ibid., 39.

12. Ibid., 8 and 120.

13. Hobson, *Uneasy Virtue,* 140.

14. Steadwell, "Introduction," 16. Research conducted during the progressive period often indicated that women made conscious decisions to become prostitutes. William Sanger's study of two thousands prostitutes, for example, indicated that personal preference was the reason most often given. See Laura Hopke, "The Late Nineteenth Century American Street Walker, Images and Realities," *Mid-America* 65 (1983): 156; Riegel, "Changing American Attitudes Toward Prostitution," 446.

15. Roe, *Great War on White Slavery,* 78. Paul Sinclair claimed on one occasion that "in two days I secured and shipped to Philadelphia eight attractive, rosy cheeked girls who were lured by the call of the stage." For a complete description of the various procurement techniques see Roe, *Great War on White Slavery,* 154; Maud Miner, *Slavery of Prostitution: A Plea for Emancipation* (New York, 1916), 85. Miner was the secretary of the New York Probation and Protective Association.

16. Bullough, *History of Prostitution,* 173; Rosen, *Lost Sisterhood,* esp. chap. 2.

17. Bullough, *History of Prostitution,* 218; Clarke, *Taboo,* 51; Connelly, *Response to Prostitution,* 67; Hobson, *Uneasy Virtue,* 152–53.

18. See John C. Burnham, "The Progressive Era Revolution in American Attitudes toward Sex," *Journal of American History* 59 (Mar. 1973): 891–96; Eric Anderson, "Prostitution and Social Justice: Chicago, 1910–1915," *Social Science Review* 48 (1974): 206; Clarke, 58–61; Connelly, *Response to Prostitution,* 67.

19. Addams, *New Conscience,* 4.

20. Addams, *New Conscience,* 4; Feldman, "Prostitution, the Alien Woman and the Progressive Imagination," 192.

21. "The White Slave Traffic," *Girls* 15 (1912): 58.

22. *Report of the Boston Florence Crittenton League of Compassion for 1912,* Boston Public Library.

23. *Girls* 16 (1913): 49.

24. "Work in St. Louis," *FCM* 7 (1904): 262.

25. *Girls* 13 (1910): 141.

26. "Extracts from the 1912 Report of the Mother Mission, N.Y.C.," *Girls* 16 (1913): 55.

27. *Girls* 15 (1912): 114.

28. "Photographing Evil," *Girls* 15 (1912): 116.

29. Crittenton, "President's Letter," 572.

30. "Brother of Girls," *Girls* 13 (1910): 12.

31. See Hobson, *Uneasy Virtue*, 160; Judith Walkowitz, "The Politics of Prostitution," *Signs* 6 (1980): 125.

32. "Editorial," *FCM* 7 (1905): 225.

33. *Girls* 13 (1910): 69.

34. Emile D. Stonehill, "A Midnight Rescue and a Narrow Escape," *Girls* 12 (1910): 161.

35. Barrett, "Country Girl in the City," 118.

36. "Moral Reform," *Girls* 15 (1912): 24.

37. Kneeland, *Commercialized Prostitution*, 263.

38. "Work Among Professional Prostitutes," *Girls* 16 (1913): 61.

39. "Report of Mrs. Kate Waller Barrett, President Florence Crittenton Mission," *Girls* 15 (1912): 83 and "The White Slave Conference at Mountain Lake Park," *Girls* 15 (1912): 82.

40. "Of Interest to Women," *FCM* (1906): 472.

41. "The White Slave Traffic," *Girls* 15 (1912): 58.

42. *Detroit News,* 16 Feb. 1915, p. 1, National Florence Crittenton Mission Folder, KWB Papers, LC.

43. *Girls* 15 (1912): 42.

44. Addams, *New Conscience*, 24. See Lubove, "Progressives and the Prostitute," 311; Brandt, *No Magic Bullet*, 29.

45. "No One Told Her," *Girls* 17 (1914): 92. According to Allan Brandt, sex education during the progressive period was "highly superficial and euphemistic," but even this assault on traditional female reticence was controversial. *No Magic Bullet*, 29. It was not atypical for a young woman to have little knowledge of sexuality, venereal disease, and pregnancy, see Alexander, *"Girl Problem,"* 28.

46. *Girls* 13 (1910): 116. See Riegel, "Changing American Attitudes Toward Prostitution," 45; Connelly, *Response to Prostitution*, 134.

47. Roe, *Great War on White Slavery*, 53.

48. See Stead, *If Christ Came to Chicago!* 245; Addams, *New Conscience*, 101; Roe, *Great War on White Slavery*, 224.

49. "What of the Prodigal Girl?" *Girls* 16 (1913): 105.

50. *Girls* 13 (1910): 69.

51. See "Editorial," *FCM* 7 (1905): 225.

52. Judith Walkowitz termed prostitution a "paradigm for the female condition" in "Politics of Prostitution," 125. See Hobson, *Uneasy Virtue*, 5 for a similar viewpoint.

53. See Pivar, *Purity Crusade,* 106; Burnham, "Essay," 6–9; Addams, *New Conscience,* 209. An enlightening discussion of prostitution as a question of urban social control is Paul Boyer, *Urban Masses and Moral Order in America, 1820–1920* (Cambridge, 1978): 189–204.

54. Addams, *New Conscience,* 105.

55. Ibid., 145.

56. *Affiliated Branches, 1914,* 139–40.

57. Miner, *Slavery or Prostitution,* 245. See also Riegel, "Changing American Attitudes Toward Prostitution," 447; David M. Kennedy, *Birth Control in America: The Career of Margaret Sanger* (New Haven, 1970), 58; Lubove, "Progressives and the Prostitute," 324.

58. Kate Waller Barrett, "Equal Standards of Morals," *FCM* 8 (1906): 833 (a reprint of an address delivered before the National Council of Women in Toledo).

59. Anderson, "Prostitution and Social Justice," 223.

60. Kneeland, *Commercialized Prostitution,* 173.

61. See Miner, *Slavery or Prostitution,* 250; Burnham, "Progressive Era Revolution," 888.

62. "Mrs. Tyler's Report," *Annual Report of the Boston Florence Crittenton League of Compassion, 1913,* 17, Boston Public Library.

63. See Addams, *New Conscience,* 52; Stead, *If Christ Came to Chicago!* 244; Pivar, *Purity Crusade,* 104.

64. Edholm, *Traffic in Girls,* 66–86. See also "The Age of Protection," *FCM* 7 (1905): 108–9.

65. See Odem, *Delinquent Daughters,* 4–5.

66. Roe, *Great War on White Slavery,* 80–81; Addams, *New Conscience,* 26. For an excellent discussion of immigration, see John Higham, *Send Them to Me* (New York, 1975).

67. Feldman, "Prostitution, the Alien Woman and the Progressive Imagination," 194. See Miner, *Slavery or Prostitution,* 31; Kneeland, *Commercialized Prostitution,* 101; Roe, *Great War on White Slavery,* 101.

68. The Fargo, North Dakota, home reported in 1910 that of 72 girls the home served, 43 had been "Americans," "Annual Report of Fargo Home," *Girls* 13 (1910): 125. The Los Angeles home reported in 1912 that of forty-six girls served, twenty-seven were "Americans," *Girls* 15 (1912): 77. The situation was similar in other Florence Crittenton homes.

69. *Annual Report, 1915,* 12.

70. Feldman, "Prostitution, the Alien Woman and the Progressive Imagination," 193–99.

71. Addams, *New Conscience,* 34.

72. See "Personalities—Dr. Kate Waller Barrett," *World's Work* 49 (1924): 70.

73. Kate Waller Barrett, "The Immigrant Woman," in *Immigration—Some New Phases of the Problem,* ed. Frank B. Lenz (Published by the American Sociological Society and the Committee of One Hundred, Federal Council of Churches of America, 1915), 12. Frances Kellor also sympathized with immigrant women (see Fitzpatrick, *Endless Crusade,* 140–45).

74. Department of Labor, Bureau of Immigration, *Annual Report of the Commissioner General of Immigration to the Secretary of Labor, 1914* (Washington, D.C.: GPO, 1915): 14–15; Feldman, "Prostitution, the Alien Woman and the Progressive Imagination," 199.

75. Feldman, "Prostitution, the Alien Woman and the Progressive Imagination," 386.

76. "International Council of Women Quinquennial Meeting, Minutes," 13 May 1914, #30-3 and 30-4, KWB Papers, U.Va.

77. Bureau of Immigration, *Annual Report of the Commissioner General of Immigration to the Secretary of Labor, 1914*, 381–86.

78. See *Biennial of the Proceedings of the National Council of Women, Washington, January 1916, and the Executive Meeting, New York, June 1916; With Report of the International Congress of Women, San Francisco, California, November 1915*, Library of Congress, and *Biennial Report of the National Council of Women of the United States, Report of Its Biennial Meeting, held at Washington D.C., December 8, 9, 10, 11, 12, 1917*, Library of Congress.

79. *Biennial Report of the National Council of Women of the United States*, 384–85.

80. *FCM* 8 (1906): 308; 7 (1905): 308. See also Barrett, "Immigrant Woman," 12; *Girls* 13 (1910): 124; "The Deportation of the Immigrant Girl," *Girls* 15 (1912): 86.

81. Kate Waller Barrett, "The Deportation of Immigrant Girls," *Proceedings of the National Conference of Charities and Corrections, 1912*, 558; *Greensboro Daily News*, 18 Feb. 1925.

82. See U.S. House of Representatives, "International Agreement for the Repression of the Trade in White Women," *White Slave Traffic*, H.R. 47, 61st Cong., 2d sess., 1909–1910, 13–18.

83. Bullough, *History of Prostitution*, 183. On the Mann Act, see David J. Langum, *Crossing Over the Line: Legislating Morality and the Mann Act* (Chicago, 1994), esp. 15–71.

84. #2-81, KWB Papers, U.Va.

85. Undated Address, Florence Crittenton Mission Folder, KWB Papers, LC; "The White Slave Trade," *Girls* 15 (1912): 58.

86. "The Government Needs the Help of Our Organization," *Girls* 15 (1912): 85.

87. *Girls* 17 (1914): 12.

88. "Work in the Civil Courts," *Affiliated Branches, 1914*, 136.

89. Ibid., 137.

90. "The Work in New York," *Girls* 14 (1914): 135.

91. "30th Annual Conference, Detroit," *Girls* 17 (1914): 11.

92. *Girls* 15 (1912): 26. According to *Girls* 15 (1912): 43, the Baltimore home offered to provide a place to live for all 800 inmates in houses of prostitution in that city.

93. Wilson, *Fifty Years' Work*, 180.

94. Frank B. McClain, Mayor, Lancaster, Pennsylvania, to Kate Waller Barrett, 21 Mar. 1914, National Florence Crittenton Mission Folder, KWB Papers, LC.

95. *Girls* 17 (1914): 45.

96. *Annual Report of the Florence Crittenton League of Compassion, Inc., 1912,* 11, Boston Public Library. See Peiss, *Cheap Amusements.*

97. See Kunzel, *Fallen Women, Problem Girls,* 58–59.

98. "Pleasure Resorts," *Girls* 15 (1912): 89.

99. Ibid., 90.

100. "Protective and Rescue Work at Expositions," *Affiliated Branches, 1914,* 139–40.

101. Ibid.

102. "Rescue Work at St. Louis," *FCM* 6 (1904): 251–54. The term "fraternities" is the formal name for women's college sororities. All are fraternities except Gamma Phi Beta.

103. #2-78, KWB Papers, U.Va.

104. #2-79, KWB Papers, U.Va.

105. "Kind Words About Young Women," *FCM* 6 (1904): 101.

106. Portland Board Minutes, Aug. 1904, Oregon Collection.

Chapter 6. The Great War and After

1. Typescript of a Kate Waller Barrett speech, #29-9, KWB Papers, U.Va.

2. Ibid., #29–11.

3. *Affiliated Branches, 1918–1919,* 29. The Boston home folded 20,745 dressings. *Annual Report of the Florence Crittenton League of Compassion, Inc., 1917,* 17, Boston Public Library (hereafter cited as *Annual Report, 1917*).

4. Chicago Board Meeting Minutes, Feb. 1918, box 3, folder 1, Anchorage Collection. See Emma Octavia Lundberg, *Unto the Least of These: Social Services for Children* (New York, 1947), 216.

5. Chicago Board Meeting Minutes, Apr. 1918, box 3, folder 1, Anchorage Collection.

6. See various undated newspaper clippings, #29-13, KWB Papers, U.Va.

7. "Achievements of Women Result of Men's Influence," undated newspaper clipping, #29-14, KWB Papers, U.Va.

8. Ibid.

9. Hobson, *Uneasy Virtue,* 165.

10. "Makes Plea for Girls," newspaper clipping, 1 Oct. 1917, #8-22, KWB Papers, U.Va.

11. Fred D. Baldwin, "The Invisible Armor," *American Quarterly* 16 (1964): 432–33; Brandt, *No Magic Bullet.*

12. Allen F. Davis, *Spearheads for Reform: The Social Settlements and the Progressive Movement, 1890–1914* (New York, 1967), 226.

13. See Raymond B. Fosdick, "The Program of the Commission on Training Camp Activities with Relation to the Problem of Venereal Disease," *Social Hygiene* 4 (1918): 71–76; Walter Clarke, "Social Hygiene and the War," *Social Hygiene* 4 (1918): 259–305; Clarke, *Taboo,* 80.

14. Fosdick, "Program of the Commission," 75. See also Baldwin, "Invisible Armor," 434.

15. Clarke, *Taboo,* 75.

16. Baldwin, "Invisible Armor," 438. See Jane Deeter Rippin, "Social Hygiene and the War Work with Women and Girls," *Social Hygiene* 5 (Jan. 1919): 125–36.

17. There is a letter on this stationery in the National Florence Crittenton Mission Folder, KWB Papers, LC.

18. Lundberg, *Unto the Least of These,* 218.

19. A copy of Stecker's letter appeared in *Girls* 20 (1917): 11.

20. "War Work in Florence Crittenton Homes," *Girls* 20 (1917): 1.

21. *Affiliated Branches, 1918–1919,* 19. In some cities, such as Mobile, Alabama, the war work led to the organization of a new Florence Crittenton home.

22. See Hobson, *Uneasy Virtue,* 165–75; Freedman, *Their Sisters' Keepers,* 147.

23. "War Work in Florence Crittenton Homes," *Girls* 20 (July 1917): 3.

24. Ibid.

25. "Crittenton Work Head Reports on Work," newspaper clipping, 28 Jan. 1919, #2-96, KWB Papers, U.Va.

26. Chicago Board Meeting Minutes, 4 Oct. 1917, box 3, folder 1, Anchorage Collection.

27. *Annual Report, 1918,* 10.

28. See Barrett address, "Minutes of the Conference of the National Florence Crittenton Missions, Held at Atlantic City, New Jersey, May 30–31, 1919," *Affiliated Branches, 1918–19,* 102.

29. "Brings Message of Cheer," newspaper clipping, 28 Jan. 1919, Library of Congress, National Florence Crittenton Folder, KWB Papers, LC.

30. Typescript of a Kate Waller Barrett speech, National Florence Crittenton Mission Folder, KWB Papers, LC.

31. Ibid.

32. *Affiliated Branches, 1918–1919,* 100.

33. Ibid.; Wilson, *Fifty Years' Work,* 59; *Annual Report, 1917,* 111.

34. Chicago Board Meeting Minutes, Dec. 1918, box 3, folder 1, Anchorage Collection.

35. Ibid., 6 Sept. 1917.

36. See, for example, *FCM* 1 (1899): 13; Wilson, *Fifty Years' Work,* 58.

37. *Affiliated Branches, 1918–1919,* 49.

38. Ibid., 80.

39. "Minutes of the Conference of the National Florence Crittenton Missions, Held at Atlantic City, New Jersey, May 30–31, 1919," *Affiliated Branches, 1918–19,* 30–31.

40. Ibid., 101.

41. *Forty-Fifth Report of the National Florence Crittenton Mission and Its Affiliated Branches for the Year 1927* (hereafter cited as *Affiliated Branches, 1927*), box 2, folder 7, Florence Crittenton Collection, SWHA.

42. *Affiliated Branches, 1918–1919,* 101.

43. See, for example, "President's Report," *Affiliated Branches, 1918–1919,* 12.

44. Mr. and Mrs. Thomas Arnold to the National Florence Crittenton Mission, 4 June 1928, box 12, folder 6, Florence Crittenton Collection, SWHA.

45. Camille P. Davied to Kate Waller Barrett, 23 July 1920; 31 July 1920; 30 Aug. 1920, box 12, folder 6, Florence Crittenton Collection, SWHA.

46. See some handwritten notes entitled "Some Lessons We Should Learn," National Florence Crittenton Mission Folder, KWB Papers, LC; *Report of the National Florence Crittenton Mission and Its Affiliated Branches for the Years 1922–1924* (hereafter cited as *Affiliated Branches, 1922–1924*), box 2, folder 7, Florence Crittenton Collection, SWHA.

47. A Kate Waller Barrett letter to an unknown person evidently written in 1917, National Florence Crittenton Mission Folder, KWB Papers, LC.

48. *Florence Crittenton Bulletin* 1 (1925): 2.

49. Ibid.

50. Ibid.

51. Wilson, *Fifty Years' Work,* 81.

52. "Winsome Babies Will Get Most from Flag Day Contributions to Florence Crittenton Home," undated newspaper clipping, #8-24, KWB Papers, U.Va.

53. "Crittenton Home Planning Bazaar," newspaper clipping, 24 Nov. 1922, #2-11, KWB Papers, U.Va.

54. *Girls* 20 (1917): 11, 13.

55. Walter Trattner, *From Poor Law to Welfare State: A History of Social Welfare in America,* 2d ed. (New York, 1979), 216.

56. See *Affiliated Branches, 1922–1924; Forty-Sixth Annual Report of the National Florence Crittenton Mission and Its Affiliated Branches for the Year 1928* (hereafter cited as *Affiliated Branches, 1928*), box 2, folder 6, Florence Crittenton Collection, SWHA. See also Wilson, *Fifty Years' Work,* 68.

57. "Report of the President," *Affiliated Branches, 1922–1924.*

58. *Affiliated Branches, 1928,* 5.

59. *Report of the National Florence Crittenton Mission and Its Affiliated Branches for the Year 1919–1920* (hereafter cited as *Affiliated Branches, 1919–1920*), box 2, folder 6, Florence Crittenton Collection, SWHA.

60. See Trattner, *From Poor Law to Welfare State,* 217–19. Clarke A. Chambers has pointed out that men usually managed Community Chests. Chambers, "Women in the Creation," 22.

61. "Report on the Audit of the Florence Crittenton Home, April 1–December 31, 1920," United Community Services of Metropolitan Detroit Files.

62. Wilson, *Fifty Years' Work,* 74. See also *Florence Crittenton Bulletin* 1 (1925): 1; Robert South Barrett, *The Care of the Unmarried Mother* (Alexandria, Va., 1929). On social work in general during this period see Lubove, *Professional Altruist,* 119–71; Clarke Chambers, *Seedtime of Reform: American Social Welfare and Social Action, 1918–1933* (Ann Arbor, 1963). For a discussion of the specific Crittenton situation see Kunzel, *Fallen Women, Problem Girls,* 121–22. The Chicago home

tried to break with the National Florence Crittenton Mission, see "Financial Committee Report, November 15, 1917," box 3, folder 1, Anchorage Collection.

63. *Florence Crittenton Bulletin* 2 (1926): 5.

64. *Annual Report, 1926*, 5; Minutes of the Meeting of the Committee on Case Co-operation, 22 Jan. 1919, box 8, folder 12, UCSC.

65. See Trattner, *From Poor Law to Welfare State*, 212–17; Lubove, *Professional Altruist*, 119; Kunzel, *Fallen Women, Problem Girls*, 1–64. I contend that Kate Waller Barrett possessed a more modern viewpoint than Kunzel attributes to her.

66. "Minutes of the Conference of the National Florence Crittenton Mission Held at Atlantic City, New Jersey, May 30–31, 1919," *Affiliated Branches, 1918–1919*, 106.

67. "Minutes of the Conference of the National Florence Crittenton Mission Held at Atlantic City, New Jersey, May 30–31, 1919," *Affiliated Branches, 1918–1919*, 117.

68. Children's Bureau, *Illegitimacy as a Child-Welfare Problem*, pt. 2, 189, 43–44.

69. Ibid., 68; Children's Bureau, *Children of Illegitimate Birth*, 3, 165.

70. *Annual Report of the Detroit Florence Crittenton Home, 1926*.

71. *Affiliated Branches, 1918–1919*, 29, 21–22.

72. *Florence Crittenton League of Compassion Annual Report, 1926*, 5.

73. *Affiliated Branches, 1926*, 63.

74. Mrs. T. E. Robertson, "Keeping a Mother and Child Together," Annual Convention, 1926, *Affiliated Branches, 1926*.

75. *Affiliated Branches, 1927*.

76. R. G. Mith and Harry Gauss, "Serologic Survey of the Denver Florence Crittenton Home," *Journal of the American Medical Association* 78 (1922): 535–36; *Affiliated Branches, 1922–1924*, 48. For example the results of one group of tests at the Kansas City Home were 110 positive and 116 negative.

77. *Affiliated Branches, 1922–1924*, 99.

78. *Affiliated Branches, 1925*, 68; Mith and Gauss, " Serologic Survey," 535.

79. Gen. Hugh Cummins, *The Florence Crittenton Missions and Their Relation to Public Health*, 1925, a pamphlet in the National Florence Crittenton Mission Folder, KWB Papers, LC.

80. Brodie, *Contraception and Abortion*, 262–68.

81. "Birth Control," *Girls* 20 (1917): 7–9. See *Survey* 37 (18 Nov. 1916): 161–65; *Survey* 37 (23 Dec. 1916): 345–46.

82. *Forty-Fifth Annual Report*, 31, box 2, folder 7, Florence Crittenton Collection, SWHA. The debate continues to the present. Dr. Donald McKinney, executive director of Florence Crittenton Home Services in Little Rock, Arkansas, chided Ann Landers for writing that "for some abstinence is not a realistic alternative, and for those I recommend condoms." Dr. McKinney indicated that abstinence should be the only alternative. *Spokesman Review* (Spokane, Wash.), 26 Sept. 1994.

83. See *Affiliated Branches, 1918–1919*, 80, 85; Wilson, *Fifty Years' Work*, 190.

84. "Report of the Acting President," *Girls* 20 (1917): 8; *Girls* 20 (1917): 9.

85. For a discussion of this aspect of progressivism see Ashby, *Saving the Waifs.*

86. *Affiliated Branches, 1918–1919,* 86.

87. *Girls* 20 (1917): 8.

88. *Affiliated Branches, 1918–1919,* 87.

89. Kate Waller Barrett to all Florence Crittenton Girls, 10 Dec. 1919, National Florence Crittenton Mission Folder, KWB Papers, LC.

90. *Affiliated Branches, 1922–1924,* 82.

91. "Data in Regard to the Erection of a Cottage at Ivakota Farms for Colored Girls," box 19, folder 12, Florence Crittenton Collection, SWHA.

92. Kate Waller Barrett to Whom It May Concern, 20 June 1919, box 19, folder 12, Florence Crittenton Collection, SWHA.

93. Ibid.

94. See "Report of Ivakota," *Affiliated Branches, 1919–1920,* 45.

95. *Affiliated Branches, 1922–1924,* 81.

96. See Lyman Beecher Stowe, "Training City Boys for Country Life," *Outlook* 102 (1912): 540.

97. Ibid., 537.

98. Lexington, Kentucky, Home to Kate Waller Barrett, 31 Jan. 1924, box 19, folder 14, Florence Crittenton Collection, SWHA. Regina Kunzel has noted that Ivakota Farms' purpose was to protect residents of Florence Crittenton Homes from association with delinquent girls. This quotation seems to indicate that the opposite was sometimes true. See Kunzel, *Fallen Women, Problem Girls,* 55.

99. *Affiliated Branches, 1927,* 35. See also *Affiliated Branches, 1926,* 37.

100. *Affiliated Branches, 1926,* 38.

101. *Affiliated Branches, 1919–1920,* 48.

102. *Affiliated Branches, 1927,* 40.

103. *Affiliated Branches, 1926,* 114.

104. *Affiliated Branches, 1925,* 126.

105. Ibid.

106. *Affiliated Branches, 1918–1919,* 86.

107. Ibid., 113.

108. Ibid., 115. Few individuals are blessed with names that coincide so well with their chosen profession.

109. Ibid., 84–85.

110. Reba Barrett Smith, "Description of Work at Ivakota," newspaper clipping, #3-11, KWB Papers, U.Va.

111. *Affiliated Branches, 1919–1920,* 46.

112. Ibid.

113. *Affiliated Branches, 1926,* 38.

114. Smith, "Description of Work at Ivakota."

115. Ibid.

116. Ivakota Farms, *Affiliated Branches, 1918–19,* 80.

117. "Enthusiastic Over Ivakota," newspaper clipping, Nov. 1921, #3-11, KWB Papers, U.Va.

118. See Wilson, *Fifty Years' Work,* 197; *Affiliated Branches, 1918–1919,* 11; #27-1, KWB Papers, U.Va.; "Personalities—Dr. Kate Waller Barrett, Sociologist," *World's Work* 49 (1924): 69.

119. *Affiliated Branches, 1919–1920,* 4.

120. *Greensboro Daily News,* 18 Feb. 1925.

121. "Lure to Get Husbands," #38-1, KWB Papers, U.Va. Barrett also spoke out against "extreme tango dancing" and "gowns that have no proper place anywhere," newspaper clipping, #58-13, KWB Papers, U.Va.

122. Kate Waller Barrett, *The Sanctity of Marriage,* a pamphlet in box 4, folder 1 of the Florence Crittenton Collection, SWHA.

123. "Unhappy Marriage Better than None Says Dr. Kate Waller Barrett," *Boston Post,* 1 Feb. 1924, #58-15, KWB Papers, U.Va.

124. Ibid.

125. "Sociologist Says She Has Cure for Divorce," *Newark (N.J.) Evening News,* 30 Jan. 1925, #58-9, KWB Papers, U.Va.

126. John J. Wicker to Hon. Claude A. Swanson, a night letter, 7 June 1924, #46-15, KWB Papers, U.Va.

127. There is a copy of Barrett's speech in the #46-21, KWB Papers, U.Va.

128. Harry F. Byrd to Kate Waller Barrett, 21 Feb. 1925, #46-47, #46-48, KWB Papers, U.Va.

129. #55-70, #55-71, KWB Papers, U.Va.

130. Jane W. Bancroft, "Kate Waller Barrett: A Tribute to the Late President of the Florence Crittenton Homes," #55-54, KWB Papers, U.Va.

131. Governor E. Lee Tinkle to Charles D. Barrett, 25 Feb. 1925, #56-144, KWB Papers, U.Va.

132. *Florence Crittenton Bulletin* 1 (1925): 1, box 2, folder 7, Florence Crittenton Collection, SWHA.

Conclusion

1. Barrett, *Care of the Unmarried Mother,* 42.

2. Prindle, "How Shall We Reach the Street Girls?" 39.

3. "Work in the District of Columbia," *FCM* 8 (1906): 931–32.

4. Joseph P. MacCarthy, ed., *Mary Magdalene: Hope for the Erring and a Sociological Study* (Kalamazoo, Mich., 1906), 133.

5. Emerson, "Place of the Maternity Home," 772.

6. Gordon, *Pitied but Not Entitled,* 175.

7. Joe Klein, "Monumental Callousness: Political Demagoguery—Not Reality—Is What Has Driven the Debate About Welfare Reform," *Newsweek* 128 (12 Aug. 1996): 45.

8. Freedman, *Maternal Justice,* 352, makes this point regarding Miriam Waters. See Kunzel, *Fallen Women, Problem Girls,* 116.

9. Wilson, *Fifty Years' Work,* 139.

10. Sklar, *Florence Kelley,* xiii.

11. Gordon, "Family Violence," 454.

Epilogue

1. Barrett, *Care of the Unmarried Mother,* 49.

2. According to Rickie Solinger, the trend among social workers was towards the idea that "motherhood" itself was not possible outside of marriage—that the unmarried mother was not an acceptable mother. See Solinger, *Wake Up Little Susie,* 16–38.

3. Peter Romanofsky, ed., "Florence Crittenton Association of America, Inc.," *The Greenwood Encyclopedia of American Institutions: Social Service Organizations,* vol. 1 (Westport, Conn., 1978), 306–11.

‏ ‎⚜

Bibliographic Essay

Primary Sources

Kate Waller Barrett's claims to the contrary, the record-keeping practices of the National Florence Crittenton Mission were often only rudimentary; the mission seldom kept file copies of Crittenton letters and saved only scattered items of incoming correspondence. Workers destroyed a great many records and documents in later years to avoid having to reveal their confidential contents to relatives and others seeking birth information. However, the national organization and Barrett did maintain sufficient files to provide researchers with a fairly complete picture of the NFCM's operation. Bits and pieces of documentation from several local homes aided me in making generalizations regarding the local situation.

The Florence Crittenton Collection, Social Welfare History Archives, University of Minnesota, covers the period from the mission's founding until the 1970s and includes items from several local homes as well as from the national. The NFCM annual reports, reports from local homes and national officers, and financial statements proved invaluable, as did local home folders containing sample programs, admission forms, rules, menus, and items of a similar nature that helped to reconstruct what life was like in the FC institutions.

The Kate Waller Barrett Papers, Library of Congress and University of Virginia, are Barrett's personal papers and shed light on both her NFCM activities and her many other reform and organizational pursuits. The papers at the University of Virginia are copies of some of those deposited at the Library of Congress, but where possible I have cited the University of Virginia holdings because that collection is more completely indexed. Barrett's papers include many newspaper clippings chronicling her accomplishments and those of the NFCM. Unfortunately, the clippings seldom include the date or the newspaper's name, and

251

while it is possible to approximate the time period, this is not always satisfactory. Several rough drafts of Barrett's speeches are informative but are also frequently undated.

The Florence Crittenton Anchorage Collection, University of Illinois, Chicago Circle Campus, was crucial to this project because it documented the activities of a local home. An incomplete set of Crittenton home board meeting minutes revealed the problems the board confronted as well as the nature of day-to-day home operation. While sometimes local boards glossed over difficulties in reports to the national, these minutes include frank discussions of inmates, staff, and board actions. The collection also includes complete financial reports, as well as several Anchorage publications. The board meeting minutes often contain the full names of inmates, in which case I have used only the first name.

Board meeting minutes for the Portland, Oregon, home are deposited in the Oregon Collection, University of Oregon, Eugene. While the minutes cover a relatively few years, longtime board secretary Cornelia Rockwell was both a forthright and an articulate reporter. The minutes include valuable information on clients, fundraising, and the board's relationship with the National Florence Crittenton Mission.

The Boston Public Library holds copies of all of the Annual Reports of that city's Florence Crittenton League of Compassion, Inc. for the years this study encompasses. The Boston organization was one of the larger FC operations, and its annual reports are a rich source, containing many pictures of the home, inmates and their children, workers, and home activities. Financial reports, as well as annual reports from circles, the superintendent, and the matron are included.

The Detroit Florence Crittenton organization continued to operate a large hospital into the 1980s, and Detroit was home to Crittenton efforts that included early rescue work and eventually a home for unwed mothers, a kindergarten, and day-care facilities. The United Community Service Case files, Archives of Labor and Urban Affairs, Wayne State University, Detroit, Michigan, contain formal case records. Unlike the board minutes and annual reports in Chicago, Portland, and Boston, the Detroit records follow families throughout their contact with the Crittenton organization, sometimes over a period of several years. The notes workers included provide important insight into the way they viewed their clients. These records also offer clues as to the clients' viewpoint through the accounts of client actions and notes regarding client statements. I have referred to the cases using the numbering system the social workers used.

The Burton Historical Collection, Detroit Public Library, contains a quantity of Florence Crittenton information. D. D. Spellman and Mary Heartwell, two prominent Crittenton workers, are represented in this collection, which includes a number of Crittenton pamphlets, fundraising letters, programs, circle information, and newspaper clippings.

The McClung Collection, Lawson-McGhee Library, Knoxville, Tennessee, includes a few items touching upon the Florence Crittenton work. Annie McClung was active in rescue work, and among her papers are notes on the early organization of an FC board and a copy of the Knoxville home's articles of incorporation. A group of clippings from the Knoxville newspapers concerning one of Charles Nelson Crittenton's visits to that city was especially useful.

Florence Crittenton activists wrote a number of books that are essential to any study of the mission's history. Otto Wilson's *Fifty Years' Work with Girls, 1883–1933: A Story of the Florence Crittenton Homes* (Alexandria, Va., 1933) is a convenient compilation of several sources. The volume contains Charles N. Crittenton's autobiography, *Brother of Girls*. The title suggests the tone of the work, and every home was supposed to own a copy to serve as an inspiration for FC inmates. Kate Waller Barrett's *Fourteen Years' Work Among Erring Girls* includes an autobiographical sketch and accounts of the NFCM's organization and early years. Wilson added a history of the mission's first fifty years as well as brief histories that each local home sent for inclusion in the volume. There are also photographs of a number of homes.

Traffic in Girls and the Florence Crittenton Missions by Charlton Edholm (Chicago, 1893) was one of the earliest tracts praising Crittenton work. Edholm was an official in the Women's Christian Temperance Union and an avid Crittenton supporter. (Some sources indicate that her name was Mrs. Charlton Edholm, but a number of Crittenton references indicate that Charlton was her first name, and a picture in Otto Wilson's book is labeled "Charlton Edholm.") Her book featured a discussion of the origins of the first Crittenton missions, suggestions on steps to end white slavery, and several former Crittenton inmates' statements.

Although Charles Crittenton founded and financed the early homes, Barrett influenced the operation of each home. Her pamphlet, *Motherhood: A Means of Regeneration* (1904) put forth the philosophy that was a central tenet of Crittenton work. In *Some Practical Suggestions for the Conduct of a Rescue Home* (Washington, D.C., 1903), Barrett offered a blueprint for rescue-mission operation from finding a suitable matron to appropriate attire for inmates and everything in between.

The NFCM publications, the *Florence Crittenton Magazine, Girls,* and the *Florence Crittenton Bulletin,* were the most important available source. The magazines printed articles on all facets of Crittenton operation and philosophy and are vital to any attempt to assess FC workers' view of their contribution. Some volumes began with the March issue, so the volume numbering system varies. Many articles had no titles.

To grasp the hysteria that accompanied the white-slavery scare and to assess the prodigious research and investigation that followed, there is no substitute for anti-vice crusaders' works. *The Great War on White Slavery, or Fighting for the Protection of Our Girls* (1912) was a prime example of this literature. Clifford G. Roe, the Illinois attorney instrumental in prosecuting white-slavery cases, and B. S. Steadwell, president of the American Purity Federation, wrote the book partly to serve as a warning to prospective white-slave victims and partly to urge people to join the anti-vice campaign. George J. Kneeland's *Commercialized Prostitution in New York City* (New York, 1913), was the product of the John D.

Rockefeller–led vice investigations in that city. Jane Addams, in *A New Conscience and an Ancient Evil* (New York: Macmillan, 1912), provided the consummate progressive interpretation of the prostitution problem, especially among immigrants. Maud Miner, *Slavery of Prostitution: A Plea for Emancipation* (New York, 1916), is an account by a probation officer who had contact with many New York City prostitutes and with the Florence Crittenton mission in that city.

Progressive-era reformers conducted a number of studies of unmarried mothers and their children that are relevant. Percy Gamble Kammerer's *Unmarried Mother: A Study of Five Hundred Cases* (Boston, 1918) provides important information, as do the several studies conducted under the auspices of the Children's Bureau, Emma O. Lundberg and Katherine F. Lenroot, *Illegitimacy as a Child-Welfare Problem*, part 2, *A Study of Original Records in the City of Boston and in the State of Massachusetts* (1921); *Illegitimacy as a Child-Welfare Problem, Part 3: Methods of Care in Selected Urban and Rural Communities* (1924); Ethel Waters, *Study of Maternity Homes in Minnesota and Pennsylvania* (1926); and A. Madorah Donahue, *Children of Illegitimate Birth Whose Mothers Have Kept their Custody* (1928).

Secondary Sources

There is a vast amount of historical literature dealing with the progressive period, in part due to progressivism's diverse groups with sometimes divergent interests. I have concentrated on those aspects of progressivism that combined evangelical fervor and humanitarianism with organization, science, and efficiency. Clyde Griffen's article "The Progressive Ethos," in *The Development of an American Culture,* ed. Stanley Coben and Lorman Ratner (Englewood Cliffs, N.J., 1970), influenced my thinking on these aspects of progressivism. Samuel Haber's *Efficiency and Uplift: Scientific Management in the Progressive Era, 1890–1920* (Chicago, 1964), does an excellent job of pointing out how scientific methods and facts influenced progressive reformers. John C. Burnham's essay in John D. Buenker, John C. Burnham, and Robert M. Crunden, *Progressivism* (Cambridge, Mass., 1977), offers a revealing discussion of progressivism's fusion of moral idealism with bureaucratic organization, a progressive impulse particularly evident in the history of the National Florence Crittenton Mission. David P. Thelen, *The New Citizenship: Origins of Progressivism in Wisconsin, 1885–1900* (Columbia, Mo., 1972) remains a key work for its exploration of progressive "insurgency." Daniel Rodgers, "In Search of Progressivism," *Reviews in American History* 10 (Dec. 1982): 113–32 offers an excellent review of the literature, and Arthur S. Link and Richard L. McCormick's *Progressivism* (Arlington Heights, Ill., 1983) is a good synthesis. James T. Kloppenberg, *Uncertain Victory: Social Democracy and Progressivism in European and American Thought, 1870–1920* (New York, 1986) discusses the intellectual underpinnings. My entire concept of progressivism owes much to LeRoy Ashby's excellent chapter in *William Jennings Bryan: Champion of Democracy* (Boston, 1987). Two recent studies were particularly important. Ellen Fitzpatrick's *Endless Crusade: Women Social Scientists and Progressive Reform* (New York, 1990) provides insight into progressivism, gender, and reform. Robyn Muncy, *Creating a Female Dominion in American Reform, 1890–1935* (New York, 1991) is invaluable for pointing out how active women reformers were during the period of the current study and for providing benchmarks for assessing Dr. Kate Waller Barrett's career.

The history of Florence Crittenton people parallels that of social workers in general, as discussed by Roy Lubove in *The Professional Altruist: The Emergence of Social Work as a Career, 1880–1930* (Cambridge, Mass., 1965), which remains the standard account. Clarke Chambers, *Seedtime of Reform: American Social Welfare and Social Action 1918–1933* (Ann Arbor, 1963) and John H. Ehrenreich, *The Altruistic Imagination: History of Social Work and Social Policy in the United States* (Ithaca, 1985) are useful. Clarke A. Chambers, "Toward a Redefinition of Welfare History," *Journal of American History* 73 (Sept. 1986): 407–33 and "Women in the Creation of the Profession of Social Work," *Social Service Review* (Mar. 1986): 1–33 provide significant insights. Regina Kunzel, "The Professionalization of Benevolence: Evangelicals and Social Workers in the Florence Crittenton Homes, 1915 to 1945," *Journal of Social History* 22 (Fall 1988): 21–44 and more fully in *Fallen Women, Problem Girls: Unmarried Mothers and the Professionalization of Social Work 1890–1945* (New Haven, 1993) analyzed an evolution in Crittenton attitudes, although I think she underestimates Barrett's role in this transition.

Studies of philanthropy and welfare illuminate the Florence Crittenton experience. Robert H. Bremner's pioneering study, *From the Depths: The Discovery of Poverty in the United States* (New York, 1956), discusses the recognition of many of the problems that Crittenton workers also faced. Linda Gordon, *Pitied But Not Entitled: Single Mothers and the History of Welfare* (New York, 1994) is a seminal work that sheds light on both Florence Crittenton workers and their charges.

For a helpful discussion of the progressive fear and dislike of the urban environment, see Paul Boyer, *Urban Masses and Moral Order in America, 1820–1920* (Cambridge, Mass., 1978) and Kenneth L. Kusmer, "The Functions of Organized Charity in the Progressive Era: Chicago as a Case Study," *Journal of American History* 60 (1973): 657–78.

Progressive responses to the problem of delinquency and dependence are discussed in admirable fashion by LeRoy Ashby in *Saving the Waifs: Reformers and Dependent Children, 1890–1917* (Philadelphia, 1984); Steven J. Schlossman, *Love and the American Delinquent: The Theory and Practice of "Progressive" Juvenile Justice, 1825–1920* (Chicago, 1977); David Rothman, *Conscience and Convenience: The Asylum and Its Alternatives in Progressive America* (Boston, 1980); and Joseph M. Hawes, *The Children's Rights Movement: A History of Advocacy and Protection* (Boston, 1991). James T. Patterson, *America's Struggle Against Poverty, 1900–1994* (Cambridge, 1994) is useful on mothers' pensions.

Historians writing about progressive reformers have frequently addressed the question of "social control." Linda Gordon's essay, "Family Violence, Feminism, and Social Control" in her *Women, the State, and Welfare* (Madison, Wisc., 1990) discusses this perspective as it relates to women and social welfare, and her "Family Violence, Feminism, and Social Control," *Feminist Studies* 12 (Fall 1986): 453–78 and "Black and White Visions of Welfare: Women's Welfare Activism, 1890–1945," *Journal of American History* (Sept. 1991): 559–90 also discuss this. Other helpful items are Lois Banner, "Religious Benevolence as Social Control: A Critique of an Interpretation," *Journal of American History* 60 (June 1973): 23–41; William Muraskin, "The Social-Control Theory in American History: A Critique," *Journal of Social History* 9 (Summer 1976): 559–69; Walter I. Trattner, ed., *Social Welfare or Social Control?* (Knoxville, Tenn., 1983); and Eileen Boris, "Reconstructing the 'Family': Women, Progressive Reform, and the Problem of Social Control," in *Gender, Class, Race, and Reform in the Progressive Era,* ed. Noralee Frankel and Nancy S. Dye (Lexington, Ky., 1991), 73–86.

Since most Florence Crittenton workers and their charges were women the large women's history literature applies. Most historians would agree that any discussion of nineteenth-century women begins with Barbara Welter's seminal article "The Cult of True Womanhood: 1820–1860," *American Quarterly* 18 (1966): 151–74. The Carol Smith-Rosenberg, Kirk Jeffrey, and Charles Rosenberg articles cited at the end of chapter 1 were relevant to this study. A number of other journal articles are noteworthy, including John T. Cumbler, "The Politics of Charity: Gender and Class in Late Nineteenth Century Charity Policy" *Journal of Social History* 14 (1980): 99–112; Susan Porter Benson, "Business Heads and Sympathizing Hearts: The Providence Employment Society," *Journal of Social History* 12 (Winter 1978): 301–12; Anne M. Boylan, "Women in Groups: An Analysis of Women's Benevolent Organizations in New York and Boston, 1797–1840," *Journal of American History* 71 (Dec. 1974): 497–523; and Mary Ryan, "The Power of Women's Networks: A Case Study of Female Moral Reform in Antebellum America," *Feminist Studies* 5 (Spring 1979): 66–87. Maxine Van de Wetering, "The Popular Concept of 'Home' in Nineteenth-Century America," *Journal of American Studies* 18 (Apr. 1984): 5–28 helps explain the Crittenton reverence for the home and family, as does Christopher Lasch, *Haven in a Heartless World: The Family Besieged* (New York, 1977). Kathleen D. McCarthy, "Parallel Power Structures: Women and the Voluntary Sphere," in *Lady Bountiful Revisited: Women, Philanthropy, and Power,* ed. Kathleen D. McCarthy (New Brunswick, 1990) helped me to understand how Barrett and her colleagues tried to gain power through their reform activities.

I believe that there are many similarities between Barrett's career and Sheila Rothman's picture of the "protestant nun," *Woman's Proper Place: A History of Changing Ideals and Practices, 1870 to the Present* (New York, 1978). I also found Christopher Lasch's discussion of Jane Addams in *The New Radicalism in America 1889–1963: The Intellectual as a Social Type* (New York, 1965) helpful in my attempts to understand Barrett and her motivations. There were parallels between Crittenton work and prison reform described so well in Estelle Freedman, *Their Sisters' Keepers: Women's Prison Reform in America, 1830–1930* (Ann Arbor, 1981). I owe much to Freedman's important "Separatism as Strategy: Female Institution Building and American Feminism, 1870–1930," *Feminist*

Studies 5 (Fall 1979): 512–29 for my conception of Barrett and other Florence Crittenton workers as female institution builders. Of the many works on women and nineteenth-century reform, I have particularly benefited from Barbara J. Berg, *The Remembered Gate: Origins of American Feminism* (New York, 1978); Karen J. Blair, *The Clubwoman as Feminist: True Woman Redefined, 1868–1914* (New York, 1980); Ruth Bordin, *Women and Temperance: The Quest for Power and Liberty, 1873–1900* (Philadelphia, 1981); Barbara Leslie Epstein, *The Politics of Domesticity: Women, Evangelism, and Temperance in Nineteenth-Century America* (Middletown, Conn., 1981); and Lori D. Ginzberg, *Women and the Work of Benevolence: Morality, Politics and Class in the Nineteenth Century United States* (New Haven, 1990). Glenna Matthews has discussed the relationship between the domestic sphere and the public sphere in *"Just a Housewife": The Rise and Fall of Domesticity in America* (New York, 1987) and *The Rise of Public Woman: Woman's Power and Woman's Place in the United States, 1630–1970* (New York, 1992). Nancy Cott's *The Grounding of Modern Feminism* (New Haven, 1987) is a must for any discussion of women in American society during this period.

There is clearly a relationship between Florence Crittenton efforts and changing behavioral patterns of especially working women that Kathy Peiss, *Cheap Amusements: Working Women and Leisure in Turn of the Century New York* (Philadelphia, 1986); Christine Stansell, *City of Women: Sex and Class in New York 1789–1860* (Urbana, Ill., 1987); and Joanne Meyerowitz, *Women Adrift: Independent Wage Earners in Chicago, 1880–1930* (Chicago, 1988) discuss. The so-called girl problem was one ramification of these changes and is analyzed in Mary E. Odem, *Delinquent Daughters: Protecting and Policing Adolescent Female Sexuality in the United States, 1885–1920* (Chapel Hill, N.C., 1995) and Ruth M. Alexander, *The "Girl Problem": Female Sexual Delinquency in New York, 1900–1930* (Ithaca, 1995). Since the delinquency label was often a result of women's sexuality, these studies are of paramount importance for FC mission history.

Gender as a lens for historical analysis is discussed in Linda K. Kerber, "Separate Spheres, Female Worlds, Woman's Place: The Rhetoric of Women's History," *Journal of American History* 75 (June 1988): 9–39 and Karen Offen, "Defining Feminism: A Comparative Historical Approach, *Signs* (14) Autumn, 1988): 119–57. No study of the Florence Crittenton movement can avoid the topic of maternalism: Seth Koven and Sonya Michel, "Womanly Duties: Maternalist Politics and the Origins of Welfare States in France, Germany, Great Britain, and the United States, 1880–1920," *American Historical Review* 95 (Oct. 1990): 1076–1108; Elieen Boris, "Regulating Industrial Homework: The Triumph of 'Sacred Motherhood,'" *Journal of American History* 71 (Mar. 1985): 745–63; Mary G. Dietz, "Citizenship with a Feminist Face: The Problem with Maternal Thinking," *Political Theory* 13 (Feb. 1985): 19–37; and Theda Skocpal, *Protecting Soldiers and Mothers: The Political Origins of Social Policy in the U.S.* (Cambridge, 1992). Recent works that link maternalism and reform reinforce my notion that Barrett and the NFCM used maternalism as a foundation for their reform philosophy and actions. See especially, Molly Ladd-Taylor, *Mother-Work: Women, Child Welfare, and the State, 1890–1930* (Urbana, Ill., 1994); Estelle B. Freedman,

Maternal Justice: Miriam Van Waters and the Female Reform Tradition (Chicago, 1996); and Katherine Kish Sklar, *Florence Kelley and the Nation's Work: The Rise of Women's Political Culture, 1830–1900* (New Haven, 1995).

Historians have not yet paid sufficient attention to African American women and social welfare. Two classic works by W. E. B. Du Bois are still the starting place: *The Negro American Family*, Atlanta University Publication No. 13 (Atlanta, 1908) and W. E. B. DuBois, ed., *Efforts for Social Betterment Among Negro Americans*, Atlanta University Publication no. 14 (Atlanta, 1909). Historians owe a debt to Darlene Clark Hine for her pioneering works: "'We Specialize in the Wholly Impossible': The Philanthropic Work of Black Women," in *Lady Bountiful Revisited: Women, Philanthropy and Power*, ed. Kathleen D. McCarthy (New Brunswick, N.J., 1990); Darlene Clark Hine, ed., *Black Women in United States History* (Brooklyn, 1990); and Darlene Clark Hine, ed., *Black Women in America: An Historical Encyclopedia*, 2 vols. (Brooklyn, N.Y., 1993). There are similarities between the activities of white middle-class philanthropists and their African American counterparts: Eileen Boris, "The Power of Motherhood: Black and White Active Women Redefine the 'Political'," in *Mothers of the New World: Maternalist Politics and the Origins of the Welfare States,* ed. Seth Koven and Sonya Michel (New York, 1993), 213–45 and Anne Firor Scott, "Most Invisible of All: Black Women's Voluntary Associations," *Journal of Southern History* 56 (Feb. 1990): 3–22. Cynthia Neverdon-Morton, *Afro-American Women of the South and the Advancement of the Race, 1895–1925* (Knoxville, Tenn., 1984) provides useful insights. Jacquelyn Dowd Hall's *Revolt Against Chivalry: Jessie Daniel Ames and the Women's Campaign Against Lynching* (New York, 1979) remains a first-rate study of stereotypical ideas of African American women's sexuality and of one attempt by black and white women to cooperate in achieving a reform goal.

There is also a large body of scholarship dealing with prostitution and rescue homes. David J. Pivar, *Purity Crusade, Sexual Morality and Social Control 1868–1900* (Westport, Conn., 1973) discusses the antecedents to the white-slavery scare, and Allan M. Brandt, *No Magic Bullet: A Social History of Venereal Disease in the United States Since 1880* (New York, 1985) is an excellent account. Vern L. Bullough, *The History of Prostitution* (New Hyde Park, N.Y., 1964) is a good starting place. More recent works are Mark Connelly, *Response to Prostitution in the Progressive Era* (Chapel Hill, N.C., 1980); Judith R. Walkowitz, *Prostitution and Victorian Society: Women, Class and the State* (Cambridge, 1980); and Ruth Rosen, *The Lost Sisterhood: Prostitution in America, 1900–1918* (Baltimore, 1982). I found Barbara Meil Hobson, *Uneasy Virtue: The Politics of Prostitution and the American Reform Tradition* (New York, 1987) especially enlightening. Of particular interest was Hobson's discussion of the relation between feminism and attempts to reform prostitution policy. John C. Burnham's several articles cited in the text helped me to tie progressive fear of prostitution and vice to the larger issues of progressivism. Other useful articles are Robert E. Riegel, "Changing American Attitudes Toward Prostitution, 1800–1920," *Journal of the History of Ideas* 29 (1968): 437–52; Egal Feldman, "Prostitution, the Alien

Woman and the Progressive Imagination, 1910–1915," *American Quarterly* 19 (1967): 192–206; Roy Lubove, "The Progressives and the Prostitute," *Historian* 24 (1962): 308–30; Judith Walkowitz, "The Politics of Prostitution," *Signs* 6 (1980): 123–35; and Laura Hopke, "The Late Nineteenth Century American Street Walker, Images and Realities," *Mid-America* 65 (1983): 155–62. John D'Emilio and Estelle Freedman discuss sexuality, illegitimacy, and prostitution in their pathbreaking *Intimate Matters: A History of Sexuality in America* (New York, 1988), and Ellen DuBois and Linda Gordon analyze women's views of sexuality in "Seeking Ecstasy on the Battlefield: Danger and Pleasure in Nineteenth-Century Feminist Sexual Thought," *Feminist Studies* 9 (Spring 1983): 7–26. Kathy Peiss and Christina Simmons, eds., *Passion and Power: Sexuality in History* (Philadelphia, 1989), is useful. A recent comprehensive study is Timothy J. Gilfoyle, *City of Eros: New York City, Prostitution, and the Commercialization of Sex, 1790–1920* (New York, 1992). David J. Langum, *Crossing Over the Line: Legislating Morality and the Mann Act* (Chicago, 1994) discusses the legal ramifications of the Mann Act.

On rescue work and related social-reform activities, see Steven Ruggles, "Fallen Women: The Inmates of the Magdalen Society Asylum in Philadelphia, 1836–1908," *Journal of Social History* 16 (Summer 1983): 65–82 and Michael W. Sedlak, "Young Women and the City: Adolescent Deviance and the Transformation of Educational Policy, 1870–1960," *History of Education Quarterly* 23 (Spring 1983): 1–28. Peggy Pascoe's *Relations of Rescue: The Search for Female Moral Authority in the American West, 1874–1939* (New York, 1990), discusses rescue work in the West with special emphasis on Chinese women, Mormon women, and Native Americans. Pascoe makes a real contribution to the literature on rescue work, and her idea of a "search for moral authority" goes far toward solving the problems of social feminism and/or social control explanations of rescue work. Marian J. Morton's *And Sin No More: Social Policy and Unwed Mothers in Cleveland, 1855–1990* (Columbus, 1993) offers a look at Cleveland's Florence Crittenton organization, as well as other Cleveland institutions designed to aid unmarried mothers. Regina Kunzel's *Fallen Women, Problem Girls: Unmarried Mothers and the Professionalization of Social Work 1890–1945*, already mentioned, provides considerable valuable information regarding the Crittenton organization, changes in approaches to the problem of unmarried mothers, and the role of gender in the professionalization of social work. Rickie Solinger, *Wake Up Little Susie: Single Pregnancy and Race Before Roe v. Wade* (New York, 1992) concentrates on the period after the current study but offers valuable insights into maternity homes and to later views of the unmarried mother. Regina Kunzel, "Pulp Fictions and Problem Girls: Reading and Rewriting Single Pregnancy in the Postwar United States," *American Historical Review* 100 (Dec. 1995): 1465–87 contains an excellent discussion of case records as a source for historians studying unmarried mothers and prostitutes.

Index

Harnessing the Power of Motherhood was designed and typeset on a Macintosh computer system using PageMaker software. The text is set in Sabon and the titles are set in Caxton. This book was designed and composed by Sheila Hart and was printed and bound by Thomson-Shore, Inc. The recycled paper used in this book is designed for an effective life of at least three hundred years.